THE MAKING OF A CHILD OF DESTINY

THE ANDRETTA TILLMAN STORY

BRIAN K. MOORE

DOUSI PUBLISHING

Spring, Texas
Est. 2013

The Making of a Child of Destiny

Copyright © 2014 by Brian Kenneth Moore

All rights reserved. No part of this book may be reproduced, distributed, or transmitted in any form or by any means, or stored in a database or retrieval system, without the express written permission of the publisher except for the use of brief quotations in a book review.

ISBN-13: 978-0991635504

Library of Congress Control Number: 2014934814

First Printing, May 2014

Printed in the United States of America

Inquiries should be addressed to:
Dousic Entertainment Publishing
Spring, Texas.77379
www.dousic.net

Disclaimer

All the material contained in this book is provided for educational and informational purposes only. No responsibility can be taken for any results or outcomes resulting from the use of this material.

While every attempt has been made to provide information that is both accurate and effective, the author does not assume any responsibility for the accuracy or use/misuse of this information.

In Loving Memory

☙❧

I write this book in memory of my friend and partner - the late, great Mrs. Andretta Tillman. You taught me so much about the music industry and how to continuously draw on the internal will to achieve and fulfill our destiny. For that, we say thank you.

To the memory of Dwight and Shawna Tillman, because of Ann's love for you, we were able to accomplish what others said could not be done.

To the memory of others who have touched my life, my Grandmothers Lizzie Banks and Armelda Moore; my sisters Louise and Sharron; all of my uncles, aunts, and cousin of The Moore, Banks, Wooden, Smith and East Lawn Drive families that are resting in the arms of God.

I dedicate this book to my wife Cassey for her love and support; to my children Brian and Bryanna; to the children of Andretta and Dwight Tillman, Armon and Christopher; to my father Reverend B.T. Moore, Sr. and his wife, Ada; to my mother, Elizabeth Banks; to my brothers Gregory Moore, Booker T. Moore, Jr., Tony Moore; to my sisters Beverly Caulfield, Armelda Thomas, and Sheila Moore; to my in-laws Sam and Macy Wooden; and to all of my aunts, uncles, cousin, nieces, nephews, and friends. You know who you are.

Acknowledgments

Special thanks to the Brown, Tillman, Knowles, Rowland, Luckett, Davis and Roberson families. Nikki, Nina, Beyoncé, Kelly, Ashley (Tamar), Latavia, Latoya, Lonnie Jackson, Tony Moore, David Brewer, Lynn, Sha Sha Daniels and the guys of Tayste (TuTu, Harlan, Mitch, And A.J.) Thanks you guys for being a part of a wonderful journey to Destiny.

Thanks to Atiya & Ingram, Keisha, and the Dousic Family for your support and understanding. Thank you all from the bottom of my heart.

Foreword

When Brian "Kenny" Moore told me that he was going to write a book about how my mother created the group Destiny Child, I was surprised, relieved, and doubtful. A book on the truth of how Beyonce, Kelly, LaTavia, Ashley, and the rest of the girls became a part of this story was a long time coming. Yet, Andretta Tillman was not here to tell it. So, who better to give the intimate details about the truth of what went on behind the scenes; what better person was there to step up and talk about the journey in such a personal and compelling way, but her friend and partner, Kenny.

The business world knows him as Brian K. Moore. Beyonce, Ashley, and the other girls called him uncle watermelon head. The management team referred to him as Kenny Mo. To me and my younger brother, Chris, he has always been pops as long as I can remember. Although pops was like a father to us, he was my mother's rock of support, confidante, friend and "make it happen" business partner. Who would have known that over 17-years later, we would be looking back and reminiscing the bitter-sweet memories, the dreams, the joys, the heartbreaks, the setbacks, the sacrifices, the lives lost and the victories that so few knew of, let alone willing to tell the truth about.

From the time I was around nine years old, our home was filled with little girls singing and dancing and grown folks telling them how to move. Some faces came and left, but the few who were mainstays and there from the very beginning were almost like part of the family. Kelly even lived at our house for a while. Some may wonder who I am or even who my mother was because the story has changed numerous times over the years, and with those changes there was less and less of her contributions being mentioned. I am Armon Tillman, Andretta's eldest child and just as much as this is the true story about my mother's life and her legacy, it is also about how Destiny's Child start was right in our living room, backyard, and garage. Likewise, this book sets the record straight and brings out the many truths that have been hidden for far too long.

Moore worked with Andretta as her partner up to the time of her death. He worked with Beyonce, Kelly, LaTavia and the others from the time they were nine and ten years of age, and was a staple of the management team during the many name changes that took place from Girl's Tyme to Destiny, to ultimately Destiny's Child. He experienced the many trials and triumphs first-hand as he was co-manager and partner of Tillman Management. Although the name later changed to Music World Management, he remained and continued to work alongside Andretta and Mathew Knowles playing a major role in the strategic development and success of Destiny's Child until he finally walked away from it all.

After leaving the camp, and shortly before bridging his diversified music industry background with technology serving for over 20-years with a fortune 500 tech company, Moore worked as vice president of operations for Eastlon's records management and music portfolio. Like the energy and work ethic that he and Andretta shared which made them effective business partners, today Moore lives, breathes, and eats in the worlds of Music and Technology. He is the president/founder of DOUSIC Entertainment LLC formed in February 2011 and the creator of the DOUSIC concept. DOUSIC aspires to be one of the world's leading social media and entertainment content companies, with unparalleled expertise in the development, production and marketing of digital media, to a global audience across its distribution and media platforms. This Buffalo, New York-born gent who was raised in the Mississippi (Greenwood) Delta, attended Mississippi College.

It was no doubt that it was divinely meant for Andretta Tillman to meet Brian K. Moore. It was also destined that the group become a major force in the music industry under their direction. The reason being is that of the driving forces behind both of their lives, their calling, and their life-experiences. Andretta faced a plethora of complexities and challenges; but her "why" was much greater than the struggles she faced. Her drive to reach the promise was so strong that she refused to let it die, and it just so happens that Beyonce, Kelly, LaTavia, Ashley and even Michelle Williams, although she became a part of Destiny's Child after Andretta, today are the beneficiaries of that unyielding and relentless force that refused to give in to failure.

Moore does a remarkable job at uncovering the facts with astonishing details of events that are often talked about but shrouded in a dark cloud, whereas the light of truth is hardly recognizable. In the book, he unravels the myths that have been accepted, by providing specifics surrounding various situations and circumstances. One excellent example is that of how Mathew Knowles actually became involved with Destiny's Child in the first place and ultimately a part of the management team and of Music World. He also explains why and how Beyonce became the lead singer for the group, and the circumstances surrounding the group's name changes.

Destiny's Child was one of the best-selling girl groups of all time, and Beyoncé is one of music's greatest icons. Yet, that did not happen in a vacuum and it certainly did not happen at the hands of Mathew Knowles as many may have been led to believe. There had been several questions left unanswered and many hidden truths. However, in The Making of a Child of Destiny: The Andretta Tillman Story, Moore discloses the "unknown" facts which had a tremendous impact on Andretta's life, and the success of Destiny's Child. He presents compelling and in-depth information leaving it to the reader in the end to be the final judge.

This is a relevant story and a liberating one for many who were involved in some way or another. The world through the years have heard whispers of setbacks including the Star Search loss, but no other text out there until now has even come close to lifting the veil and capturing the highs, lows, sacrifices, wins and losses of the journey leading to the beloved group we now call Destiny's Child. As the saying goes, "You shall know the truth, and the truth shall set you free." Regardless of what anyone believes or thinks about the whole subject matter, this book will most definitely captivate you and address the question of what really happened. The truth just is…undisputedly, and it was just a matter of time before it was told.

Moore's passion shines on every page, particularly when he ventures off on side-trips through happier times in young Destiny's Child development. It's filled with romance, drama, comedy, tragedy, ingredients necessary to open your eyes, so that the next time you see Beyoncé or any of the girls from the group; you will appreciate what they went through to be where they are today. Above all, you will learn of a profound love, a love so strong, that could not and would not let the dream die regardless of who did in the process. Many readers will immediately be able to identify and relate to wanting something so bad, to feeling so obligated to keep going no matter what, to loving so hard that regardless of what it costs you, you just keep going.

This is not just a book, it's an experience where Andretta in the spirit, guides the reader through her life and love of something that was and is so much greater than herself. She comes alive within these pages to answer those questions that were left unanswered for the girls, as well as to help each of them and the other people involved move on with their lives and finally live and walk in their true purpose. In doing so, she can finally rest in peace comfortably knowing that the truth was finally told, her destiny reached, and her name placed in the annals of history that the world may recognize the light shining brilliantly behind the "stars" that we see.

From all of us who love Destiny's Child — thank you, Brian Kenneth Moore, for finally speaking up and allowing yourself to be a conduit and a means of access for one of the most incredible love stories ever, to be told, The Making of a Child of Destiny: The Andretta Tillman Story.

I shouldn't have doubted that you could do it, not for a minute!

Armon Tillman
Son of Dwight and Andretta Tillman
Houston, Texas

Table of Contents

DESTINY FULFILLED 1
MEET THE BROWNS 9
THE EARLY YEARS 17
WHEN LOVE CALLS 45
A BRIGHT FUTURE 77
WHAT DREAMS MAY COME 109
THIS IS MY DREAM 131
LOVE LOST 151
MOVING ON 167
DO DREAMS COME TRUE 181
ALL IN THE FAMILY 193
HERE WE COME 203
A LOOK INTO THE FUTURE 231
TAKING THE LEAD 261
GOT TO GIVE HIM MORE 305
NO TIME TO CRY 339
LET'S MAKE IT HAPPEN 375
HARD TO GET, EASY TO GO 409
OUR SECOND CHANCE 445
PLAY IT AGAIN 467
DRUMS STOP, BUT THE BEAT GOES ON 495
SOMETHING KEEPS CALLING ME 535
About the Author 569

APPENDIX 571

DESTINY FULFILLED

"We did it! We finally did it! We actually made it happen!"

As I looked upward toward the top of the Toyota Center's dome, water welled up in my eyes, and all I could think about was if only she were here to see that all of the sacrifices and hard work was not in vain. Little girls eight, nine, ten back then, but today, stars in a beautiful galaxy of people as far as the eye can see. All are here to behold what my friends had been telling me would be the last tour for Destiny's Child; possibly the last time they will ever share the stage together as a group.

With bitter-sweet memories running across my mind, I could not help but to flash back to yesteryear and wonder to myself, do they really know the sweat and the tears it took to get them to this very moment? Do they fully understand the tough times endured by many or the sacrifices made to make this very night possible? Most importantly, do they realize the lives that were lost on this tragic but wonderful journey?

Glimpses of bold colors of red, gold, purple and hints of green, here we are back where it all began – Houston, Texas. The night was August 20, 2005. It was about

90-degrees outside. It was hot and humid, but inside of this home to the Houston Rockets, it was much hotter than outside. In fact things were heating up fast! I finally got up the nerves to go see the girls perform. It had been about eight years since I had seen any of my old team let alone any of the girls in the flesh. Yet, here I was confronted with my own truth. As each song played, I recalled moments in time that pierced my soul like a knife. I cried, I laughed, and I deeply reflected. With each song came a remembrance of those who labored; a realization of the pain and heartache that many faced and an appreciation of it all.

Thinking back to the time I stepped into the picture and the day I walked away, as I looked up to hear and see the energy, the lights, the roaring crowd, I was so proud. Although there were moments where it hurt badly, that day through the tears of joy, I can honestly say it felt so good to finally accept that I was a part of this. It feels so good! And yes! "We" finally did it."

As the stage came up, there stood three young women who were no longer little girls; and two of whom I watched grow up. Little-by-little the hurt, the bitterness, and the pain were transformed into pride, appreciation, acceptance, and more importantly an inner knowing that I played a significant role. The song that kicked everything off was, "Say My Name." Yet, there were many names that one could shout out, and some that certainly went across my mind: Dretta, Lonnie, Mathew, Arne, T-Mo. Each time I heard, "Say My Name," I thought out loud, "Ash, Bey, Nicki, Nina, Kelly, Tavia, Toya, Uncle Watermelon Head, Baldy Locks, and Pops."

While others were jamming to the beat and grooving to the chants of, "Say My Name," I was in many moments at one time while listening with an attentive ear and watching them perform, dancing in unison and working that stage. I shook my head because all of the coaching, the long hours of practice, the changes, the girl talks, the drama, and all the names that could truthfully fill in the blanks to, "Say My Name," there were some really great times.

Back then they were "snotty-nosed heffas" running around during cookouts where we grown-folks gathered around laughing and joking and doing what grown folks do. The children of the families ran and played and did what children did. It was a much needed release for them because although they were young, they worked just as hard as the adults if not harder and were faced with challenges that most children their age were not confronted with. No matter how we as managers, parents, producers, or friends tried to shield them and protect them from the harsh realities of the world, some were inevitably touched by real ugliness and we as a team had to confront it head on and help them move beyond it.

Both good and bad, those times will never be forgotten no matter how many names are omitted from the history. One memory of an unforgettably fun time was after one of the shows, where we all went back to Dretta's, and Tayste was telling me, "Man, K-Mo, Bey keeps stealing our stuff!" It was too funny! Big A.J., Mitch, Harlon, and Tu Tu- they were all characters. A.J. was the church singer. Mitch was the quiet one. Harlon, well, he was the brains, the dancing sex symbol and Ralph Tresvant knock-off. Finally, there was Tu Tu, Dretta's brother and cocky lead singer. I don't know who was worse; but one thing for sure, they all were really exceptional singers and each had a great sense of humor.

"Say My Name, Say My Name." As the song was coming to a close, I just laughed to myself thinking back to the crazy times. We called each other every name under the sun, but at the end of the day, we had lots of fun.

There were always ups and downs along the way; and sometimes those downs seemed to overshadow the ups. I was sad to hear that Girl's Tyme, the group that ultimately became known to the world as Destiny's Child, formed and managed by Andretta Tillman from a group of about thirty young girls who showed up one day at a local recreational center hoping to get picked to become a part of a singing group, would be parting ways to pursue their perspective solo careers after this tour. I wasn't sad that they were dismantling. I was saddened because Dretta was not here for the journey.

Although she was the one who without a doubt not only put her money where her mouth was, she also gave many pep talks of the need to stay strong and to keep going. She reminded the team that the show must go on no matter what. It was Dretta who provided a platform and laid a strong foundation for these girls, and she knew a star when she saw one. You had to show up and show out or go home. That's the way it was.

I was sad that she was not sitting in the audience watching them rock that stage like nobody's business and like grown-ass women who knew exactly how to handle themselves. She would be proud. The crowd was going mad as they were laying it down! Who could have imagined that little Girls Tyme, a cross between TLC and En Vogue would put on their big-girl drawers to ultimately go on to sell more than forty-million records worldwide and a year later receive a star on Hollywood Boulevard's Walk of Fame? Who would have imagined the sacrifices made that started in nineteen eighty-nine would eventually render this level of success and this wide of a following and fan base? Dretta knew. She had an intuitive nature about her. If she said it, you could take it to the bank. No one can argue the point against the fact that she indeed was a launching pad and catalyst to their success; and for her to miss out on this night was disheartening to say the least.

By the time they got to, Lose my Breath, the place was on fire! What a show! What a magnificent performance. I was so proud of them. That was one hell of a night, and to think, I was a part of it from almost the beginning. It's been a long time, and as the show was wrapping up, I wondered, "Do they really know what happened? Do they really know what's ahead?" Time will tell.

To know where you're going, it's important to know where you've been. While some may say that the past doesn't matter, it is very much relevant. When phenomenal success is achieved, those who labor from the very beginning understand the blood, sweat, tears, and even sacrifices to achieve a dream and claim your destiny! So the past does matter, because it is the very time and season which lays that critical foundation upon which everything else is built.

No matter how high the acclaim we reach, we can never forget those fallen heroes who made it possible for us to be where we are today. In light or the dark and God only knows, one's destiny is always fulfilled. Yet, it is up to us to remember and acknowledge that without those helping hands, compassionate hearts, and hard work, there would not be a platform on which to stand. While many winds do blow, our greatest triumphs lie in the winds that blew to lift us up, to make us stronger, and resilient. Our greatness comes not alone and not merely by believing in ourselves, but rather a combined force where self-belief is matched with others believing in us. Therein are we able to truly reach our destiny.

A child of destiny gives birth to a dream that never died with the dreamer, but lived through a believer who believed that destiny could be fulfilled. So it is, we have indeed come a very long way and through many trials; but we must never forget those who helped us to make it this far. You can never forget those who made contributions no matter how small or great, because regardless, they too played a part in your destiny!

"Say my name, say my name…" Every time you hear that song, there is one name that we shall never forget – Andretta Tillman; and this is her story.

MEET THE BROWNS

They say the apple doesn't fall too far from the tree. I guess that depends on what apple you're talking about and which tree. There can be two very different trees in the same back yard and a whole bunch of apples. That certainly was the case when it came to Dretta and her family. Although Whitehouse, Texas only had a population of close to seven thousand people, the Brown family made up a good portion of the residents. Dretta's family was so large that when all the children and grandchildren came over for dinner or holidays, they would often gather around the picnic tables under the big tree in the front yard.

The house was surrounded by nothing but woods. There were no neighbors for about two miles, so they could make all the noise they wanted and never had to worry about disturbing the peace, at least not anybody outside that big old slave-looking, ancestral, plantation house. Although it sat on several acres on top of a hill, you could see the ground through the floor. The Browns may have had land, but they were dirt poor.

There was no division between house Negroes or field Negroes; you just had a bunch of Negroes in one house. If anyone from out-of-town happened to drive down Troup Highway, it would not have been out of the ordinary to think that it was a family reunion going on.

Dretta's family was not the only large Black family in Whitehouse though. There were the Pettigrews, the Bowies, and the Stewarts. It was a whole lot of them there Negroes too, and in many cases it was hard to say who was who because in those families they were all mixed up. That's a tough one to figure out, so we will leave that one right where it is.

Back then it was not unusual for couples to have large families, especially in the South. The people in Texas were either tilling the land or having babies or a little bit of both. The crops included the kids, or at least that is what one could think. Brookshires Grocery Store and the Piggly Wiggly made a small fortune from all the mouths that had to be fed. The Gizmo didn't do so badly either. It was one of the first Black-owned restaurants, owned by the Johnson family since the nineteen forties.

People stayed busy. There was no such thing as idle time. No matter the day of the week, there was always something going on over at the Brown's household. Rain or shine Mrs. Brown had her hands full and she was never

The Making of a Child of Destiny

without something to do. The amount of stress she endured made her hard. Therefore, Sunday services at New Canaan Baptist Church and listening to her children sing in the choir was the calm in the midst of a storm.

However, Mondays were not always stormy. The sun came out to shine its brilliance this thirty-first day of March nineteen fifty-eight when another apple was picked from the Brown Family Tree. Lighting up the room and exposing herself to the world for the very first time was a little, yet strong and courageous baby girl who came to be known as Andretta Brown. She was the eighth child of twelve born to Jimmie and Effie Lue Brown. Aside from Ann, the Browns birthed Charles, Jeanette, Glenda (Mop), Arvonette, Jann, Larrell, Mary Joe (May Jo), Lornando (Tu Tu), Brenda, Lucretia, and Jimmie Jr. (Bo). From that first day in the hospital, Andretta's mother knew that it was God's grace and favor shining upon her, and she quickly begin to call little Andretta, Ann for short.

Ann was born during a very significant time-period, especially for Black America. During the 1950's, the Civil Rights Movement started and the South quickly became a very heated area of the country. Ensuing from an incident in Topeka, Kansas, The U.S. Supreme Court ruled that legal segregation was unconstitutional, and therefore ruled in favor of Brown vs. The Board of Education. Rosa Parks refused to give up her seat in the colored section of a bus in Montgomery, Alabama sparking the historic Montgomery Bus Boycott. As a result, four African American churches, as well as the homes of Dr. Martin Luther King, Jr. and E.D. Nixon were bombed by four angry whites infuriated over the boycott.

In Mississippi, Emmett Till, the fourteen year old Black boy from Chicago, Illinois was beaten to death for allegedly whistling at a white woman. Nine students became the first Black youth to integrate the Little Rock Central High School and were blocked entry by the National Guard, making it necessary for the intervention of Texan born President Dwight D. Eisenhower to get involved and order Federal Troops to escort them into the school. These students from Little Rock, Arkansas became known as the Little Rock Nine. Around the same time, Dr. King helped to form the Southern Christian Leadership Conference (SCLC) also becoming its first president to lead the fight for civil rights. The Civil Rights Act of 1957 was passed by Congress and The U.S. Commission on Civil Rights was established. The U.S. Department of Justice also began to investigate cases where Blacks were being denied the right to vote.

While in the South things were like an inferno with fighting throughout, the Midwest played their own part in the quest for racial equality. One of the biggest turning points for not only Blacks, but for all people in America also happened in the 1950's. Playing a tremendous role in the racial integration of popular music, Berry Gordy, Jr. founded Motown, a record company that gave rise to many industry greats such as Marv Johnson, Smokey Robinson and The Miracles, Mary Wells, The Marvelettes, Diana Ross and the Supremes, The Jackson 5, The Four Tops, Marvin Gaye, The Temptations, The Spinners, Gladys Knight and The Pips...the list goes on and on.

Along with the emergence of Motown, racial tension and political upheaval were the news of day. All of these factors created an atmosphere where Andretta would have no choice but to become an influential figure herself in world history. So, it was no surprise that the Motown Record Corporation of Detroit would eventually have an amazing impact on her life. In her mother's arms, some eleven hundred miles away in this small town near Tyler, Texas, Ann's destiny was simply waiting for her to walk in.

From her early years onward, she had no problems comprehending sound. Her family was inclined toward music and her rearing was filled with song. Not only was her family big, their bones were big and so were their voices. Dretta's brothers and sisters were very talented but she had something special - an intuitive insight that was so profound she could look at you and tell whether or not you would be a star.

Yet, Ann's father didn't see her in the same light that her mother was able to see her. He was an alcoholic and a gambling man. He may not have been a rolling stone, nor laid his hat in many homes, but there was speculation of another child being born outside of his union with his wife. His problem with drinking and gambling was a major factor and often left the burden on Mrs. Brown to carry. If you couple that with what was going on in the world, it might explain why she had the sort of sense of humor where she could easily make you the brunt of a joke, but never crack a smile. She was a short dark-skinned woman, one of those old throwbacks and Harriet Tubman types who would shoot you if you breathed too loud, then stand on the front porch with a sawed off shotgun in one hand and a Virginia Slim in the other and dare you to say anything. If you asked her a question, it better be a good one, and when she answered, it was right-to-the-point. Small talk was not a part of her modus operandi.

She was firm and you rarely saw her laughing at her home on Troup Highway where she ruled with an iron fist. Ann and her family moved from the top of the hill to the bottom of the hill when Ann was about 12-years of age. It was the same plot of land, just a reconfiguration of the living quarters. Whether it was up the hill or down the hill, it didn't matter. Mrs. Brown didn't play. Her children and grandchildren could tell you, "She was off the chain!" Yet, through her hard shell and somber facial expressions, Mrs. Brown had a soft spot when it came to her Andretta.

THE EARLY YEARS

Growing up Ann loved music, the arts, and nature. She was a very idealistic child and easy to get along with, as long as she was in charge. She enjoyed writing and used it as a way to release her deeper feelings. Although at times, she may have been a difficult child for any other parent to contend with, Mrs. Brown's ability to love her child and give her the necessary freedom through quiet observation went a long way to bringing a smile to both of their faces. Mrs. Brown understood Ann, therefore she was able to effectively balance between protecting her and giving her space in the midst of the countless colorful childhood adventures. Ann was one of few people who made her mother smile, and this is one of the reasons why Mrs. Brown had a deep appreciation for her little Ann.

Time passed by quickly and Ann was beginning to blossom. She learned her way around the kitchen pretty well often helping her mom and older sister. Soon, Ann was in the kitchen cooking and baking on her own, and rather enjoyed it as well.

Ann was always a daydreamer and free spirit; but as she was approaching high school, she was becoming even more active and enthusiastically ambitious. While she had great leadership skills, she could sometimes get a little impatient if anyone tried to interfere with her getting something done. She had that type of personality where she required freedom to move about and as long as you did not get in her way she was cool. Dretta had an incredibly large heart and would do anything in the world for her friends and family. She had no problem making friends, and there was no one that didn't like Andretta Tillman.

It didn't take Ann long to get through the anxieties of transitioning from Junior High to High School. Freshman year breezed by and chides of "fresh-meat" were short-lived. Tyler, Troup, and Whitehouse residents were still celebrating Robert Taylor winning a gold and silver medal at the summer Olympics. He won gold for the 4 x 100 meter relay. It was a proud moment for Tyler residents, especially those who graduated from the Emmett J. Scott High School that closed down two years after Robert graduated. If they could not brag about anything else, they were definitely able to boast of a local Black hero.

Sophomore year went by just as fast. Ann's sister Glenda, who had graduated two years prior, got married to Raymond Stewart. Weddings were a common activity. Whether she was singing or attending, it seemed like there was a wedding every year or every other year, and if it wasn't one of Ann's siblings jumping the broom, it was another family friend.

By her second year in high school, Ann knew for sure that she wanted to go to college and major in Communications placing an emphasis on Television Broadcasting. She had her mind set on evolving into one of the most successful news anchor women of her time. A natural communicator, popularity was a given. Her teachers adored her. Her classmates looked to her for guidance. Her friends followed her example.

Junior year was filled with fond memories, school bus jam sessions, Kittenette practice, and knuckles upside the head. Ann crooned on the bus rides to school. Because of how far apart the houses were, both high school and lower grade students rode the same bus. Ann often had to keep her younger brother Tu Tu in line whenever he acted up. That boy could not keep himself still and at nine years old, he was into everything. She'd yell his name out one time and if he didn't stop she would give him a good whack with her middle finger knuckle over the head, then go right back to singing her song. Tu Tu would always threaten to tell Mrs. Brown, but she didn't pay him any mind. She knew he was a handful. Ann kept many of the younger children on the bus in check, and it was all for the better.

She attended the graduation ceremonies for the class of seventy-five to support some friends that would soon be going off to college. It's funny how things change and how quickly the tables turn. One minute you're getting your locker slammed shut in the freshman hall. The next you are preparing to be the new senior class walking the halls of Whitehouse High School.

Ann drifted off in a daydream as she was listening to the class Alma Mater.

"All hail to Whitehouse High School;
All hail to you.
For truth and knowledge;
We will 'ere be true."

"Always in our memories.
Ever in our hearts.
We will remember;
Dear Whitehouse High.
W-H-S"

James Stewart, Ann's classmate, was sitting next to her and they were waiting for Esterlean and some other people they knew to walk across the stage.

"Hey James, this is going to be us next year."

"I know, Ann. It's hard to believe, right?"

"You know, I was listening to the school song, and I was just thinking. I'm actually looking forward to graduating so I can do my thing."

"You say that now Ann, but next year you gonna be crying like Esterlean."

"Shut up James," Ann said laughing and lightly hitting him. "I ain't no crybaby and I ain't your damn girlfriend! I'mma be partying my ass off all the way to college. Then hit the books."

"If you say so."

"I am going to get my communications degree, and make some real money doin' the news. Ya'll gonna be like, uh, there's Ann. I am going to have my shit together."

"I believe you."

"And you can go on and fix cars or whatever the hell you gonna do," she said laughing. "But it's all good."

"Hey Ann, here comes Esterlean."

Ann and James stood up as Esterlean's name was called. There were several people graduating that Ann knew, but she mainly showed up because of her friendship with James and Esterlean. Ann and Esterlean were in some of the same school activities.

"Hey Ann, what are you going to do after this?"

"I'm going home, James. What were you and Esterlean thinking about doing?"

"Some of them are talking about a graduation party. I am not too sure about the details. I think they are talking about hooking up with some of the others from Tyler."

"Well, I'm just gonna go home. We still have another week of school left so I guess I'll see you on Monday."

"Alright Ann, see ya later."

The last week of junior year was uneventful, but thought-evoking for Ann. She cleared her locker out and walked the junior halls in much anticipation and reflection. She had finally made it to her last year of high school. Ann knew that senior year would be very different. Before, she was very focused on her grades and had been somewhat disinterested in boys.

Ann was athletic, on the drill team and cheerleading squad, and very active overall, but she wasn't necessarily one who primped or vied for the attention of boys. She was just like one of the guys or one of the girls. No one was threatened by her. She could get along with anybody. Although she had a great build, she didn't make ado about stuff like the Miss Brick House contest. James' younger twin sisters on the other hand grabbed that title every time. It was at the end of her junior year when Ann started to look at things a little differently and pay more attention to her feminine side.

School finally let out and summer break was a welcomed arrival. Yet, Dretta still had to pull out a can of whoop ass on Tu Tu. That boy was hard-headed. She stayed on him and pretty much kept him out of trouble the entire summer. Between July and August, she was busy with cheerleading camps and drill team practices. She occasionally hung out at Lincoln Park with some of the other teenagers. Everybody she knew had a boyfriend or girlfriend. Yet, she wasn't dating anyone and it didn't seem like there was a boy in sight that was even a potential. Ann was often a third or fifth wheel. To Ann's group of friends that didn't matter because Ann was fun to be around, plus they were all friends. She always gave great advice and was honest about it. She didn't sugar-coat anything, but was sensitive to the feelings of others.

Ann was a lot more mature in her thinking than a lot of teenagers her age. She could fit in with just about any group, but she often held deep emotions inside. For her it wasn't all about partying and the guys. She didn't look at boys her age that way. She was close to her mom, and she spent a lot of time in church and singing in the choir. On many occasions you could catch her humming along to the song Mrs. Brown often played, "Oh, Happy Day." Ann helped a lot with the housework and preparing meals. On Sundays at the Brown's home, there were large dinners. After church, they ate like nobody's business and

Ann's brothers and sisters who were married and had already moved out would make their way over. The family gathered around singing, eating, laughing, and talking.

Summer finally came to a close. Ann was ready for summer to be over and for school to start. She knew that the sooner she faced her senior year, the sooner she could graduate and get on with her life. The last big jam before school started back was Glenda's twenty-first birthday. Come September, school would be back in session and Ann would finally have her turn walking down senior lane.

It was the morning of the first day of class. Whitehouse Wildcats here she comes. Ann spent this morning like no other morning – primping. She was determined to show a feminine side of herself. She insisted that this year she will actually go out on a date. Last year there were several hook-ups on Saturday nights at the Starlight or Apache Theatres; however Ann would occasionally go with her friend Brenda, James and some of the others teens in Whitehouse.

As previously mentioned, Whitehouse, Texas was filled with large families, but the main ones were the Browns, the Stewarts, and the Pettigrews. Of course there were the Bowies too and they were right up there with the other large families. Brenda was a Pettigrew. She and Ann had been best friends since sophomore year. James is a Stewart. The Stewarts and the Pettigrews are related.

During her earlier high school years, Ann was sort of tall and awkward looking. In photos you would notice her, but she was often the one slouching when standing next to girls who were shorter than she was. Ann stood close to six feet tall, yet was a very shapely young woman. She had what many would refer to as big bones. In the past, Ann didn't focus much on her physical attributes.

"Mom, I'm out the door."

"Alright."

Ann went into the kitchen to give her mom a hug and kiss on the forehead. Mrs. Brown was sitting at the table, smoking a cigarette and having a cup of coffee. Her mother looked at her and gave her a funny look.

"Who are you trying to impress?"

Ann looked at her mom and smiled. "What do you mean?"

"Look at you. You're apparently trying to get somebody's attention?"

Ann chuckled, hesitated a moment, then twisted in front of her mother. "My future husband."

"Get your little fast tail ass on out of here girl."

"Yep!"

Ann's mother was in no way worried about Ann and boys, at least not yet. She had not seen anyone hanging around calling themselves liking her and Ann didn't even talk about anyone that she even remotely liked in that way.

"No baby you look fine. Have a good first day."

"See you mom, love you. I'm out!"

"Okay baby."

Ann left the house in a pair of low cut jeans fitting her like a glove and a colorful blouse. Her outfit accentuated her full curves. Her big afro was well shaped and complemented by a pair of hoop earrings. This was definitely a different showing than last year and the years before.

The bus arrived at school. Ann looked forward to her chance to finally walk down senior hall. Only a few years ago many of the students were saying hello for the first time to who started out as strangers. Now in a few short months, they will be saying goodbye to some really great friends. Alas, Ann was now at the top and at once able to claim the privileges of being a senior. Her dreams were closer in sight and in no way felt like a dream but more rather her reality just beginning to take shape. There was no one else to look up to. She was one of the upperclassman that all others would see as their examples. She was a senior! As they say – the shit.

As Ann would soon be preparing to graduate from Whitehouse High School, her younger sister Arvonette would be making her first marks as a freshman. It seemed like as one Brown graduated another followed right behind. Mrs. Brown was proud of her children, all of whom were pretty active in school. Between church, home, and school she kept them busy. "An idle mind is the devil's workshop," was Mrs. Brown's motto. "So I'mma keep their little asses busy!" She was not like old Mother Hubbard who had so many children she didn't know what to do. Mrs. Brown, who most of the children referred to as Buck, probably because all the bullshit stopped right there, handled her business.

She often was mama and daddy because Jimmie Brown was a, "drunk-ass fool." There were many-a-times when you would hear Mrs. Brown saying, "Jimmie get your drunken ass up and go to bed!" The buck stops here is one of the sayings that President Truman made popular to assert that he would take responsibility for governing the country and not pass that responsibility to others. However, it didn't quite mean that for the Brown family, I'm sure. Whether it was meant as a spoof on Buck Rogers or an acceptance of "you can't get anything past mama," all of Mrs. Brown's children understood one point - "don't cross Buck, because she will whoop your ass!"

Ann's mother did not have to worry about whether or not she would stay busy. Ann was involved in many extracurricular activities. She was on the drill team, in Future Teachers of America, church choir, singing at weddings, and a whole list of other activities that kept her hands full and mind occupied. On top of that she had good friends who for the most part stayed out of trouble. Ann didn't worry about boys. The ones she knew were like brothers anyway. She couldn't even think about "doing it" with any of them. Some people might be okay with kissing cousins, but not Andretta Tillman. She was not interested in mixing things up like that.

Ann had always put books before boys, but she wanted to at least meet someone that she could say was her boyfriend. As she looked at her schedule, it was a good combination of core and electives. Ann slammed her locker shut and headed quickly toward first period. As she was making her way down the hall, someone behind her yelled out, "Dang! Do that!"

Ann turned to see who it was. There she saw walking a good distance behind her was a tall, slender, good-looking Black student wearing a checkered blue and white shirt and a pair of slacks. He had a little swag to him. Ann looked at him and smiled coyly. She realized as he got closer that it was Ruben Hill.

"4-sho." Then turned back around and ran off to class.

"Oh, it's like that huh?"

"Yep, gotta get to class."

"You just gonna blow me off like that!"

"Catch you on the rebound. Gotta go."

The warning bell rang. "Shit!"

Ann took off quickly to make it to her class on time. Being late was not the first impression that she wanted to make with her teachers. She didn't like to be disruptive and had a pet peeve about being late. Just as she sat in her seat, the teacher walked in and the final bell rang. Ann was a good student and most of her teachers favored her. She was respectful in class, was always prepared, and took responsibility to turn in quality work. Ann was a leader. Senior year would prove to be no different in that regard.

The first day of school was about meeting the teachers, seeing who was in what classes and gearing up to start an amazing year. Ann was sitting in Teacher Occupations Class with Brenda laughing, talking, and comparing notes from the day. They were in several classes together this year. When the two of them get together, they can talk for hours.

"Girl, you know Ruben is crazy."

"What did he do?"

"He wasn't even smooth about it either."

"Tell me."

"I was running trying to get to class and at first I didn't know it was him. He was …"

Just as Ann and Brenda were getting into their conversation the teacher started doing an attendance call. "Carnell Beasley, Marva Beasley, Gaye Bowie, Andretta Brown…"

"Here."

"Dorothy Caldwell… Karen Holt…Rosie Lottin, Dorothy Mackey, Thelma Mitchell, Beverly Pettigrew, Brenda Pettigrew…"

"Yes, I'm here."

"Glenda Pettigrew…James Stewart, Kaye Stewart…"

Ann and Brenda were sitting next to each other. Ann looked around then whispered something to Brenda and they both started laughing quietly.

"There sure are a lot of Black folks in here."

Then they continue to laugh even more.

Some of the students were just looking around at each other as the teacher continued doing roll call. She was reading off the names on her list but never looked up.

"Charlene Reed, Susie Shaddox, Trina Stephenson, Patsy Swindle…"

There were repeated echoes of "here, present, or yes." Finally most students were accounted for. You could tell by the group in the room that it would be a pretty lively class. The students in this class were also members of a national organization called Future Teachers of America

(FTA). This was a national organization that provided many of the students the opportunities related to the teaching profession. The class was an avenue that provided senior students the chance to grow their experiences through local projects, service projects, monthly programs and participation in district and state conventions. There were not too many strangers in the class or the senior chapter of FTA. Pretty much it was the same group of kids. They were well acquainted with one another already.

During the school day, Ann realized that there were some very familiar faces. Some she knew, some she only heard of, and others she didn't know at all. Either way, she was content with her classes and was happy to see that she had close friends in most of them. She continued to see Brenda throughout the day.

Ann's best friend Brenda was somewhat tall, but not quite as tall as Ann. She had brown paper-bag colored skin, the complexion that might barely make it through the Jack and Jill Club. However her nappy hair would raise a few questions.

"Girl, my black ass wouldn't be allowed to walk on the same street they were having one of those ca-tilly ons..." This is the kind of thing Ann would say.

"Hell, I gotta mama they call Buck with a bunch of damn kids as dark as the ace of spade. My daddy gets so pissy drunk, you got to lead his drunk-ass to the toilet so he don't piss all over the place. What would we look like waltzing up there being all high and mighty?"

Ann and Brenda could find just about anything to laugh at and or poke fun about. Ann was a tough cookie and didn't take things so seriously. She had a great sense of humor and knew how to laugh and have fun. Brenda on the other hand was a little more on the sensitive side. She had squinty eyes and big teeth. They didn't stick out, they were just big. She was athletic, but pretty. She was a cool person to be around and a very good friend to Ann.

Between football games, basketball games, parades, and their social calendars, there was always somewhere to be. As the school year progressed, both Ann and Brenda's schedule became very hectic with their school commitments and extracurricular activities. Football season was coming to a close and everyone was preparing for the big game and the homecoming dance. Dress up days, maroon/white days and pranks - there was hardly a student not showing some sign of school spirit. It was already the week of homecoming and things were hopping at WHS.

Several students and faculty members were helping to gather wood for the bon fire that was scheduled for Thursday night. Brenda was nominated for homecoming queen, and of course Ann was one of her biggest cheerleaders. As students walked the halls of WHS you could

The Making of a Child of Destiny

see the spirit building. Carnell, Lawrence Williams, and Terry Bowie were hyped up for Friday's game.

Hump day passed, the bon fire went over without a glitch, and Friday morning the gymnasium was packed with students from all four years cheering on the Wildcats! "Go Wildcats go!" Willie Wildcat made his appearance and the students waved school banners and their signs created especially for the game.

Whitehouse's homecoming queen was to be crowned before the game and at half time the band and drill team would perform. As people were taking their seats in the stands, Brenda was getting geared up to see what the outcome of homecoming queen would be.

"You ready, Brenda?"

"Yes! How do I look?"

"Great!"

"Okay, here goes."

The bull horn sounded and the nominees for Whitehouse homecoming queen ran out to the field. All you could hear was whistling, cheering and a whole lot of noise. Ann was on the sidelines in her drill team uniform watching Brenda. Then the moment had arrived…

"The Whitehouse High School nineteen seventy-five, seventy-six homecoming queen is…"

The drums rolled and Brenda's knees were shaking. Ann was nervous for Brenda.

"The nineteen seventy-five, seventy-six Whitehouse homecoming queen is…Jana Harbeson."

Brenda was not voted the homecoming queen, but she was a part of the court along with another white girl named Christy Cole. You couldn't tell who was more disappointed – Ann or Brenda. When she came back from off of the court, Brenda could see that Ann was pissed off.

"You know, I don't get it."

"What do you mean?"

"See first of all, Brenda you lucky you my friend. Because what I really wanted to do was go out there and snatch that crown and sash off her ass."

"Ann you are crazy."

"No! See this is what I really don't get. Whitehouse can have Black and white every damn thing else, but when it comes to homecoming queen, there's only one, and some white bitch is always winning."

"I wondered that too."

"See that's some racist ass shit to me Brenda, and you know it. What! Ain't no Black good enough to win homecoming queen?"

"I hear you Ann."

"Shit! Bullshit!"

Brenda was in band and Ann was on the drill team. During the half time of the homecoming game, both Ann and Brenda performed. It was a great game. Afterwards many of the Black students started to congregate at different places. The next day Brenda was escorted to the homecoming dance by James where they announced the queen and her court. Several students went to the dance not with any specific date, but in groups. Ann was one of those students.

Homecoming came and went, the Tyler Rose Festival was a blast and the Whitehouse High School Band and drill team took part in the Rose Parade. WHS band ended up winning a trophy for outstanding band in the AA Class. They also won outstanding Drum Major and Outstanding Majorette Line. The school hosted the nineteen seventy-five, seventy-six regional twirling competition. Whitehouse High School was putting WHS on the map with back-to-back wins. The band received the highest possible rating at the Regional IV University Interscholastic League Marching Contest.

The girl's varsity basketball team came in first in the district, and the junior varsity team tied for first in the district and won the title of 14 AA Co-Champs. Brenda and her sister Beverly both played on the varsity basketball team. Brenda was number forty and played guard. Her younger sister who was only a sophomore wore number thirty-one and was an all-district guard. Brenda would always complain to Ann about how tough Coach Button was, but it paid off in the end and the memories created were all-in-all some really great ones. Ann could remember games and losing her voice screaming for the Wildcats.

"Hustle Marva! Rebound, Linda!"

All of the girls on the basketball team were good players. Wanda Taylor, Dorothy Mackey, and Linda Richardson were each all-district forwards. Even the non-starting players were good enough to start. Ann frequently demonstrated school spirit and was very supportive of school activities and her classmates. But, you could see a streak of her mother come out of her when things weren't quite right or fair.

The weather in Texas was not as drastic as in the Midwest. Whitehouse didn't see all four seasons. So although Christmas was right around the corner, the Kittenettes and the Majorettes didn't have to worry about sub-zero temperatures and snow during their performance in the Whitehouse Parade that took place every December. Those dreaming of a white Christmas in this area of the country were better off packing it up and going somewhere North.

Ann loved Christmas time. The Brown family was not big on a lot of gifts because they couldn't afford it. A pair of socks to go with their new shoes about summed up what the modest Christmas tree would be surrounded by. The highlight of Christmas was the meal and Buck's deep fried turkey. The Brown family ate until it hurt, and New Years was more of the same.

Just like Christmas, New Year's was a family affair. As the year nineteen seventy-six crept in, celebrations were round and about. The entire Brown family gathered that Thursday at Mr. and Mrs. Brown's for dinner and another opportunity to partake of that famous turkey. There was always more than one prepared. It had to be because of the size of the family. There is no turkey like Texas turkey. It's the tenderest turkey one could eat. Everyone pretty much chipped in to cook and created a spread with all the holiday trimmings.

December and January was a favorite time of the year for many of the families in Whitehouse. So each year as it comes and goes, there is a little melancholy that soon followed the close of one year and the beginning of another. In a twinkling of an eye and hardly before the bridge in Silent Night sung by the carolers singing their songs of joy, all of the Christmas decorations and beautiful lights on Broadway Street were replaced with cupid and his bow and arrow and petitions of "Be My Valentine." Songs like I Saw Mommy Kissing Santa Clause were quickly usurped by the sweet sounds of Sam Cook.

"Cupid, draw back your bow, and let your arrow go, straight to my lover's heart for me…" Then those were replaced with a more heightened sense of spiritual awareness and the preparations for various church revivals. The cycle repeated year-after-year. The stores reflected the changing seasons, even if the weather did not.

By now the holidays had long gone, and the weather was great as New Canaan Baptist Church Choir made their way to a church revival in East Texas. There were several churches in attendance. Ann sang a solo and threw down. She sang her butt off. The spirit of the Lord was upon the place and it was on fire as she sang "I'm Going Up a Yonder." No one could say that God wasn't moving that day in Texas.

There were hours of singing, preaching and Holy Ghost spirit. Then after the service the congregation gathered and socialized afterwards for several more hours. The church was packed. Children were running around and members of various churches were intermingling and just having a good 'ole time. Ann had just finished talking with one of the other choir members and was on her way downstairs where the food was being served, when she was unexpectedly approached by someone she didn't recognize.

"Hi, there, how are you? I must say you have a voice like an angel."

Ann turned around to see who was talking to her. As she looked up, standing in front of her was this six feet, two inches tall, about two-hundred, thirty pound fine

Black man with a sexy voice. He was wearing a brown double breasted suit and a killer pair of Stacy Adams. Staring at him from head to toe, when she looked up again she had to clear her throat and blink her eyes to make sure it wasn't a dream. She thought to herself, "Lord thank you for beautiful Black men, damn he's fine. Ooh Father forgive me… In the name of the father, the son, and the Holy Ghost…"

It must have seemed like an eternity before she could get her composure to realize that he actually had said something to her. While she was getting herself together, the man just looked at her and smiled. That of course made Ann even more nervous to say the least. However, she did finally manage to respond.

"Oh, uh, thank you. That is very nice for you to say."

"No really. You have a beautiful voice."

This man who Ann had never seen before in her life was flanked in front of her as if he belonged there and was making it be known that where he stood was his territory. His boldness was what was blowing Ann's mind. His carriage gave her the impression that there was more behind his words. The way his eyes penetrated hers had her flustered and at a lost for words. For someone who had always been self-assured, Ann didn't know what to do with herself. For a moment she thought she was going to "pee her pants."

Ann kept shifting back and forth, and it was apparent that she was nervous. She was trying to figure out what to say to break the silence when he spoke up again.

"I'm Dwight…Dwight Tillman."

"Hi, Dwight Tillman, it's very nice to meet you."

Ann just continued to smile, looking very awkward and feeling out-of-place. She was not sure what else to say. Her silence, which appeared to her to be an eternity, was almost unbearable. She could feel herself heating up from embarrassment.

"Does the voice have a name that comes with it?"

"Oh, yes, I am so sorry. My name is Andretta."

"Well Andretta, that's a nice name and I think you just saved my soul."

Ann burst into this loud nervous laugh. Some of the other people, who were gathered in their social circles talking, stopped and looked over at Ann and Dwight. He didn't flinch, but Ann shrunk down a little and said softly, "Sorry."

Dwight took his tongue and his teeth over his bottom lip and continued to stare deeply at Ann. Although no one was really paying either of them any attention after the initial outburst, for Ann everything seemed so big and overwhelming as if everyone were watching them.

"Ok I've heard it all now! That one threw me. Tell me, how did I save your soul?"

"Lawd have mercy girl, you can sang!"

They both started laughing. It was apparent that there was a connection. As they talked more, Ann began to relax and came back to her self. They walked downstairs to where the food was being served and continued their conversation. People walked up said hello, some hugged Ann or shook Dwight's hand and left them to it. Dwight's sense of humor was refreshing and it made Ann feel right at home with him.

"Why haven't I seen you before?"

He looked at Ann and smiled. "I don't know, why haven't you? You tell me."

"Stop playing with me. Where are you from?"

"Troup. Where are you from?"

"Whitehouse."

"So if you are in Whitehouse and I live in Troup, then why don't we know each other?"

As Dwight toyed with Ann, they both laughed at the playful exchange. He was smooth and laid back with his approach. Yet, Ann continued to try to get her composure. She knew she wanted to meet someone, but she did not envision it happening like that way.

"So what does Andretta do?"

"What do you mean what do I do? I go to school."

"Tyler Junior College?"

Ann looked at Dwight with wide eyes. "No, Whitehouse."

"Stop playing."

"I'm not!"

"No way, you're kidding, right?"

"No for real. I'm a senior at Whitehouse High School." Ann said smiling.

"You tryin' to get me in trouble."

Dwight could not believe that Ann was still in high school. She carried herself with a little more maturity and he could not imagine that she was not his age.

"What do you mean I'm tryin' to get you in trouble? What is it that you do, Mr. Tillman?"

"I go to school too."

"Where?"

"You really wanna know?"

"Yeah, I do."

"Prairie View."

"Prairie View A & M University?"

"Yep!"

"Wow! A college man, huh? What year are you?"

"A junior."

As Ann and Dwight continued talking, they learned a lot about each other. The more they talked the smaller the age gap became between the two of them. The chemistry was definitely there. After a little while, some of the churches were beginning to leave and the crowd was dwindling down. Ann was waiting on many of her choir members and they didn't look like they were ready to go anytime soon, so she and Dwight continued to talk.

"What is your major?"

"Education. I'll probably be a teacher or something. You know my dad is the sheriff in Troup, but my mom is a teacher. So I guess they expect me to teach or something."

"Is that what you want to do?"

"Well…"

"Honestly, is that what you want to do?"

"For real?"

"Yes, for real."

"Well what I really want to do is music. I want to be like Berry Gordy. You know give others the opportunity who can sing, a chance to shine. I want to have several acts that I manage…make some real money you know?"

"Wow, that's good. So why don't you?"

"Cause I need help."

"You will get the help Dwight, just start working on it."

Dwight looked at Ann and smiled. "I'm working on it now."

Before Ann had a chance to respond, her sister came up to her to see if she was ready to go. Ann and Dwight exchanged telephone numbers. He mentioned to her that maybe they should hook up soon. Ann agreed and then she left.

WHEN LOVE CALLS

After Ann left the church, Dwight just stood there smiling and shaking his head. He then headed out the door. He was on spring break from school and had another week before classes resumed. After the current semester, Dwight had only two more semesters to go before graduation. He was scheduled to graduate in May of the following year. Therefore, as long as he did what he needed to do, he would be among Prairie View A&M University's May graduating class of nineteen seventy-seven.

Dwight was at the phase of his college matriculation process where he needed to seriously consider lining up a job that would be able to support him and eventually a family. He wanted to get married at some point in his life and those thoughts would every now and again cross his mind. Although he dated a few girls off and on in high school, there was nothing really serious; plus no one ever seemed to measure up to his parents' expectations.

Although Dwight was moving in the direction of a teaching career, he was also set on following his passion for music. He realized though that because of R.J. and

Wanda Marie Tillman's strict upbringing and their deep interest in his decisions where his career was concerned, that he would have to be careful in terms of how he went about following his dream. His father was no-nonsense, a man-of-steel character who rarely showed emotions. He definitely wore the pants in his household. His mother, a very petite woman, was able to present a more dignified and cultured demeanor. She was a very likeable math teacher and woman of civic responsibilities. Education was very important to Dwight's parents. There was never the option of not going to college, it was always just a matter of where. When it came to dreams, to his parents, they better make logical sense. Music, no matter how much you loved it, was something to enjoy during your pastime. It was not a sensible career choice.

Prairie View A & M University, an HBCU (Historically Black College/University) was almost two hundred miles away from Tyler, Texas. For education, Dwight could not have picked a better school. He played both basketball and football in high school, but as a promising running back and line backer on defense for Troup High, he actually attended college on a football scholarship. While his parents were extremely proud of his athletic abilities and anyone who walked into the Tillman household would see both his and his brother's medals and trophies spread across the mantel, Dwight also excelled academically. He was a member of the Honor Society, on the yearbook staff and was voted Mr. Troup High School. He was a letterman and jock to say the least and he and his brother Keith were two very sought after young men in Troup, Texas. They were of good stock as many would say.

Dwight's athletic performance was equally impressive in college until an ear surgery ended his college football career, and the option for him to play pro football. Impact to his ear would be too risky, so he had to give it up. Funding the rest of his college education was not necessarily a hardship for his parents. Between Dwight's academics and his parents' careful planning of the children's college education, he was able to continue his schooling at Prairie View without the football scholarship.

Unlike the Browns, the Tillmans were a very affluent family in Troup. Mr. Tillman worked for the Texas Highway Department and was the Mayor Pro Tem for the city. As a matter of fact he was the first Black man to hold such a position there. Mr. and Mrs. Tillman only had two mouths to feed, so their expendable income was far greater than Mr. and Mrs. Brown's. Also, not to mention, the Tillmans were much more fiscally responsible. Jimmie Brown's gambling was a major issue and often put the

Brown family in financial upheavals. The hopes of winning big often came with very little reward.

No matter what class you place the Tillman family or the Brown family in among the Southern Negro families, one thing for sure was that both had great kids. Thus, Ann was not defined by her parents, her station, or her societal class. She made her own mark from the way she lived her life. As was Dwight, she was highly respected among her peers. There was no such thing as someone being better than her; and she uncompromisingly carried herself with that sort of air.

After Ann returned from the revival that Saturday night and after church services at New Canaan on Sunday, many of the family members as usual gathered over at the house. Mary Jo and Glenda were sitting on the couch. Ann asked her sisters if they had heard of any Tillmans in Troup, Texas.

"Do either of you know any Tillmans that went to Troup High School?"

"Why, was that who you were talking to last night?"

"Yeah. I was just curious."

"I've heard of some Tillmans. I think some are around my age, but I'm not sure though."

"Huhm. Okay. What about you May Jo?"

"I think I do remember a Curtis Tillman who used to play football. I think he was all-state or something. Wait! I think I do remember hearing about a Keith Tillman too. I'm almost sure one of them graduated the same year as me or the year after."

"What about a Dwight."

"No, Dwight doesn't ring a bell. But like I said Keith or Curtis does. But Dwight…Uh Uh…That name doesn't sound familiar."

"Is that the name of the guy you were talking to at the church?" Glenda asked.

"Yes, his name is Dwight Tillman."

"Oh, okay, well he's cute anyway. Did you see him May Jo?"

"No, I was fooling around with…what's her name…you know…oh hell anyway, no I didn't see him. What he look like?"

"He's real cute. He was tall and very clean cut. When I saw him and Ann talking I was like, okey-dokey then."

"He must be a lot younger than Curtis then."

"I'm not sure. But he told me he goes to Prairie View now…He's a junior."

"Let me see. If he's a junior then he must be around mine or Mop's age."

"That's true May Jo, yeah…then…he would be close to our age."

"What…Are you interested in him or something?"

"It would be like you to ask that Mop."

"Well, hell, I'm just cuttin' through the chase, Ann. When me and Raymond started talking…shit…" Glenda chuckled as Ann was gearing up to respond.

"I don't know, he just came up to me…he was smooth though, telling me that I had a nice voice."

"Yeah, he was smooth. I give him that. I saw him when he was heading your way."

"Maybe he just really liked my voice, like he said."

Mary Jo cut across Glenda talking and quickly chimed in when Ann made that comment. She could not believe that Ann was being as naïve as she was.

"Did he ask you for your number?"

"Yes, we exchanged numbers."

"Then let me give you the skinney little sister, he is digging you!"

"Really?"

"Really!"

"Uhm, okay if you say so."

"Ann, do you know when a guy is interested in you?"

"Girl, Ann ain't had no boy interested in her. She's still a virgin."

The Making of a Child of Destiny

"Shut up May Jo!"

"Well..."

"Well what?"

"Nothin' I'm just sayin'..."

Glenda was much more settled than Mary Jo, but of course she had already been married for two years. Mary Jo was still having a good time and attending Tyler Junior College (TJC). There was a vast difference between Glenda's and Mary Jo's conversation.

"Ann, now you know college boys are interested in more than just holding hands, right?"

"How do you know he is even like that?"

Mary Jo could not help her self. She is always very blunt and sarcastic. She talks a lot too. Glenda was not able to sensibly converse with Ann without Mary Jo butting in and stating something crass or laced with some sort of bias.

"Trust me; they all are like that..."

"What May Jo is saying, Ann, is that because he is older, he has probably had more experiences and even though there is really not a big age difference between the two of you, he would maybe expect more to happen in a dating situation other than first base."

"That's not what I'm saying...What I'm sayin' is..."

Mary Jo continued speaking through her laughter.

"See what I'm saying is, he just don't want to hear your voice…he wanna feel tha funk."

"May Jo, why you gotta always take things to the max?. Ann don't pay any attention to your crazy sister."

Mary Jo stood up and started gyrating, shaking her butt and dancing with her lips puckered up as she was teasing Glenda and Ann.

"Shut up Mop you know you and Raymond got on the good foot! I don't know whatcha talking about…And I don't mean dancin' either."

They all started laughing. Mary Jo was still clowning as Buck walked in the room.

"What are ya'll laughing about?"

Mary Jo got up and danced her way out the room while wiggling her fingers toward Ann and Glenda.

"May the force be with you…"

Glenda and Ann fell out laughing. Mrs. Brown just stood there without cracking a smile, rolled her eyes up in her head, and then repeated her question with a little more force.

"What are ya'll laughing about?"

"May Jo being silly because Ann met someone."

"What do you mean Ann met someone?"

"She met some dude at the revival."

"Oh, well hell it's about time…I was startin' to get worried."

"What's that supposed to mean mama?" Ann said surprisingly.

"Just what I said…"

Once Buck said what she said, she walked out of the room eating her piece of chicken.

Ann dug Dwight. She thought he was a pretty cool cat. She was unable to keep herself from thinking about him. She knew he was going back to school the following weekend and really wanted to see him again, but she dare not call him. It just didn't seem right for her to be the one calling. So she anxiously waited for him to call. In school Monday morning, she couldn't wait to tell Brenda.

"Girl guess what?"

"What?"

"I met this dude from Troup this weekend."

"Shut up!"

"No for real."

"Is he fine?"

"Uhm Huh." Ann said smiling.

"Is he real fine?"

"Yep."

Brenda wanted all the details of Ann meeting Dwight. So Ann shared the story from beginning to end. They laughed and talked about all of the possibilities this meeting could have.

"Ann, tell me this…if you and Dwight got together, would it be like the Jeffersons or like Good Times?"

"Let's see…Oh naw girl…Hell yeah! I'll be movin' on up!"

They both laughed and headed to class. Ann was not able to concentrate the entire day. She was thinking about Dwight and trying to paint an image of him in her mind to keep a recollection of what he looked like, of what he smelled like, and how he looked into her eyes. She only saw him the one time, but she was smitten over him and wanted to get to know more about him. She was hopeful that he felt the same way.

Tuesday went by and still no call from Dwight. Ann kept picking up their old black rotary dial phone to see if there was a dial tone. Every time the phone rang, she would stand there in anticipation hoping it was him. Wednesday came, but still no Dwight. Ann was set on not calling him. Everyday Brenda asked if Dwight had called.

Thursday morning in English class, Brenda as usual asked Ann about Dwight.

"Has he called yet?"

"Nope, not yet."

"He will, don't worry."

"I hope you're right."

"If he doesn't it's his loss, anyway."

"Nu uh girl, it would most definitely be my loss…He is too fine."

Ann just shook her head and said, "Uhm Uhm Uhm…Whooh…"

They both giggled like the two teenagers they were.

Thursday after school, Ann and Brenda went to a home softball game. When Ann finally reached home it was somewhere around six o'clock in the evening. As she walked in the door, Mrs. Brown told her nonchalantly somebody named Dwight called but that he said he would call back.

"Damn!"

"What you say girl."

"Nothin' mama."

"Dwight's that boy you met at church that ya'll was talking about in there the other day?"

"Yes, ma'am."

"Uh, huhm. I spoke to him."

Mrs. Brown sucked her teeth and walked out of the room.

Ann immediately got on the phone and called Brenda to let her know that he had called.

"Girl he called."

"What he say?"

"I don't know I didn't speak with him. Mama told me when I got in."

"So then call him back."

"She said he was going to call back later."

"Well, now you know he is going to call, so you don't have to worry about it."

"I'll let you know when he calls back. But I'm gettin' off the phone so I don't miss him."

"Okay, see you tomorrow at school."

"Alright bye."

Then she hung up the telephone.

Ann had a math assignment that she needed to get done, so she went to her room to get started. Before she was even half way through she heard the phone ringing. She went flying down the stairs to grab the phone. It rang several times. "Somebody get the phone," yelled Mrs. Brown from another room. Tu Tu and Ann ran to the phone, but before she could get to it, he raced by and then answered it.

"Move boy, it ain't for you!"

"No! It ain't for you either."

Tu Tu stuck his tongue out at Ann then greeted the person on the other end of the line.

"Hello."

"May I speak to Andretta, please?"

"Who is this?"

Ann yelled at Tu Tu in the background. "Give me the phone Tu Tu!"

"Who is this…"

Ann snatched the phone out of her little brother's hand and he started teasing and mocking her. "Ann's gotta boyfriend…Ann's gotta boyfriend…"

Ann popped Tu Tu upside the head and left him yelling for Mrs. Brown who was walking out from the other room. She rolled her eyes at Tu Tu.

"Boy, stop makin' all that damn noise. Ain't nobody hurtin' you! Keep on or I'mma give you sumthin' to cry about!"

Ann finally turned her attention back to the phone call while Mrs. Brown shooed Tu Tu in the other room. That damn Tu Tu got his ass whooped all the time.

"Hello?"

"Hi, may I speak to Andretta?"

Ann immediately recognized that the voice on the other end of the line was that of Dwight. She started getting butterflies in her stomach as soon as she heard that sexy voice again.

"This is Andretta speaking."

"Do you know who this is?"

"Of course I know who it is," she said smiling.

"Can I see…?"

Before Dwight could even get the rest of his sentence out Ann responded.

"Yes. Where?"

"Some of my friends were telling me about this party happening on Saturday at some dude name Skipper's house."

"I know Skipper. He always throws the big house parties."

"Yeah that's him. Well there's a party at his house Saturday night. Can you go?"

"Hell yeah!"

Dwight gave a smooth, sexy laugh.

"Okay then, well let's meet up there and maybe afterwards we can find something else to do."

"What time are you going to be there?"

"About eight or eight-thirty."

"Okay, see you there."

They hung up. Ann started jumping up and down in excitement. She started dancing as she exclaimed, "I'm going to a party! I'm going to a party!"

She danced on back up stairs to finish her math homework.

Friday at school, Ann told Brenda all about her plans for Saturday hoping that she would be able to go out with her. She hadn't gone to one of his parties, but she thought maybe Mary Jo had gone to one or two in the past. She had always heard that Skipper threw great parties and it was the "It" place to go. Ann didn't care about the party; she was more interested in seeing Dwight.

The Making of a Child of Destiny

Tyler, Troup, and Whitehouse folks all hung out at the same places, so it was no surprise that when Ann walked into the party Saturday evening that she saw a lot of people she knew or knew of. As she, Brenda, and James walked in, she looked around to see if she noticed Dwight. He must not have been there yet. James went over to some guy he saw and they started talking. Ann and Brenda stood over in a corner up against the wall and just watched others. The party was live. You could tell that most of the people there had either graduated last year or the year before because they appeared a little older. There were some high school seniors from Tyler that Ann recognized, but not many.

Ann positioned herself where she could see the door and the room. She wanted to spot Dwight before he saw her. As she and Brenda were standing up against the wall several guys were looking over at them. Ann was wearing a pair of bell-bottomed denim jeans with a macramé tied belt and a matching short denim jacket. Underneath she had on a tight white top. The jeans looked like they had been poured on her and the only way to take them off was to peel them away from her skin. Tight jeans and hip huggers were very common among the teenagers in Ann's day.

Brenda and Ann continued to talk while periodically looking around to spot Dwight. Although Brenda didn't know what he looked like, Ann gave her a description so maybe she could spot him or someone who seemed as if they were looking for someone. Dwight came in somewhere from the back of the house so naturally Ann did not see him because she was looking at the front door and occasionally around the room. Where he stood allowed him to see her, but she couldn't see him.

As Dwight stood there just watching her, he smiled almost laughing as he was observing her talk and laugh and look around the room. It was somewhat dark in the house, but where Dwight was standing it was even darker. There was no way that Ann could see him. Dwight was sure of himself at the church, but for some reason here at the party he was not as self-assured. As he looked at Ann, he realized just how beautiful she was. Dwight loves dark, athletic women and Ann was certainly that and more.

To behold her loveliness and beauty was like a dream come true. For the first time in his life he truly felt that he was looking at a real Nubian Princess, who just might actually become his queen. Although Ann had a worldly edge, she in fact was innocent, inexperienced, and refreshingly naïve. Dwight was able to pick that up as he looked on, and that is what took his breath away.

Everyone has dreams, and high school often is the place to begin preparing for life's wonderful journey and the first step to laying a solid foundation to making those dreams a reality. Yet, for Ann and Dwight, they had to discover what dreams lie ahead as the two very different lives and births intersected at one chance meeting in time. For all intended purposes Dwight decided at the last minute to attend the service in East Texas only by suggestion of a fellow Troup High alumnus. He never even showed up, but Dwight did and a rosebud was carefully planted waiting for him to notice.

In the "Rose Capital of the World," this statuesque, graceful vision of beauty, love, and compassion was a rose like no other rose. How could he not notice her? The way she carried herself, the way she looked, and her bright and luminous smile was enough to make him believe that it would never rain. As long as he could be blessed with the presence of her beauty even only as an onlooker, the sun perhaps would always continue to shine.

Dwight stared at Ann for about ten minutes before making his presence known. He was hypnotized by her big beautiful brown round eyes that kept calling out to him, "Come, come!" Of course, he knew that this was only in his mind. Yet the mind is a very powerful thing and the perceived yearning of her call is what pulled him out of the dark corner from where he discreetly stood by watching her. When Dwight came out of the darkness he stumbled and almost lost his footing. What caught Ann's attention was not the fact that Dwight almost fell, but rather the sound of his voice as he politely apologized to the person's foot on which he stepped trying to get to Ann. "Excuse me."

Ann looked over in the direction from which Dwight was coming, and gave a big smile as soon as she saw him. She nudged and whispered to Brenda, "Here he comes."

When Dwight finally arrived at Ann and Brenda, he was a little ruffled but quickly gained his composure. "Hi there, how are you?"

"I'm good. Glad you made it. I was starting to worry."

"No, I've been here for a minute."

"So, what...You were somewhere in a corner watching me or something."

Dwight could only smile because she actually hit the nail on the head.

"Now why would I do that?"

"Because, you strike me as the type of guy that would actually do something like that."

Dwight just rubbed his hand over his face as if wiping the masquerade off of it. They both smiled at each other for a moment, and then looked away momentarily in embarrassment.

"Oh, Dwight, this is my friend Brenda. Brenda this is Dwight."

"Hey, nice to meet you, Dwight."

"You too."

"I told Brenda about you."

"Oh? I hope it was all good."

Brenda teased Dwight a little. "Well…"

Then all three of them laughed.

James finally came back over and Ann introduced James to Dwight. The four of them talked for a while, took turns dancing with each other, and participated in the soul train line. Eventually Brenda and James somehow faded into the background and the rest of the night it was Ann and Dwight. She vaguely re-collects an agreement to get a ride home from Dwight. However, the night was ever young and Ann did not have to be home until midnight. Yes, she had a curfew, and that is what brought Dwight back to the reality that Ann was still in high school.

He didn't have a curfew. He lived on the college campus and when he did come home on break, he moved about as he saw fit. While respectful of his parents' home, they viewed him as a man and didn't question him about his "personal life" per say, until he brought someone home. The Tillmans only had two boys, but they both had a midnight curfew as well when they were in high school. So, Dwight understood and respected the fact that Ann had a curfew. Although at this phase in his life, he had a certain amount of freedom; he was set on getting Ann home in time. That was just something he would definitely honor without question.

The way Ann and Dwight were getting on they could have stayed out all night laughing and talking. Of course, Ann understood "Buck will tear that ass up." It didn't matter how old her children were it was ingrained into their psyche.

"If you live under my roof, you go by my rules."

There was no negotiation, democracy, due process, or psychology. There was Buck-ology, Switch-ology, and Belt-ology. Mrs. Brown ran a tight ship and it was pure dictatorship.

"You do as I say, and not as I do!"

Ann needed no reminders of her mother's approach to parenting; she had witnessed enough with her older brothers and sisters. For her it didn't matter how wonderful Dwight was and how sweet his words were, the ever present echo in her head was, "A hard head makes a soft ass."

This was Bucks favorite line when her children misbehaved.

It was a quarter 'til eleven. Ann and Dwight left the party and started to make their way toward Troup Highway. They took the scenic route to Ann's and arrived at about eleven fifteen. He parked his nineteen sixty-nine black and white Malibu out front. It was the same car that he and his brother shared in high school, but it became his when he went off to college. Ann asked Dwight to wait a minute and she would be right back. She ran through her front door to let her mother know that she had made it home.

"Hey mama, I'm home. I'm just outside talking."

"Alright."

Ann ran back out to the car and hopped in the front seat. It was dark outside. There was nothing but woods, stars and the moon. It was nice sitting in the car. They didn't disturb anyone and no one disturbed them. As she sat there with Dwight, she realized that she had never been alone with a guy before in this type of situation. This was all new to her. Dwight was very manly. It's as if she had known him for years. She naturally felt safe and secure with him. Between the church and the party, they spent a lot of time communicating. This was simply another opportunity for them to learn even more about each other before Dwight had to drive back to school the next day.

Ann and Dwight wanted to make the best of the time they had to get to know each other. They spent a couple of hours outside just talking asking some tough questions to one another before they said goodnight.

"What do you plan on doing when you graduate from high school?"

"I plan on going to college. It looks like TJC."

"What will be your major?"

"Communications, with an emphasis in television broadcasting."

"Uhm, Interesting."

"Why is that?"

"Well, I would have thought you would do something that had to do with music."

"I like music, but that comes naturally. I really want to be a TV Anchor."

"Nothin' wrong with that."

"You're asking me all the questions, let me ask you some."

"Go ahead, whatcha wanna know?"

"Well, you're in your third year at college, what do you plan on doing when you graduate?"

"What I plan on doing and what I want to do are two different things. I plan to apply for teaching jobs. I am not sure how available they are in this area, so I may end up having to apply in some larger cities like Houston or Dallas."

"I remember you telling me at the church that your dream was to be like Berry Gordy. You said you wanted to manage music acts."

The Making of a Child of Destiny

"Yes, that's what I want to do. One day, I will be a famous record executive just like Berry Gordy…make lots of money, and buy you the biggest and most beautiful house you could ever dream of having."

Dwight looked right at Ann and started smiling as he continued.

"We will have a couple of sons…you know…"

"What makes you think I want all boys? I want at least one girl."

They started laughing as they were fantasizing and describing their fictitious lives. Although they just met, it didn't seem too far off a reality for either of them when they took the time to really think about it.

"All right now! I stand corrected." Dwight said smiling.

"Boy, you're crazy. You just a Casanova aren't you?"

"Naw. Just a dreamer."

"On the serious side though, what sort of girl are you looking for to settle down with?

"Somebody like you."

"You don't even know me…What do you mean? What am I like?"

"Well, you're smart. You are talented. You have a great sense of humor. You seem to have your head on straight…It ain't like I'm at a psycho convention when I'm with you. You know…I mean you're decent. You know what I'm saying?"

"Hell, I don't know about that. You come to my house it's like a crazy house."

"Why you say that?"

"I have a lot of brothers and sisters. Some of them are already married and moved out though."

"How many are there."

"It's twelve of us."

"Damn girl, yo mama and daddy were busy."

"Shut up, Dwight." Ann said laughing as she tapped him lightly on his arm.

"For real tho. That's a lot of damn kids."

"How many is in your family?"

"It's just two of us, me and my brother."

"What's his name?"

"Keith."

"Oh, so Keith is your brother?"

"Yeah, why you say it like that?"

"My sister Mary Jo, well we call her May Jo, but anyway, she mentioned a Keith and Curtis."

"Curtis is my cousin…So what ya'll got, a Mary Jo, Bobbie Jo and Billie Jo?" Dwight said laughing.

"Hell, it ain't no Petticoat Junction in Buck's house."

The Making of a Child of Destiny

"Buck? What the hell! Is that's your mama's name?" Dwight said laughing.

"You wrong for that. Hell naw. That's what most of my brothers and sisters call her."

"That's some messed up shit."

"What's your mama's name? Yo mama probably got some name like Claudine or something proper like that."

"No, it's cool."

"So what is it?"

"Her name? Oh, it's Wanda."

"Wanda what?"

"Wanda Marie."

"Oh, okay that's not so bad."

"So they call your mama Buck? What's her real name?"

Ann started laughing before she could even get it out. Dwight laughed seeing Ann laugh. She could hardly get her mom's name out for laughing.

"What's so funny?"

"Her name is Effie Lue."

Dwight looked at Ann trying not to bust out laughing again. He put on a feigned serious face, then asked, "Is that what you gonna' name our baby girl?"

"I love my mama, but hell naw."

They both sighed from all the laughing. Then Dwight went back to something that Ann had said to him.

"Wait a minute! You said your sister mentioned my brother and cousin. What brought that about?"

"Oh yeah, last week after church, I asked two of my sisters if they ever heard of any Tillmans. Like I said, May Jo had, but my sister Glenda, we call her Mop… Mop hadn't heard of any Tillmans."

"Mop? Damn! So what, ya'll were talking about me?"

"Yep, real bad. They said guys your age ain't lookin' to just hold hands."

"Well, I have to be honest. I did want to kiss you."

Ann blushed. This was definitely a very different scenario. Dwight looked Ann straight in her eyes, and then slowly leaned forward.

"May I kiss you?"

She nodded her head shyly and the two begin to first kiss gently. Then the kisses became more intense. Ann felt warm. She experienced sensations that she had never experienced before. The close proximity was affecting her in some interesting ways. Dwight and Ann had been necking for about ten to fifteen minutes in the front seat of the car, before they gently pulled their lips apart. They looked into each others eyes for a brief moment, and then he lightly tapped her on the nose and gave her a warm smile. Ann put her head down in embarrassment.

"Did I tell you how beautiful you look?"

"Yes several times."

"You know I have to drive back to school tomorrow afternoon, right?"

"Yes, I thought about that."

"When can I see you again?"

"How about at church tomorrow?"

"New Canaan right?"

"Yep. When do you have to drive back?"

"I want to be heading out before dark. It takes about three and a half hours."

"You are a long way away."

"Not too far to come and see you."

"Oh, if it's like that then…"

"So what time does your church start?"

"About ten forty-five."

"Okay, so it's a date."

"Yes, so I better go on in."

"Yeah, before your daddy come out with his shotgun."

"Jimmie Brown ain't the one you need to worry about, it's Effie Lue…"

"Old Buck huh?"

Dwight chuckled. "Buck ridin' like that?"

"You wait 'til you meet my mama."

"Hell, just talking to her on the phone was bad enough."

"You didn't tell me that, what did she say?"

"Naw, for real, I'm just jivin' you. She was cool."

"I know my mother…she probably asked you a thousand questions."

"Yeah, she did, but it's all good."

Dwight and Ann talked for a few more minutes then wrapped their evening up about one thirty in the morning. Once she got in the house Dwight pulled off. Ann got a glass of water, and prepared herself for bed and church with excitement of seeing Dwight once more before he left town. By the time she actually got into her bed, she was tuckered completely out.

Morning arrived too soon. Ann slept longer than usual. She was tired, but she knew that she needed to get up so she could be ready for church on time. Regardless as to how late you stayed out or whether or not you made curfew, Mrs. Brown expected you to be at church. Everyone living in Buck's house went to church most Sundays, even Jimmie Brown. If he drank too much the night before, it was still rise and shine for him as well.

Ann mentioned to her mother that Dwight was coming to church. Mrs. Brown was serving her husband breakfast, while he was sitting at the kitchen table eating his food and drinking a cup of coffee.

"Who's Dwight?"

"It's this guy I met, daddy."

"What he do?"

"He's a student at Prairie View."

"Ah, what he want with you?"

"What kind of stupid question is that Jimmie?"

"He in college, Ann's in high school…That's not a stupid question woman."

Mrs. Brown rolled her eyes and mumbled under her breath.

"If your ass wasn't in the juke joint all damn night, your Black ass would have seen't her sittin' in the car."

Mr. Brown didn't hear his wife, but Ann did and just shook her head. This was normal interaction. When Jimmie Brown had been drinking, he could be something to deal with. Sometimes the girls would have nothing to do with him and Buck was not amused in the least.

Mrs. Brown was not much of a hugger or touchy feely type of woman. I imagine her lifestyle and marriage to Mr. Brown had its share of ups and downs. There were hints of infidelity where at least one child was born outside of the marital union. Mrs. Brown carried her share of burdens. Yet, church was the one place and time she could lay her burdens down. She did that faithfully and it didn't hurt that the church was just about a mile down the road.

The Brown family arrived at church. Ann greeted some of her older brothers and sisters who also went to the same church, but no longer lived at home. About five of her siblings already had their own families and households to run. It seemed just about every year another Brown was getting married and moving out. Yet still, no matter how old you are, there is no place like home…mama's home that is.

Reverend D.C. Brown delivered an amazing sermon and although Ann didn't sing a solo, the choir got down. New Canaan had a jamming choir and everybody could "sang." Dwight was in the congregation nodding his head and tapping his feet. He lit up when the music played. Church let out about one o'clock. Dwight met Mr. and Mrs. Brown and a few of Ann's siblings. Mrs. Brown just stared at him for a long while. Mr. Brown just nodded his head.

"Good young man, good young man."

Ann and Dwight walked outside as he was heading back to Troup to have dinner with his parents.

"So that is Jimmie and Effie Lue, huh?"

"Stop talkin' bout my mama and daddy!"

The Making of a Child of Destiny

Dwight smiled at her. Neither one of them wanted to part ways, but they knew it was time to say goodbye, at least for now.

"So, I gotta go, I'll call you though."

"You can write me too you know."

"Alright, but I might not need to, it's not that far away."

Ann wrote down her address for Dwight and also took his school address. They hugged, and then Ann went back into the church while Dwight drove away.

About a week passed by before Ann heard anything from Dwight. When he finally called, she spent over an hour on the telephone talking to him. That became the first of many phone calls she received from him. Ann was getting on everybody's nerves tying up the phone line. All she cared about was talking to Dwight.

Over the course of the next month, Ann and Dwight were regularly talking on the telephone and even managed to send a couple of letters back and forth. She was so into Dwight that time had gotten away from her and it wasn't until she and Brenda had a conversation that she realized in just a little over a month, she would be graduating from high school. In reflection, Ann was proud of herself. She finally met someone, and that person was beginning to occupy a very big part of her life.

A BRIGHT FUTURE

The time had finally arrived for Ann to graduate high school. In one week it would be time for her to take that ultimate high school walk. Coming into those doors of Whitehouse High she walked the freshman halls with hope and anticipation. She graced the senior halls with surety and a sense of obligation to be an example for those who were treading behind. Now, here she was entering a new phase of her life. It had been a journey filled with wonderful memories and lessons. It was a training ground preparing young minds to conquer the world and sharpen their swords to become the new leaders, the new entrepreneurs, the new politicians, the new teachers, the new mothers and fathers - the new future. Once she crossed that platform and reached the other side with diploma in hand, real life would inevitably set in. It would then be her time and her turn to make dreams come true – hers and perhaps others.

The final week before graduation was a hectic one filled with trivial pursuits such as hair styling, trying on clothes, buying makeup, arranging social activities and parties, and other matters of a young woman about to embark upon an important expedition. All the while down the road not so far way, Dwight was engrossed in final exams and last minute details for his trip back to Troup for the summer. Replaying in his mind were the numerous telephone conversations with Ann and the letters he kept tucked away for safe keeping, which for him were remnants of her exuberate personality, sense of humor, and radiant smile. It was just two short months ago, when he left Whitehouse. He took with him warm feelings of an apparent mutual attraction. Yet through indepth conversations and a profound cleverness of the pen, seeds of love were deeply planted in the fertile ground of their hearts, and what started out as an unceremonious acquaintance has now started to blossom into a budding love affair.

Long distance romances can be filled with complications and complexities. Albeit for Ann and Dwight, their separation was only contrived in the mind of those who had not a clue of what was germinating in the dark, simply waiting to burst forth for all the world to see. In less than seven days the light would shine brightly on their growing affections for one another. Dwight too was preparing to see his damsel as she took her final walk at Whitehouse High School.

Back in Smith County, Ann and other schoolmates were putting together last minute graduation party details hoping perchance that this would be the one night they could defy the midnight curfew rule and just celebrate the good 'ole fashioned way. Mrs. Brown might have been okay with bending the rules this time, since after all it was a reason to celebrate. As Ann stood there in line with her fellow seniors, flashes of the many years at Whitehouse Junior High and Whitehouse High School went flashing through her mind. She spent over one third of her life thus far in school.

Thoughts of Mr. Hancock and geography class, Miss French's P.E. class, pep rallies, football games, dances, spirit week, softball games in the country, drill team competitions, cheerleading tryouts, Brenda's band competitions and basketball games, and all of the other memories that made something compulsory worth-the-while came flowing forth.

As the commencement exercises began, many students were recognized for their outstanding achievements. Black students however were more concerned about how well they faired overall. Included in the top ten were David and Beverly who were also Rotary Award winners and voted most likely to succeed. Brenda and James captured the Most Beautiful and Most Handsome title. Ruben and Andretta were consider the Class Favorites and won the highest votes for Best Personality. David and Brenda were Best All Around, while Beverly and Carnell were the Best

Dressed. Andretta claimed the Most Talented, and Most School Spirit went to Carnell and Andretta.

As the music started to play, row-by-row, the students frocked in maroon and white stood up waiting on their name to be called for that one moment in time. It wasn't Esterlean Stewart, Marilyn Bowie, David Brown, Raven Pettigrew or Carl Caldwell. It wasn't Linda Childress, Wayne Mitchell, or Bobby Caddell. This time, it was James Stewart, Brenda Pettigrew, Andretta Brown, Ruben Hill, Carnell Beasley, David Williams, Beverly Walker, Larry Caldwell, and Gaye Bowie. This time it was Jerry Sikes, Vivian Stewart, and Alfred Garrett standing there proudly in their caps and gowns singing in unison for one last time, the Whitehouse Alma Mater.

"All hail to Whitehouse High School;
All hail to you.
For truth and knowledge;
We will 'ere be true."

"Always in our memories.
Ever in our hearts.
We will remember;
Dear Whitehouse High.
W-H-S"

The Making of a Child of Destiny

For these graduating seniors, Mrs. Brewer would no longer insist them on returning their books to the library on time. There would be no more sit-downs with Mrs. Davis or Mrs. Tucker to decide which classes are best to take for the next quarter. There would be no more trips to Mr. Smith's office when it was necessary to see the principal. They wouldn't see Tommy Mitchum or Bud Hurst sweeping the halls or emptying the trash cans. Ann wouldn't be reminded to snap the moves in drill practice by Ms. Terry or reminded that there is even practice by Ms. Linda Johnson. Mrs. Ray would no longer be there to tell them at what temperature to pre-heat the oven or how much flour to put in the mixture.

High school provided its own sense of security. But after this day, the security of Whitehouse High School would be no more. It was time for the graduating class of nineteen seventy-six to face the world as adults.

After all names have been called, all awards presented, Head Marjorette and Top Ten Honors Student Gayla Morrison presented these words to remember:

"The Senior Class of seventy-six has made it to the top.
From our 'hellos' to our classmates to our 'goodbyes' to our friends,
we take on activities and responsibilities.
In our class meetings we have elections and decide on projects.

After the new wears off of our rings and jackets,
we began to make decisions for our future.
Through all the cheers of a crowded gym to the silence of a diploma,
another year has ended.
These brief years of school life will fade but the memories of them never will.
As we go our separate ways, we all will be the same in one big way;
we are the graduating Seniors of Nineteen Seventy-Six."

After the speech, applause filled the air, maroon and white caps went up, and tears streamed down the cheeks of proud parents and students alike. There sat Mr. and Mrs. Brown proud of their daughter and of the fact that another Brown received their high school diploma. As Ann walked over to her parents and family members who were present to show their support and celebrate in a very proud moment, Dwight walked over and greeted everyone.

"Oh my gosh! You made it."

"Ann, you know I wouldn't have missed this day girl."

"Wow! I'm so glad you came."

Mr. and Mrs. Brown hugged Ann on this rare occasion.

"I know we won't see you probably for the rest of the night. But we discussed the rules, right?"

"Yes ma'am."

"Alright baby. Have fun with your friends and be safe. Call me when you are in the room."

"Yes, Ma'am. See you later daddy, and thank you."

"Alright baby-girl."

"Well, little sis, me and Raymond are leaving too. We'll see you at the house. Oh and Dwight, keep an eye on my little sister."

"You bet."

"Okay Mop, talk to you later."

All of the other family members, who attended the graduation, hugged and congratulated Ann, and then walked out of the gymnasium. Ann pulled Dwight over to where Brenda and some of the other classmates were. Brenda, James, and some of the others had already met Dwight, but most of her other friends had not met him. Ann was popular so of course, those who had never seen her with a guy in this type of arrangement were wondering who this dude was. As the evening progressed, and the need arose to introduce Dwight, it became crystal clear that he had already placed himself in the "boyfriend" category.

The rest of the evening Dwight submitted himself to hanging out with a bunch of high school graduates. He was ever-present, but he gave Ann the room to be herself with her group of friends. He understood all too well that graduation night presented a somewhat intimidating freedom, but freedom all the same. Ann had a lot of fun and what was even more exciting for her was that she also shared it with her "boyfriend."

The summer of nineteen seventy-six was probably one of the most liberating summers there was. Ann and Brenda were college-bound and in the fullness of their transition to womanhood. They both enrolled at TJC and were still "thick as thieves" as they say. However, this particular summer there were fewer outings with the guys and the girls from Whitehouse, but many more rendezvous with Dwight. Ann and Dwight were officially dating and an item. They went to the drive-in movies together and like many other couples, made out. They went roller-skating. They had picnics together and took long walks in the park. The summer was filled with young love. They spent just about everyday together and Ann's family could see this was Ann's first love. For Ann, however, it did not take long for her to figure out that Dwight was the only one for her.

Dwight spent many days at Ann's house late at night sitting outside talking, watching the boob tube and the other sort of normal things people do when they are in love. However, it wasn't until the fourth of July barbeque/Dwight's twenty-first birthday party at Dwight's house that Ann met his parents. This was the day Dwight finally got up the nerve to take his girl to meet the Tillmans. Ann had already heard countless stories about how Mr. and Mrs. Tillman was a tough crowd to win over, but that did not stop Ann from accepting the invitation to celebrate Independence Day with her beau.

She graced the Tillman household wearing a long spunky and fun summer dress, and wore her hair up in an afro-puff. When they arrived at the house, Dwight's parents were out back, but his brother Keith had ran into the house to grab something for his dad who was barbequing.

"Hey, big brother!"

"Hey man, this is Andretta."

"Call me Ann. It's nice to meet you."

"Good to meet you too."

"So you're the reason why I never see my big brother, huh, since he's been home from school."

Ann smiled. "I guess so."

"Well, man, pops is waiting on this out back, so I better get back out there."

"Alright, man, but don't mention that I'm here yet, we'll be out in a minute."

"No problem."

Ann made her way by the mantel and started looking at family photos, reading all the awards, plaques, and trophies. "Wow, look at this. You must have been really good."

"I was alright."

"This is a lot of stuff here. Huhm…your parents must be proud of you and Keith."

"Yeah, you could say that."

Dwight grabbed Ann by her waist and led her to the direction of his room.

"Come here."

"Where are you taking me?"

"You'll see."

Ann and Dwight spent about fifteen minutes in his bedroom looking at pictures, high school yearbooks, and knick knacks. His room was exactly the same as it was when he was in high school.

"You know, you are starting to grow on me, don't you."

Ann just smiled as Dwight leaned over and kissed her. They kissed deeply for a few moments then made their way out back where his parents and brother were. Dwight's parents were expecting several of his friends at this barbeque because the usual Fourth of July celebration was also combined with Dwight's twenty-first birthday celebration. They had an idea that he would be inviting a female friend, but they did not anticipate it being anything serious.

As Ann and Dwight headed out the back door to the backyard, his parents smiled as they saw him coming hand-in-hand with a very attractive young woman. Dwight walked over to his mom and hugged her and kissed her on the cheek. He hugged his dad who reached and patted him on the back like men often do.

"Hey there son."

"Hey dad."

"Glad you finally made it."

"Yeah…Mom, dad this is Andretta."

"Hi there Andretta it's nice to meet you."

"It's nice to meet you Mrs. Tillman."

"Andretta, this is my dad."

"How you doing sir?"

"…And you already met Keith."

Keith nodded and smiled. Things were a little awkward because it had been a while since Dwight brought a girl home, and it was apparent that Mrs. Tillman was sizing Ann up. No matter how stiff things were, Dwight knew that it would start to loosen up a bit once his cousin Curtis and some of the old crew showed up. TC, Nobel, and Abe were friends from high school. They would also probably be bringing some people with them, not to mention Mr. and Mrs. Tillman invited who they wanted to see there as well.

This year was a big celebration and Mrs. Tillman had a certain level of social acumen. Therefore nothing was lacking. Keith was a live wire. He was very resourceful in making Ann feel at home.

"So Ann, Dwight said you just graduated recently."

"Yeah, I did, Keith."

"Oh, so from what college?"

"Mom, Ann hasn't started college yet. She just graduated from high school."

Mrs. Tillman looked in the direction of her husband. "Oh, okay. You're kind of young aren't you?"

Ann chuckled, and then Dwight grabbed Keith and the two of them got up. He told Ann he will be right back and left her there with his mother. Then they headed into the house.

"Well…I'm eighteen…I guess that would make me legal."

"Perhaps, I guess it does. So where will you be going to college?

"Tyler Junior College."

"Oh…" Mrs. Tillman looked over at her husband again.

"So what will you major be?"

"Television broadcasting."

"Well, that's nice."

"Dwight tells me you're a teacher."

"Yes, I am."

Mrs. Tillman quickly shifted the questioning off of herself and back to Ann.

"So, Andretta right?"

"Yes ma'am."

"Do you have any brothers and sisters?"

"Actually I have several. Seven sisters and four brothers."

"Oh, you come from a large family I see."

"Yes ma'am."

"I couldn't imagine your mother working with all those children."

"Well, actually my mother does work. She cleans houses."

"Oh, I see. What about your father?"

"My father is a carpenter, mechanic. I guess you could say jack-of-all trades. He does what he has to do."

"Oh. It must be really crowded in your house."

Ann thought to herself, "What in the hell is your problem lady asking me all these damn questions." Then she spoke up with firmness in her voice, but a smile on her face.

"Well, in truth Mrs. Tillman, several of my brothers and sisters have already gotten married and moved out of the house and into their own. It used to be a lot of us in the house at one time, but we were used to it. We've always had a full house. I like it that way because it's always somebody to talk to."

"I suppose you're right. Well excuse me dear; let me go check on…"

As Mrs. Tillman was getting up to go over to where her husband was flipping the meat on the grill, Keith and Dwight returned just as several guests were making their way around to the backyard. Curtis gave Keith and Dwight five.

"Hey, what's happening?"

"Nothing much man."

"Look at you. How's the birthday boy?"

"I'm good, been chillin' with my girl, you know."

Ann was sitting over where she and Mrs. Tillman had been talking. Dwight and Curtis came over to where she was and Dwight introduced the two of them. Soon other guests also began to arrive and by late afternoon things were getting pretty entertaining. There was a lot of laughter, hugging, drinking, dancing, clowning around, and reminiscing of yesteryear. Dwight's mom and dad watched the interaction between Ann and Dwight. They could tell that their son really liked this girl. It didn't really make a difference to Ann or Dwight who approved of their relationship or who did not. They were falling in love and that's what was important.

By six-thirty Ann, Dwight, Keith, and others closer to their age, left the Tillman house and headed over to Lindsey Park to watch the fireworks. The Tyler Jaycees held the event every Fourth of July. People came and paid to park their cars, buy refreshments, and watch the fireworks. This year was an extra special celebration as it was America's bicentennial year. They were celebrating two hundred years of independence. Therefore, it was a lot more going on this particular year as opposed to other years.

Once the explosive finale ended several people continued to hang out, while others quickly got into their cars and left. You could see several couples cuddled up next to each other. Ann for the first time got a glimpse of what some of her high school friends felt when they would hang out at Lincoln Park. Yet, the truth is Ann felt that it was much better when you had someone you loved to hang out with. It felt good.

"Alright man, me and Ann are about to take off."

"Alright bro."

"Hey see you later man, it was good to see you. I'll see you again before you head back."

"Fo sho, cuz."

"See you next time Ann."

"Alright Keith, see you guys later."

Ann said bye to everyone else including the few girls that were there as well. She and Dwight got into the car and took off. It was about midnight when Dwight finally got around to taking Ann home. I guess some habits are hard to break. Ann let her mother know that she was home, and she and Dwight just sat outside at the picnic table under the tree for a while. They kissed, they talked, and they laughed. Whenever the two of them spent time together, they could not keep their hands off of each other. However, neither of them let things go too far. However, time did often slipped away from them.

The rest of July flew by, and August almost just as fast. It was nearing the time for Ann and Dwight to go back school. This time both would be in college; Ann a freshman and Dwight a senior. Yet starting school also meant being separated again, and this time would not be nearly as easy as before. Ann and Dwight went for a long ride the last week before the fall school term and spent hours together talking.

"Girl, I am going to miss you. I wish I could take you with me."

"I know, but look on the bright side, Thanksgiving will be here before you know it, and we will get to see each other again."

"Not soon enough."

"Don't remind me, you gonna make me cry." Ann paused for a moment, and then continued. "You'll have school to keep you busy."

"Just don't be going out with some other dude tryin' to rain on my parade."

Ann started to baby talk to Dwight. "Is my baby getting jealous?"

Dwight smiled and lightly pinched Ann's nose. "Naw, I'm just saying. You my girl so don't forget that."

"Me and Brenda will just be hanging out more until you get back."

"We'll call each other and write…"

"You better."

"You not going to forget me are you?"

"Now Dwight! What do you think?"

Dwight's face moved closer and closer to Ann's face and his voice got gentler. "Are you sure you're not going to forget about me now that you are a college girl?"

He started to kiss Ann softly on the lips. "Yeah I'm sure, Dwight, I not going to forget you."

They toyed with each other back and forth as they kissed. It was dark outside and Dwight's car was parked in the boonies somewhere. He continued to softly kiss Ann. Then they started to play pitty pat with their tongues as they kept kissing. With each kiss Dwight's tongue went softly further inside of Ann's mouth. After a while the kisses got more passionate. He lightly stroked the side of her neck, then her back. He kissed and played with her ear with his tongue and gently kissed her right below her ear. "Ooh" Ann said quietly as the feeling caught her by surprise.

Dwight continued to kiss her neck and nibble on her ear. He whispered in her ear.

"Are you okay?"

Ann answered him quietly and innocently. "Yes."

He took her chin and slowly lifted her head so that her eyes could meet his. As he stared deeply into her eyes and gently kissed and nibbled her lips, Ann started to tremble. Dwight began to kiss her again. With each kiss their tongues met one another's. Dwight pulled her head up again so that his eyes would connect with hers.

"I want you." He whispered to her. Ann did not respond verbally, instead she leaned forward to kiss him and grabbed his head so as to lay it on her chest. He began to gently kiss her chest, and then made his way up to the front of her neck under her chin. He slowly moved his mouth back to the side of her neck, then back to the spot below her ear. Ann was getting warmer as he slowly and lightly moved his hand down the back of her neck and down her spine as he continued to tongue-kiss her ever so deeply.

Dwight touched Ann's upper arm as light as a feather's touch. He then slowly moved his hand over to her collar bone outlining it with his pointed finger as he kissed her. He then swiped his hands gently down her chest plate, then gently grabbed and massaged her supple breasts. As he caressed and cupped her round tenderness, her nipples became erect and ready. There was no resistance at all coming from Ann as Dwight began to explore every part of her voluptuous body. She was becoming even more hot and ready as his hand slowly slipped down to her navel then to the crotch of her shorts. He rubbed his hands up and down between her legs. Ann squirmed sensually inviting him with her movements to continue.

As he kissed her, he raised his hand to the waistband of her shorts, and unfastened them. He took his pointed finger and started to circle her navel then finger climbed his hand up her shirt. He slowly lifted her bra to touch her bare breasts. Dwight released the seat to go back as he continued to embrace and kiss her neck. He moved his mouth to her breast and began sucking them softly then more fervently. Catching Ann completely off guard his hand slipped into her panties and he lightly tickled her pearl tongue.

As he pulled her shorts down he could feel her wetness and her body tingling to every circular motion on her clitoris. Ann moaned as he slipped his middle finger into her vagina. The more she moaned the more he filled her up. Dwight took Ann's hand and mapped it down toward his manhood. He unhooked his button and unzipped his pants and took her hand and wrapped it around his long, thick, and hard penis encouraging her to stroke it from base to tip. He slid his finger from her, then grabbed her butt and moved her even closer to him. He then turned her completely on her back and mounted her. As he slowly began to penetrate her passion fruit, she gasped when he finally with one swift, thrust himself inside her. Ann let out a shrill.

"Look at me." He said softly.

Ann opened her eyes and the two stared at each other intensely as Dwight continued to thrust himself in and out, in and out, in and out. "I love you, Andretta."

Tears rolled down her eyes but she didn't say a word at first. She showed him with her body how much she wanted him to be only hers. "You are the one Dwight."

When he heard the softness of her voice and the sweet surrender of her body to his, he went deeper and deeper inside of her. She moaned and groaned as her body moved naturally and rhythmically in time with his. "ah…ah…ah…ahm…" She moaned.

Ann was hot with passion. Sweat poured off of him as their bodies glided against each other. You could hear them panting and their hearts palpitating loudly the nearer they got to a climactic ecstasy. The feeling overtook them. As they reached the peak of sexual excitation, Dwight ejaculated inside of Ann, and they both let out almost in unison a vibratory sound that shook the car, and then exhaled. He continued to hold her tightly for a moment, gently kissing her forehead, then her cheek, then her nose, and then her lips.

Dwight rolled off of Ann and onto his back with his eyes closed. Then he grabbed her close to him again and kissed her on the top of the head. Ann shyly looked up at him. "This was my first time Dwight."

He kissed her on the nose. "I know."

"We didn't use protection."

"I know, don't worry, it'll be okay."

Ann believed him. In that moment, there was nothing Dwight could say that would make her doubt him. She had given herself completely to him and didn't regret it one bit. If Dwight had to separate himself from her, he wanted to leave her with something to think about. But little did he know, for Ann, this day would never be forgotten because he was the man who took her virginity.

As Ann and Dwight fidgeted to fix their clothes, conversation resumed but in a much more mellow fashion.

"I better get you home."

"Yeah I know."

"You okay."

"Yes, I'm good."

"You sure?"

"Yeah."

"Okay."

Dwight started the car, and then drove away from the lonely road in which not one soul was nearby for miles. When the two of them pulled up in front of Ann's house, she smiled at him and he gently kissed her. "Goodnight, Babe."

"Goodnight."

"I enjoyed you tonight."

"Me too."

Ann walked on in the house, briefly looking back and waving to him. As she entered the house, she was glad that no one was in the main area. She whispered to her mother through the bedroom door that she was home and quickly headed up to the bathroom. As Ann tended to herself, she noticed a little blood in her panties. She now understood what it meant to "Have your cherry popped."

The next couple of days Dwight and Ann spent together doing fun things like going to the zoo, walking on Broadway Street, and going out to eat. The last day they were meant to spend together, Dwight surprised Ann with a heart pendant necklace that was only half of a heart. On it were the words "Dwight" engraved on it. He pulled out the other half of the heart, which had "Andretta" engraved on it. They both wore the hearts representative of their incompleteness without each other.

It was finally time for Ann to start TJC and for Dwight to head back to Prairie View. Classes started for Ann on the twenty-third of August. Dwight's classes resumed on the thirtieth; but he needed to get back a few days earlier to get himself organized. He was able to drive Ann to her classes and pick up her the first couples of days. After that, they had to part ways so that Dwight could now focus on his last year in college and secure a job.

September and October were uneventful. Ann was missing Dwight tremendously and went through a brief period of grief. No one seemed to notice that some things had changed in her because everybody was busy getting on with their life. Ann was struggling to focus because she was lovesick. Her load of classes and the work required of her at TJC was much more than high school. Unlike Whitehouse, there were no teachers insisting she do her work. What she turned in and how seriously she took her academic career was a matter of personal responsibility and accountability. She either wanted to succeed or not.

By mid-September, Ann snapped out of the funk. She was relieved to get her period and made the decision to be responsible and accountable for both the personal and academic areas of her life. Brenda and Ann maintained their friendship while at TJC. They still hung out, but both were focused on school and realized that they had their own lives to manage. They were transitioning, and with life's changes, come its own set of emotions.

Neither Ann nor Dwight managed to write, but the number of phone calls made up for that. Hearing each others voice was enough to ease the loneliness caused by them not being able to touch one another. Both Dwight and Ann understood that it was only for a time and soon they would be able to hold each other again.

Finally Thanksgiving break came! Dwight rushed over to see his girl! Ann was not expecting him because usually he would call. This time he had not. As far as she knew he would be by on Wednesday. Dwight drove into town and went straight to her house. Prairie View only gives Thanksgiving Day, Friday, and Saturday off. However, Dwight finished up things he needed to do and left on Tuesday after classes. So while Ann was expecting him to get there on Wednesday, his intent was to surprise her and come to town a day early.

When he knocked on the door, Mrs. Brown answered. She had some sort of uniform on and he could gather that she might have just gotten off work. Ann was not there; she had not made it home from school yet, but her mother expected her shortly. Mrs. Brown invited Dwight in to wait for her, so he obliged. He was nervous because Mrs. Brown was not friendly, nor did she ever smile; so he didn't know how to take her. Mrs. Brown didn't care whether Dwight felt comfortable or not. Her concern was her daughter and what his intentions were with her.

Although she did not say much to either of them, she was not a fool and knew what was going on. She wanted to make sure that Dwight's intentions were in the right place.

"So, what is going on with you and Ann?"

"I like Andretta a whole lot, Mrs. Brown."

"Yeah okay, so what's going on?"

"I'm not sure what you mean?"

"You know what the hell I mean. No need in playin' the fool, Dwight. So let me re-phrase my question. What are your intentions with my daughter?"

Dwight cleared his throat and knew that he had to man up and wasn't getting out of this situation. While he thought he was going to surprise Ann, he was the one who was caught off guard.

"Well Mrs. Brown. I like Ann a lot. Actually I can see myself with your daughter. She has all of the qualities of someone that I can see myself with."

"See I want you to be clear that Ann ain't no play thing. You understand what I'm sayin' to you?"

"Yes, ma'am, I do. And be assured I'm not playing with Andretta."

"As long as we understand each other. Also remember that she does have a father. So when you're really serious, you know what you need to do."

Before Dwight could get another word out, Ann came through the door. She was wide-eyed when she saw him sitting at the kitchen table. She looked at him then looked at her mom and back at him. She nodded to Dwight as if to say, "Is everything okay?" Dwight stood up as Ann started to address him.

"Hey, what are you doing here?"

"I came to surprise you."

"Well, I'm surprised."

Mrs. Brown looked out the corner of her eyes and snickered under her breath. Ann pulled Dwight into the living room and they sat there talking.

"What's going on?"

"Oh, nothing. I just got here and your mom said you would be here soon. So I waited."

"I know my mama Dwight. It didn't look like nothing."

"Naw, seriously. It's cool."

"Alright, well, I'm glad to see you."

"You okay?" Dwight recalled that they had not used any protection and wasn't sure what to expect. So he looked in her eyes, then her belly, then back in her eyes.

"Yeah, I'm good."

"Okay."

Dwight and Ann sat in her living room watching television. The day just went on as usual. Tu Tu ran around the house. Other family members came in and out, then in again. It was very active. They discussed Thanksgiving and how they would divide up their time between the two houses. Dwight and Ann spent the entire weekend just really hanging out. One minute they were at his house and the next at Ann's. If he wasn't over at the Browns, she was over at the Tillmans. Finally, Sunday evening Dwight made his way back to school and waited for the next time the two of them could be together.

Before they could blink it was vacation time again. Christmas rolled around and Ann and Dwight spent lots of time together. Between shopping, socializing, hanging out with friends, and attending various holiday events together, they found special moments to be together intimately. They were an item and it was not a secret that their relationship was very serious. With the bringing in of nineteen seventy-seven, Dwight spoke with his family and made it clear to them about his feelings for Ann. He also made it a point to speak with Ann's father when he was finally able to catch up with him. The degree to which their relationship had grown, it appeared that nothing would be able to tear them apart.

    Ann successfully completed her first year of college and Dwight graduated from Prairie View A & M University with a Bachelors Degree in Education. Everything was going very well, except, Dwight had not secured a job. He submitted applications for opening in Tyler, Troup, and Whitehouse from the time of his final semester in college. All of his buddies had secured positions in their perspective fields, but he had not. Dwight was getting very frustrated and even considered applying for jobs outside of teaching so that he could at least earn an income.

    His parents were on his back about getting a job in education and he became exceedingly irritable because although he had applied everywhere he could think to apply, it appeared that he was being overlooked. Dwight finally decided to focus on his dream of managing music acts and building a stable of artists. His parents were not trying to hear that nor did they support his decision. They put so much pressure on him that he could not take it any longer, and just gave up the idea all together.

The Making of a Child of Destiny

Dwight was set on moving out of his parents' home, but he relied much on their support. This upset him even more. Meanwhile, Ann started her second year at TJC. She became more focused and kept her sights on being a news anchor. While she was supportive of Dwight's situation, she stayed on task. He was not working or in school, therefore he strongly felt the emptiness of her absence. He felt that his world was falling apart.

Finally, sometime around the first week in September, Dwight received a letter from the Houston Independent School District offering him a teaching role for mathematics at Booker T. Washington High School. They wanted him to report to work beginning the January school term. They offered him a very nice salary and benefits package and agreed to pay for relocation expenses. He did not think twice; he immediately called and accepted the role. After that, he raced into town and used a little of the money he had saved up to purchase an inexpensive engagement ring. He was not moving to Houston without Andretta.

That evening Dwight went by the Browns home and picked his girlfriend up. He took Ann for a long drive and pulled over at some little quaint park-like setting. They got out of the car and went and sat on one of the benches.

"Baby, I got a job!"

"That's great, Dwight! I knew you would! I believe in you, baby. I knew you would!"

Ann was very excited for him and relieved that it finally worked out. She did not like to see him discouraged and she didn't like how his parents were on his back, pressuring him.

"But wait there's more."

"Okay. Tell me."

"Well, I was offered to teach math at Booker T. Washington High School."

"Okay…go on."

"Well baby that's in Houston."

Ann's face dropped. You could tell that she was a little taken aback. She just could not deal with another separation. She had another year before getting her Associates and it was just too much for her to think about. Dwight noticed the look on her face.

"No, baby. I know what you're thinking. But I want you to come with me. This teaching job is just the start of it. Like I said, one day, I will be a famous record executive, make lots of money, and buy you the biggest and most beautiful house you could ever dream of having. We will have a couple of sons…"

Dwight was talking so fast, he was nervous. "…oh and yeah at least one daughter… But, I want you to come with me baby…and…uh…I…I…I just want to know…"

Dwight fumbled in his pocket and pulled out a very modest engagement ring, and then got down on one knee.

"...Andretta Brown...will you be Andretta Tillman...uh...I mean...will you marry me?"

Andretta laughed and responded. "Hell yeah, I'll marry you!"

They stood there kissing and holding each other close. "You my girl. I love you. I ain't going nowhere without you."

"I love you too!"

WHAT DREAMS MAY COME

"We are gathered here today in the sight of God and the presence of friends, and loved ones for one of life's greatest rewards – the uniting of Dwight Ray Tillman and Andretta Brown in holy matrimony."

The day had finally arrived for Dwight and Andretta's wedding. On Saturday, December third, nineteen seventy-seven, New Canaan Missionary Baptist Church in Whitehouse, Texas was filled with over a hundred people attending this auspicious occasion to join together nineteen year-old Ann and twenty-two year-old Dwight both full of life and dreams. The guests smiled in hopeful anticipation as Dwight patiently waited at the altar while six bridesmaids and six groomsmen marched down the aisle, followed by the maid of honor, then by the ring bearer and the flower girls, who scattered flowers all about.

The smile that came over Dwight's face illuminated the sanctuary and the congregation stood up as the bride graciously appeared and began to make her entrance down the trail of fresh pink and red rose-petals. There was no mistaking the proud look on Mr. and Mrs. Brown's face and the exuberant joy that overflowed as yet another Brown girl, all grown up, prepared to take on one of the most important roles a woman could take on in her life. Ann was about to become a wife; but not just anybody's wife. She was about to marry a man, who's handsome, smart, accomplished, who comes from a good family, who's caring, and very protective of her. She was about to become the wife of a man who honored her and treated her with the utmost respect, but more importantly, who adored and loved her dearly.

Teary-eyed Ann cascaded down the aisle in her beautiful white gown to stand by her man, that neither miles nor class could separate. As they stood there side-by-side Reverend Brown, who watched Ann grow from a young girl, admonished them both to never forget what brought them to that very day.

"After this blessed day, two shall travel this life together. Remember that your true success, your greatest accomplishment is a testament which will stem from the love you hold in your hearts for one another. No matter what you amass in this life or no matter what challenges befall you, trust in God above and keep the love alive in your hearts. Love bears all things, believes all things, hopes all things, and endures all things. And now these three remain: faith, hope and love. But the greatest of these is love."

Keith stood tall by his big brother, as did Brenda by her best friend. The wedding party in disciplined ranks flanked on either side added support, while family and friends witnessed the exchanging of the vows and the pledging of undying love and faithfulness.

"Do you Dwight take Andretta Brown to be your wedded wife?"

"I do."

"Will you love and comfort her, honor and keep her, in sickness and in health, and forsaking all others, keep yourself only unto her being faithful as long as you both shall live?"

"I do."

"Do you Andretta take Dwight Ray Tillman to be your wedded husband?"

"I do."

"Will you love and comfort him, honor and keep him, in sickness and in health, and forsaking all others, keep yourself only unto him being faithful as long as you both shall live?"

"I do."

"So Dwight and Andretta, be that it is your intention to enter into marriage, I ask that you join your right hands. Your maid may hold your bouquet. I ask that you join right hands and in front of God and witnesses, to declare your consent, repeat after me."

"I Dwight, take you Andretta to be my wife, to have and to hold from this day forward, for better or for worse, for richer or for poorer, in sickness and in health, to love and to cherish, as long as we both shall live."

"Okay Dwight, please place the ring on Andretta's finger and repeat after me…"

"With this ring, I thee wed…"

Dwight placed the ring on Andretta's finger. She looked deep into his eyes and smiled, as the ceremony continued and she took her turn to vow to him and receive him into her life as her husband.

"I Andretta, take you Dwight to be my husband, to have and to hold from this day forward, for better or for worse, for richer or for poorer, in sickness and in health, to love and to cherish, as long as we both shall live."

"Andretta please place the ring on Dwight's finger and repeat after me…"

"With this ring, I thee wed…"

After the rings were exchanged, the congregation and everyone on the altar bowed their heads as Reverend Brown said a prayer. Once he finished, he introduced the newly married couple.

"Dwight and Andretta in so much as you two have agreed to live together in Holy Matrimony, and have vowed your fidelity and faithfulness by these vows and the joining of hands and the giving of rings, by the authority vested in me by God, I now pronounce you husband and wife."

The congregation applauded as the preacher continued.

"Dwight, you may kiss your bride."

Dwight and Andretta kissed warmly as everyone in the place cheered and clapped.

"Ladies and gentlemen, may I present to you Mr. and Mrs. Dwight Ray Tillman."

It was a lovely ceremony with the reception immediately following. However, no matter how much of a good time and cutting of the rug there was, in the back of family and friends minds was the fact that in just a few days, Ann and Dwight would be packing things up and moving from the tiny towns of Whitehouse and Troup to start their new life together some two-hundred miles away in the big city.

The wedding party along with friends and family danced and partied the night away. Ann and Dwight took a hotel room for the night and enjoyed each other for the first time as husband and wife. They could not be more happy and content. Finally, they did not have to hide their physical attraction for one another. It was now actually "legal" to have as much sex as they wanted without the fear of "getting caught."

Dwight and Ann finally headed out of town. There were a lot of details yet to be worked out, for starters, finding a place to live. The school district was paying for relocation expenses, but they would not be able to start looking until they arrived. So Dwight and Ann packed up the few belonging in the old Malibu and headed to what would now be their new home – Houston, Texas.

Upon arriving in Houston, Dwight needed to check in with the school district to complete all necessary paperwork and get things geared up for the first day of school starting the January term. He was excited about his new role and looking forward to being his own man with his wife by his side. Although Ann and Dwight were a young couple, they were fresh with ideas and excited about the journey. For the first couple of weeks they stayed in a hotel, and then found a starter place they could call their home.

The first day for Dwight to report to work in the Mathematics Department was an exciting time. As he walked the halls of Booker T. Washington High School, he was proud that he was a member of the faculty of not only the first high school that was open to Blacks in Houston, but a school where he could make significant contributions for young people. He could help them to better grasp mathematics ultimately leading them to become better problem-solvers in life. Dwight also felt privileged to be able to work under the leadership of a profoundly talented educator by the name of Franklyn Wesley. Mr. Wesley was the principal at that time and had been since around the mid to late sixties.

"Welcome to Booker T. Washington High School Mr. Tillman."

"I am honored Mr. Wesley."

"By now you know the history of the school here and it should keep your hands pretty full. We have some brilliant young minds and with the right guidance we can make a very real difference."

"Yes, sir."

"Mathematics is a discipline that is critical to the development of our children and therefore your role as faculty is most important. I am sure it will serve you well and serve our students well. Welcome aboard!"

"Thank you so much sir."

Dwight also met Langston Knowles who was the chairperson for the Department of Mathematics along with some of his other fellow colleagues who hailed from various educational institutions. Dwight's happy-go-lucky personality would prove to be a great asset for both the faculty and students alike. This was a school worthy of his time and talents.

Booker T. Washington opened its doors in eighteen ninety-three as Colored High School. Coming from a historical Black educational institution, Dwight understood all too well the importance of young people having the opportunity to see progressive role models and people that looked like them in leadership roles. It planted a seed in their subconscious mind that over time through proper nourishment could germinate and give rise to an amazing human being that could someday change the course of history.

Dwight was a product of Black educators and a Black institution of higher learning and this was his time to be able to start giving back. Although music was his heart, he knew that he was confronted with the opportunity to make an impact in the lives of a lot of young people. He had rationalized that music and math were not all that different. Both required the ability to keep time. So Dwight's style of teaching went over very well, as he made mathematics fun and his students loved him. They didn't love him because of how much he knew. They loved him because of how much he cared.

Ann and Dwight finally got settled into their first real home. Dwight had been teaching at Booker T. Washington for close to two years and Ann started working for Houston Lighting & Power Company (HL&P). Things were going very well for them. The modest home worked well, yet Dwight still had his heart set on his dream of buying his Nubian Princess a big beautiful home and having a couple of sons and…a daughter.

Mr. and Mrs. Tillman were proud of their son, Dwight. Like many proud fathers, Mr. Tillman was full of advice on investing and building up a nest egg. Dwight was respectful, but in the back of his mind, again, he was always trying to figure out a way to do both teaching and music. See, the college degree and the teaching job was for his parents. The music was for him.

For Ann, she was happy being married. Being a news anchor escaped her once she said her vows. She stopped going to school and didn't regret it. She loved being a wife and loved her new life in Houston. One of the happiest moments of her life was moving out of the country and on to the big city. School somehow did not matter to her as much as being the best wife and support to her husband. Dwight was very protective of Ann and realized what she gave up for him. He loved her very much and she loved him. They were "Inseparable." Dwight never passed up an opportunity to be romantic and loving.

Of course things were not always peachy in their marriage. Like any other couples, they had their ups and downs, and the first two years were about making adjustments. Ann was headstrong, sometimes impulsive, and liked to be in control. Dwight was moody and could sometimes be too sensitive blaming Ann for what he sometimes felt was a lack of consideration.

All and all they complemented one another very well and Ann had this knack of allowing him to feel like a man. No matter what the situation was, she took an optimistic approach which allowed Dwight to confront and overcome his fears and move about more confidently. Ann could be very possessive, but Dwight loved and appreciated this about her. So you would find that they both were equally protective of each other and somewhat possessive.

Ann and Dwight had an amazing blend of fire and water in their relationship. They were able to talk about the sexy stuff and also about hard stuff in their relationships, including how they would like things to be if something happened to one or the other.

"How was your day baby?"

"Oh it was alright. How were those bad ass kids at the school?"

"Girl you are crazy. You act like your mama."

"You know they're bad, Dwight. Anytime you get a bunch of Black ass people together, there is always something going on."

"Naw, for real, it's alright."

"Uhm, okay."

"Keith called me today."

"What did he want?"

"We just talked. He was thinking about driving up here."

"When?"

"I don't know. He was just talking about it."

"Okay."

"It's interesting though, we got to talking and it made me think."

"What?"

"It got me to thinking if anything happened to either one of us."

"Uhm. What sparked that?"

"He got to talking about how when people die, folks be acting a fool and carrying on. Can't stand your ass when you're alive, but when you die they get up on the pulpit talking about... "Oh Johnny was a good"...hell and Johnny wasn't nothing but a damn hustler and no good so and so."

Ann came and crawled up on the couch munching on some corn curls. She chuckled. "I know what you mean. Niggas be acting a fool. Don't you do that if something happened to me."

"Hell, don't you get your Black ass up there if something happens to me saying, Oh my baby, oh my Dwight. Hell, take care of my ass now."

Ann laughed. "Oh I'mma take care of you, alright." She started feeling on him.

"I was telling Keith, man look give me a short service. Don't have no damn preacher up their preachin' for three hours making everybody cry or the choir singing some depressing ass songs. And I sure in the hell don't want you up there hollering and carrying on. Do your damn job now! Know what I'm saying? Shit!"

"Yeah baby." Ann said messing around with him.

"Hell! I attended so many damn funerals when I was little. They lasted all damn day. People up there lying, talking about how much they love so and so and how much they gonna miss 'em. But hell, they wouldn't even go see about them when they were alive or you'd hear them saying the day before how they gonna kill that no good mutha fucka. Folks be lying."

Ann laughed at Dwight as he was going off.

"I feel you baby."

"Anyway girl, what we eating?"

"I thought about some fried chicken."

"Well hell then, get to frying." Dwight smacked Ann on the butt as she hopped up off the couch and headed to the kitchen. Later after the food was ready, they laughed, talked, ate, then found something to watch on television and eventually turned in for the night. Dwight kept Ann cozy and protected, while she was completely devoted to him. You could see this display of affection each morning as they had their usual banter while getting dressed and having breakfast, after which Ann would go her way and Dwight would go his until the next time they were in one another's presence. Then the whole process would start all over again the next day.

However one January morning in nineteen eighty, Ann was not her usual self. She didn't feel quite right. She had remembered feeling a little queasy the night before, but thought perhaps she ate something that didn't agree with her, so she took an Alka-Seltzer to settle her stomach then hopped into bed. Ann had been snacking a lot more lately, but she had never felt the way she was feeling at that time. She ended up calling off of work to see if the feeling passed. Yet the feeling didn't pass for several more days, so she ended up making an appointment to see the doctor.

When Ann went to the doctor, he asked her could she be pregnant. She had gotten her period, so as far as she was concerned she could not be. The first thing the doctor did do was a pregnancy test. There was really nothing else to test for because Ann's pregnancy test came back positive.

As she racked her brain on how and when at the insistence of the doctor so he could determine a due date, she finally recalled on Thanksgiving night she and Dwight went to his parents' house for dinner and ended up in his old bedroom. They made love several times that night. She remembered it well because during their own little private party, they were trying to keep quiet because his parents were at home. They laughed and joked while listening to baby-making music. That night was the subject of many conversations afterwards. Well Ann and Dwight would have plenty to talk about when she got home, because the doctor set her due date for somewhere around the fifteenth of August.

Dwight beat Ann home from work. Ann didn't get off until four-thirty. So he started dinner. When she finally walked in the door, the smell made her somewhat nauseated. She hugged Dwight and smiled. He noticed that she did not look her best, but without her saying anything realized that he was going to be a father.

"You are pregnant!"

"What are you talking about?"

"You are pregnant, and yep, I know exactly when it happened."

"How do you know?"

"Okay then, baby, what's wrong?"

"I'm pregnant…"

"I told you girl. I know you."

Dwight hugged his wife tight. He was happy that he was going to be a daddy and they would give birth to what he was hoping and praying would be their first son.

The Making of a Child of Destiny

When Dwight and Ann broke the news to family and friends, they were elated. It was a little bitter sweet though because their closest associations were back in Whitehouse and Troup. Yes, they did manage to make some great connections in Houston; it just wasn't the same for Ann without Brenda there. She came to visit, but it wasn't like being in the same city.

Ann and Dwight made it through the next several months without incident. He went to work with a little more umph in his gait, as she wobbled out the door to her job at HL&P until it was finally time to welcome the new addition to the family. Overdue but here just the same, Armon Roshaud Tillman was finally here weighing in at a little over seven pounds.

Andretta was very tired from the pushing, so after Armon was cleaned up they handed the healthy baby boy to the proud papa. Dwight was so happy. He got his first son!

"Here's your son, daddy." The nurse said handing Armon to Dwight. Andretta lifted her head up to see. He was then laid on Ann's chest. As she looked at this tiny little person, tears streamed down her cheeks. She choked out the words to her husband who only moments ago she cursed.

"We did it honey. We did it."

Dwight was also choking back tears.

"Yeah, he is a perfect linebacker, baby."

Every floor at Memorial Hermann-Texas Medical Center was buzzing on August twenty-fifth from the birth of Armon. Dwight must have gone to every floor in the hospital giving out cigars. It was his proudest moment by far – the birth of their first child.

Life changed quickly for Ann and Dwight once the baby came home. Changing diapers, suctioning mucous, fevers, eight week check ups, and well-baby care ruled. Ann quickly realized how hard it was to be a wife, a new mom, and a full-time employee. She worked it out, but it was not an easy task. Armon was growing fast. Before Ann had the chance to blink, he was already crawling around the floor cooing, "Da Da."

"Dwight! Did you hear him? He said da da!"

"Hey my little linebacker, you call my name?"

Armon just kept cooing, slobbering, and giggling. He was a happy baby and he received lots of love and attention. The birth of Armon made Dwight think more often about his dream and passion. Music was in his heart and having a baby around made the music appear much more beautiful and relevant. Their home most certainly became livelier, but little did they know what was on the horizon.

Dwight and Ann were getting used the idea of little Armon, childcare, and the overall routine of being daddy and mommy. Armon had not even turned two years old when Ann received the surprise of her life. She was once again expecting. She had been busy running around doing all the things necessary to run her household efficiently. When she finally had a moment to breathe, it occurred to her that something was missing.

"Dwight, I think I skipped my period."

"Huh?"

"Yeah, I don't recall my cycle coming this month."

"Maybe it's just late."

"No, I don't think so."

"What are you saying, Ann."

She started laughing nervously.

"What I'm saying is I think I might be pregnant again."

Dwight scratched his head and smiled sheepishly.

"Well, if you are then, I guess I will get my other son sooner than later, huh?"

Ann had a dish towel hanging off of her shoulder. She quickly took the towel and popped Dwight with it.

"If I am it's gonna be a girl!"

"Well, I can run to Super X and get a home pregnancy test…"

"Okay."

Although they didn't plan on being pregnant a second time so soon, Dwight and Ann welcomed another baby. She felt that if she was pregnant then at least the two children could grow up together. When Dwight made it back from the store, Ann took the test, and what they both found out was that indeed Ann was pregnant again. Therefore the process started all over again. Morning sickness, weigh-ins, the big horse pills camouflaged as pre-natal vitamins, cravings, and mood swings.

Dwight was a great help. Yet, he had to be because being pregnant while also having a young child was much harder, as they both soon discovered. Ann was more tired and emotional this time around. Yet, the swollen ankles, the headaches, the backaches, and the restless nights were all worth-the-while when on Monday, December thirteenth, nineteen eighty-two she was able to experience the joy of that sweet little face staring directly at her after the nine months of feeling like a kangaroo. Several hours of labor and what seemed to be endless pushing of that little booger out, completely zapped Ann.

"It's a boy!" The doctor said smiling as he placed the baby in her arms. Dwight was able to cut the umbilical cord this time. As Ann went to recovery, then on to the assigned hospital room where she slept for a few hours, Dwight went to the nursery. He held Armon up so he could look through the window of the nursery to see his little brother.

"Armon, that's your baby brother."

"Budda."

Dwight chuckled as Armon attempted to say brother. Armon tapped on the window. "Budda."

Although he really didn't know what was going on, he learned very quickly once his mother got out of the hospital that Christopher Raynard Tillman wasn't going anywhere. Armon was a very good big brother and Ann was able to help him understand very early that the Tillman world no longer revolved around just him. He had to share space with another little person. Armon helped with simple tasks such as collecting pampers. He loved his little brother and Dwight and Ann loved their two little boys.

As Armon and Christopher sprouted like trees, you could see their personalities begin to develop. Armon started talking early and was quite the conversationalist. He was a curious child and was always trying to figure things out, and wanted to be left alone to do so. Christopher was the more adventurous one and always getting into things that he shouldn't. If there was something on the floor, you better bet that he would find it and end up, you guessed it, right into his mouth.

Dwight's love for young people grew tremendously. Working at Booker T. Washington helped him to understand the importance of his work as a teacher. He grew to love the teaching profession and his boys also made him realize the importance of having strong role-models and people that you could look up to. Ann saw how quickly Armon and Christopher were growing up and started getting the baby fever again.

"Baby, I was thinking…what do you think about trying for a girl?"

"Now?"

"Yeah. You know Christopher is a little over a year and if we had another baby now they could all grow up together."

"I see your point."

"We both are working. We've been saving up for a bigger house. It just seems like now would be the time to start trying."

"Shit, you know I don't mind…"

"You nasty. I know you don't mind putting the baby there."

"Well, three would be like two in terms of work. If you are up for it, I am too."

"I want my girl and her two brothers can protect her growing up."

"Well, maybe we should start looking for that big house I promised you. I still haven't forgotten."

"Hell yeah, you know I'm ready because this little small thing is not cuttin' it anymore."

"So, I'll talk with a realtor and we can go to the bank. Let's see where we're at."

The Making of a Child of Destiny

Ann and Dwight spent the following weeks looking at houses and making whoopee. It did not take Ann long at all to get pregnant. By March of nineteen eighty-four, there was another Tillman bun in the oven; and during summer break they were moving into their big four bedroom, three bath dream home in an influential neighborhood. Their house located at 9502 Strawgrass Drive in Cypress, Texas had a huge backyard and two-car garage. At that time it was an area that was undergoing new construction of several "master-planned communities." It was a very affluent area to live. Ann was certainly right when she told Brenda that with Dwight, it would be like the Jeffersons. She was moving on up.

Dwight and Ann got moved in right before school started back. On Tuesday, October sixteenth, they welcomed their little baby girl - Shawna Marie Tillman. Her middle name Marie was named after Dwight's grandmother. She was a beautiful baby. Dwight adored his little princess and Ann dressed her up and treated her almost like a Barbie doll. At this point, they felt their little family was complete with two boys, a girl, and a great big house. Dwight R. Tillman was a man of his word. There was no doubt in Ann's mind that dreams do come true.

Things were going very well. Dwight's mom and dad were very proud of their son and grandchildren. Mr. and Mrs. Brown were equally proud and were always grateful to see Ann and her family whenever they drove back to Whitehouse. Those three children were loved and spoiled rotten. Wanda Tillman was always buying something for her grandbabies. Buck and Jimmie showered them with experiences. They ran around and played at Ann's parents' home, while they learned manners from Dwight's parents.

The holidays were always a fun time. When Christmas nineteen eighty-five came around, Armon was already five years of age, Christopher was three and Shawna was one. They were three children with very distinctive personalities, and that Shawna had everybody wrapped around her little fingers. She was a smart cookie and a very affectionate baby, who loved to give kisses. She was adorable in her little church dresses.

Ann and Dwight had a lovely family, and as she often watched her children play, she would laugh to herself at their little personalities. She was content with her family and her life. Dwight was content, but somewhere deep down there was still this burning passion inside for his music. He knew that somehow and someway that this would come to pass, and like everything else he would make that dream come true too.

THIS IS MY DREAM

School resumed after the holidays and it was hard to believe that it was January nineteen eighty-six already. Dwight had been at Booker T. Washington for nine years and in just a little while he would have been teaching math for ten years. He couldn't believe it himself. As he was with his friends, Dwight was a caring teacher and would help his students with anything he could and go out of his way to help them. So this term he developed a relationship with a troubled teen.

Dwight mentored this young man who had to get a passing grade in his class in order to graduate from Booker T. Washington High School. What Dwight discovered while working with him was that despite his reputation, he was actually a good kid. He was dealt a difficult hand he had to play and just needed a little encouragement and guidance. He was struggling, so Dwight spent extra time tutoring him and helping him to understand math better. This teenager's home life wasn't the greatest. There was not a father figure in the picture and what Dwight did not want to happen was to lose him to the streets.

Dwight could see the potential in this student and the more he got to know him the more he embraced him. Dwight could see the amount of effort the student was putting in and the significant change in his attitude and the work he was turning in. So, Dwight worked with him, giving him every opportunity to earn extra credit to bring his grade up. It was down to the wire and this kid had to score at least a high C this term in order to pass the required math and graduate.

As it came down to final exams, it really could go either way. Dwight worked with the student the entire term and he was actually doing very well in comparison to past terms. As Dwight graded the final math exams, he saw that the student was just a half a point away from the required score on the final exam to pass the class with a C. Dwight went over the test several times making sure there were no mistakes on his part. Once he realized that the student was a half a point away he was confronted with a decision that he never knew he would ever have to face and a decision that would place his compassionate being against his moral and ethical being. He was conflicted.

Dwight knew how hard this young man worked. He knew that if this student did not graduate he would inevitably give up and go back to the streets giving up his dream to go to college and lose faith in other Black men, but more importantly in himself. While any teacher might feel this is an easy decision, for Dwight it just wasn't that cut and dry. After many hours of consideration, Dwight felt the need to give this student a boost and allowed his compassion to win. He gave the half of point for effort on this student's test; but who would have ever imagined the course of events that would ultimately follow.

There were some staff members and faculty who were not able to reconcile this young man's passing score and questioned not only his grade but the amount of time that Dwight spent with him. As a result, an investigation ensued. After a long and agonizing summer, Dwight learned in August of nineteen eighty-six that his teaching career was over and he was asked to resign from Booker T. Washington High School.

He was extremely disappointed but he knew that it was the choice he made and he took responsibility for his decision. Ann was very disappointed but very understanding of his dilemma and his decision. Dwight's mother and father on the other hand were not as supportive. They ranted and raved about him never being able to find another good job in education. They bellowed about how he and Ann had a mortgage and how they had three mouths to feed. Dwight got fed up with the pressure.

"Fuck it Ann. Damn."

"Dwight look… The hell with what they say right now. You made a choice; you got fired as a result of the choice. I support you."

"I know Ann, but damn. I'm tired of trying to please my damn parents. I love them, but now I need to follow my dreams."

"Dwight stop beating yourself up. We will be fine. What about your music?"

What about his music was the question! School started back and Dwight was feeling a little empty, but hopeful. He was paid through the summer, but after that he had to quickly make some things happen. At that point Dwight wasted no time in getting started with his real passion. He inquired about what to do and started checking out various acts off the bat. He immediately went to work on building his stable of artists.

Dwight found himself on the highway back and forth from Tyler checking out acts and arranging meetings to get the couple of acts he had secured heard. By the time the end of September came, he was in business and making some things happen. Ann was very supportive and helped him in any way that she could. They worked as a team and if they could make all the other dreams in their lives come true they certainly could also make this one happen.

As Ann and Dwight were seeing some real progress, others started to believe in him and found ways to help. They were excited and the way Dwight was moving, handling his business, and on the grind, things were taking off. James Bowie, who married Brenda, Ann's best friend, had become a good friend and ear to him. Soon it didn't matter that he would not be teaching; Dwight was making waves in music and his parents had to recognize that this time, it was about him making his own dream come true and living his truth.

October rolled around and Dwight was still traveling back and forth checking out acts. He believed that Tyler, Texas had more than enough talent and he wanted to give some young people in the town the opportunity to make it in the business. So he focused specifically in that area.

On Sunday, October 26, 1986, there was a church program going on that promised to have some real talent that Dwight could check out. Dwight and Ann decided to pack up the children and drive to Tyler to go check them out. When they got to Whitehouse, Dwight ended up staying at Buck's house with the children, while Ann and her mother went to church. Ann's goal was to go check out the talent and report back to Dwight. They were jamming at New Canaan and Ann thought that there were some real possibilities. While Dwight was at the house, Raymond called to let him know that they were barbequing and since they are already in town, they might as well come on through.

When Ann got back from the church, Dwight told her what the game plan was.

"Hey Ann, Raymond called. Him and Mop are barbequing and asked us to stop by."

"Sooky-sooky now! Hell yeah. I'm hungry too."

"We need to do something about the car though. Something ain't running right with it. See if May Jo and them will let us use the car to drive over to Tyler, and if he can check it out, then when we get back we'll switch back."

Albert, Mary Jo's son was standing there listening and watching the exchange between Ann and Dwight. Ann seeing him up under them suggested to Dwight that they take him with them over to Glenda's.

"Alright. Then we might as well take Albert with us, if he wants to go."

"Was there anything good there?"

"What you mean, Dwight?"

"The acts nigga, the acts."

"Oh, Shit! Yeah you should have been there."

"Worthwhile?"

"Yeah, we'll talk about it on the way to Tyler."

Ann called Mary Jo, then she and Dwight headed over to switch cars and then on over to Mop and Raymond's house. Tyler is about thirty minutes from

Whitehouse. Ann and Dwight laughed and talked on the way to Tyler. She was able to give him some names of singers that were at the church before they pulled up in her sister's and brother in-law's house.

"Hey Shaw Shaw!" Glenda took Shawna out of Ann's arms. "How's my baby?"

"Girl take her…Little spoil ass…But that's my shoo shoo."

"Where's your car at?" Raymond asked Dwight.

"Man, it started acting up and I didn't want to take the chance on getting stuck on the highway."

"Isn't that May Jo's new car…"

"Yeah, man."

"And they let you drive it?"

"Why not, he knows I'm good."

Dwight, Raymond, Glenda, and Ann sat around laughing and talking. All of the children which included Nicole, Albert, Armon, Christopher, and Shawna played and also got their bellies full. Tu Tu was on his way home from the military so they were all excited to see him. Also, he agreed to loan Dwight some money to help out.

"Shit, I never thought Tu Tu's ass would…"

Then Ann started to sing "Straighten up and fly right… I guess the military did him some good."

"Ann, hell. You know Tu Tu is still Tu Tu." Dwight said laughing.

"He hasn't even seen Shawna yet."

Mop was looking a little puzzled. "Ann, he's seen her hasn't he?"

"I honestly don't know…I can't remember…uhm that's a good question."

"Uhm. I would have thought he has, but maybe not…Is he coming by here or meeting yaw back in Whitehouse?"

"He's going over to your mother's, Mop." Raymond said.

"Oh okay…So what ya'll have to drop Albert off, then ya'll running by Buck's then heading back on to Houston?"

"Yeah. We better head on out, it's almost eleven. Shit that drive can get long when it's late. But I got Ann and the children to keep me company so…I guess it won't be too bad."

Dwight and Ann stood up and hugged Glenda and Raymond, gathered the children and started loading everyone into the car. Glenda followed them outside so she could move her car into the spot where Dwight parked. Albert, Armon, and Christopher climbed into the back seat. Shawna sat on her mother's lap in the front seat. Dwight got in on the driver's side. They waved and then pulled off, heading back toward Whitehouse.

"Whoo, I had a really good time. I'm glad I came. Hell, I'm glad you are with me. Girl I love you, and having you with me makes it worth-the-while."

"Yeah it was good wasn't it? Well, at least you don't have to drive back by yourself. I can't wait to see Tu Tu. I don't think he's seen Shawna yet." Ann kissed Shawna on her forehead. This little baby girl was her pride and joy. She sat there stroking Shawna's head while she was sleeping on her mother's lap. The boys were in the back seat playing tap back and forth. Albert was sitting between Armon and Christopher blocking them from tapping each other.

"Hey, ya'll need to settle down back there."

"Yes ma'am." They went back to giggling and playing.

Ann and Dwight were talking and recapping the day when they came to the corner of Loop 323 and West Elm Street about five houses down from Glenda and Raymond's house. When they pulled up to the stop sign Dwight noticed a person driving recklessly looking like he wasn't going to stop.

"Oh shit! He's coming way too fast. I don't think he's going to stop!"

"Move out the way Dwight!"

"He's coming too fast, there's no where to go?"

"Ann we're gonna get hit!"

"Oh Jesus!..."

Dwight was less concerned about himself, and instead was focused on protecting Ann and the baby. As the on-coming car was speeding toward them, there was little time to do anything but brace for the impact. As he reached over in the attempt to use his body to shield his wife and daughter, the drunk driver struck the vehicle on the driver side, spinning the car completely around and smashing it almost like a sardine can.

Up the street, Glenda was pulling her car into the garage. Before she could get out of the car good and into the house, she heard a big bang. The thoughts running through her mind were, "No, not possible. It can't be." Glenda started out down the street first slowly on foot, then yelled out for her daughter Nicole to follow.

"Nicole!" As Glenda and Nicole started running up to the loop, they saw the blue Ford that Dwight was driving completely mashed in. "No, No, No, No, No!

"Oh my God! Nicole go get your dad, and call 911!"

"Oh Jesus, no Jesus! Oh my God."

Glenda saw Armon and Christopher in the back seat screaming and crying. She immediately ran to them and pulled them out the car. They appeared to only have nicks and cuts. She had them sit down over to the side, while she tried to pull Albert out the backseat who was going in and out of consciousness. Armon and Christopher were crying for their mommy and daddy.

Raymond and Nicole arrived back at the scene. Nicole walked part way down the road to direct on-coming traffic that would not be able to see that there was an accident. Raymond helped get everyone else out of the car.

As Glenda went to the passenger side, she was trying to get Ann to respond. "Ann, wake up! Ann." Ann did not respond but Glenda could see that she was still breathing. Raymond ran to help Glenda pull Ann out of the car. Glenda looked up and saw Shawna laying in the windshield half way in the car and half way out in a pile of shattered glass. The entire car was turned completely around where the side wheels were dangling over a big black hole making it difficult to get to them.

"Oh Raymond, there's the baby!" Glenda reached up to pull little Shawna from the dashboard, while Raymond struggled to get Ann out by himself. Raymond was trying to wake Ann up, but she would not wake up. As Glenda grabbed Shawna, she started crying frantically when she noticed as she held the baby in her arms, she could hear only a faint breath coming from Shawna. Her body was listless, barely holding on to life.

Raymond had gotten Ann out of the car and laid her out over in the grass. He then ran over to the driver side where Dwight's head was pressed against the horn causing it to beep loudly. Cars continued to drive by slowly. Raymond tried to get Dwight out of the car, but the door was jammed in too bad. "Dwight, man! Can you hear me?" There was no response.

"Mop, I can't get Dwight out! He's not responding!"

Raymond and Glenda were frantic and Armon and Christopher were horrified not really understanding everything that was going on. They kept crying, "I want my mommy!"

"Why won't my mommy wake up?"

Raymond grabbed Armon and Christopher up in his arms and held them trying to calm them until help came. It seemed like hours passed before the police arrived.

"Oh God, please no! Father God, please have mercy!" Glenda continued to hold Shawna in her arms who was unresponsive. Not even a cry came from her limp body. As she stood there holding Shawna and crying and pleading, she heard the last breath leave Shawna's little fragile body. Little Shawna Marie had just died in her auntie's arms.

"Oh God no! Raymond! Oh Jesus!" Glenda was crying uncontrollably breaking down when the fire department finally arrived, followed almost immediately by the ambulance. The fire department pried the door open to get Dwight out of the car. While Raymond held on to Armon and Christoper, the paramedics laid everyone else out on the grass to check vitals and to ascertain their condition. Armon and Christopher, who barely had nicks and cuts, watched in terror.

Glenda was pacing back and forth trying to cope with the situation. All of the passengers were loaded up into ambulances and transported to the hospital. Glenda rode with Shawna and the boys. Shawna was pronounced dead on the way to the hospital. Glenda was devastated. All she could do was grab her two nephews and hold them tight, trying to keep from completely losing it in front of them. She just shook her head and looked up with tears in her eyes. "Poor Ann. Oh God."

When they got to the hospital, Albert was awake, but Ann was still unconscious, but alive. However there was no news on Dwight. Raymond and Glenda did not know what was going on with him because they couldn't get to him. Glenda called Buck, Jimmie, Brenda, James, Mr. and Mrs. Tillman, Mary Jo...

"It's bad. You need to come."

"Well honey what's going on?"

Glenda kept it together long enough to let them know that they needed to get to the hospital. They didn't have all the information. They were still waiting.

"The boys are fine. We are waiting."

She just couldn't tell them that Shawna died. She got off the phone and went back in the room where Raymond was with Armon and Christopher.

He stroked their heads. "You okay babies?"

"Where's my mommy?"

"She's going to be okay Armon. We just have to wait honey."

"What about my daddy?"

Glenda couldn't cope with the questions. She left the room to cry while Raymond stood with the boys. As Glenda was coming out of the room, family members were arriving. You could hear Brenda and James walking in the door to the emergency room.

"Brenda, I ain't playing with you. Don't you take your ass in this hospital acting a fool yelling and stuff. It's tough enough. Don't make it worse. Be strong."

"Okay, James. Just be cool. Alright I hear you!"

Brenda was nervous because they knew it was bad, but just not how bad. She and James walked up to Glenda, when Glenda whispered to them that Shawna didn't make it, James broke down. James Bowie was a loner but he and Dwight were very close. So when he heard that his daughter didn't make it, he was devastated and all he could think about was Dwight, Ann and the boys.

"Oh damn!" James broke down and Brenda and Glenda had to take him from ear shot from others standing around.

"Glenda, what about Ann and Dwight."

"Well, Ann was unconscious, when they loaded her into the ambulance. We don't know about Dwight because we really couldn't get to him. It's just a waiting game right now."

Quickly the hospital emergency room was filled with family and friends. Everyone was waiting around just trying to see what was going on. Finally the doctors came out and gave reports.

"Andretta has a severe concussion. There's a lot of bruising, so she won't be able to move much. But she'll be okay. We're going to admit her for a few days. Keep an eye on her."

The family members were anxious but relieved as they continued to hear the doctor's report. "Albert, well he has a pretty bad banged up leg. He'll be okay but he probably won't be playing any more sports…Armon, Christopher…they're fine just a few minor scrapes. We bandaged those up. They can go home."

Mrs. Tillman spoke up. "What about Dwight and Shawna?"

Glenda grabbed Raymond and looked over at Brenda and James.

"Well, we will have someone come out in a moment and give you more information as it becomes available."

After what seemed to be several more hours, the hospital chaplain and two other doctors and a nurse came over. They pulled the family in a room. Glenda pulled James and Brenda in as well. One of the doctors spoke up.

"I'm very sorry. Both Shawna and Dwight suffered major internal injuries. There was nothing that we could do."

"Oh Lord!" yelled Mrs. Tillman, almost passing out.

"Neither survived the accident."

Keith jerked his hat as he took a deep breath. "Oh man!"

Family members broke down creating a panic. They took the family in the patient room where Dwight and Shawna were placed to allow them to see them. Their lifeless bodies laid there as all machines around them were turned off. "Oh my God!..Oh Ann!"

"Oh God, Why?"

The family just stood around in shock. Most of them were barely able to say a word.

Buck spoke up. "Does Ann know yet?"

"No, we haven't broken the news to her. We thought we'd rather her see family members first."

"Where is she doctor?"

The doctors directed Mrs. Brown, Glenda, and Tu Tu to Ann's room. The chaplain, Mr. and Mrs. Tillman, James, and most of the others stayed in the room with Dwight and Shawna, grieving and spending a few moments with them. "So this is it… Lord, my baby…too soon."

Mary Jo was with Albert. Nicole took Armon and Christopher into the room where Albert was sitting up and talking. Buck, Brenda, Glenda, and Tu Tu walked into Ann's room and noticed her groaning in excruciating pain. They knew that the doctors would be in shortly to break the news to her. Buck didn't say a word or show any emotion. She just kept this grave look on her face. Glenda was being the nurturer.

"Hey sweetie…You okay?"

Ann groaned in pain. "Oh…uhm…no, it hurts. Where's the children?"

"The boys are out there with May Jo." As Glenda spoke with her sister, you could see that she was extremely saddened and trying to comfort her sister the best she could. They all knew that in a matter of moments, the doctors would come in to give Ann the news about her husband and daughter.

"What? Ya'll looking like somebody d…"

Just as Ann was getting her sentence out, the chaplain, doctors and nurses came in.

"Andretta, how are you feeling right now?"

"Uhm, well how do you think I feel right now?"

"Well, we have some news for you."

Glenda and Tu Tu moved closer to Ann, while Glenda stroked her arm.

"Okay."

"Your family took a pretty hard hit."

"Yeah."

"Your boys, they're fine, they just have a few bumps. They can go home."

"Okay."

"You have a really bad concussion, so we're going keep you for a few days…You have a lot of family here who can take care of your boys, alright…so don't you worry about them."

"Your nephew, he's fine too, okay."

"What about my husband and daughter?"

Tears streamed down Glenda's face as she rubbed Ann's arm more intensely. Tu Tu lowered his head. Buck just stared straight ahead, but observing Ann out of the corner of her eyes. It was so hard for them to keep their composure.

"Well, Andretta, that's what we want to talk with you about."

"Okay."

"Your husband and daughter sustained some really bad injuries in the accident. Your husband had two broken arms... both his legs were broken and he had a crushed chest cavity. The injuries were too extensive... We're sorry but...they didn't make it, Andretta."

"Huh?"

Ann starting crying, "Huh?"

Glenda in a low tone said, "Honey they died."

"No! No! Oh God! No not Dwight! Not Shawna!" Ann screamed out painfully loud for her husband and daughter. "Shawna! Dwight! Oh Jesus! No! My baby! Ann was crying uncontrollably. "Please God no!"

"We may have to give her something to calm her," one of the doctors whispered.

Glenda, Buck and Tu Tu along with the hospital chaplain just did their best to console Ann as she continued to scream out her husband and daughter's name. "Dwight! Oh God my baby...What am I gonna do....Lord God help me...Jesus...No!"

As Buck stood there firmly looking ahead, barely showing emotion, a closer look exposed that there was a single tear rolling down her cheek.

LOVE LOST

The day of the funeral, the church was filled to capacity as family, friends, colleagues, and students came to bid farewell. Three charter buses were parked outside as the drivers waited to carry those who would leave the service with only a memory of Dwight and Shawna. There was no hollering and screaming, no preaching, no singing, just the reading of the twenty-third Psalms.

"The LORD is my shepherd; I shall not want.
He makes me to lie down in green pastures;
He leads me beside the still waters.
He restores my soul;
He leads me in the paths of righteousness
For His name's sake.

Yea, though I walk through the valley of the shadow of death,
I will fear no evil; For You are with me;
Your rod and Your staff, they comfort me.

You prepare a table before me in the presence of my ene-
mies;
You anoint my head with oil; My cup runs over.
Surely goodness and mercy shall follow me
All the days of my life;
And I will dwell in the house of the LORD
Forever."

Andretta was devastated by the loss of her husband and only daughter. While all medical indications perhaps might say that she would not physically be able to attend the funeral, Andretta got up and half way through the service to everyone's dismay, walked into the church unexpectedly to see Dwight and Shawna off.

As she walked down the long aisle, flashing through her mind were memories of the last time she took that walk. It was to celebrate a happy occasion. As she mustered up the strength to move through the constant barrage of thoughts of the "I do's," and recollections of those faithful vows she took "until death us do part," she never imagined that in less than ten years she would once again walk down that aisle only to say goodbye forever to her only true love. As she made it to the front, she looked upon their still bodies, placed her hands on her chest, and found the strength to kiss Dwight and Shawna on the foreheads and finally, the ultimate strength to say goodbye.

The Making of a Child of Destiny

Tears streamed down Mrs. Tillman's face as she bent down and kissed her son and only granddaughter on the forehead. It was a sad day and no amount of comforting could help to ease the pain. It was silent in the church, but you could hear the sniffles and cries. The family worked hard to give Dwight his wishes, no matter how hard it was. They waited to get away from the church so they could grieve freely in their own way. Mrs. Tillman could only bear five minutes before she had to leave. The service was brief and that is how Dwight wanted it. Yet, it didn't remove the truth of the profound sadness they felt.

Things happened so fast. One minute Ann and Dwight were laughing and talking about the day's events. The next minute, life changed dramatically. How would Ann be able to move on with her life? This is a question she played over and over again in her mind. "I am a widow." No amount of planning could have prepared her for the road ahead.

Ann stayed at her mother's home for a little while in Whitehouse as she recuperated. The physical scars from the accident would soon heal, yet the emotional wounds from losing her husband and only daughter may never heal. While she may be able to move forward with her life in time, she would never ever forget October twenty-sixth, nineteen eighty-six – the day when she lost her husband,

Dwight Ray Tillman at the tender age of thirty-one and her beloved daughter Shawna Marie Tillman at the tender age of two. Gone too soon, and her life would never be the same. He left this world in pursuit of his dream.

Days went by. However, the time that Ann spent at Buck's house allowed her to have her mother with her, which is the place that most little girls go when they are hurting. Mrs. Brown offered her fragile little girl, who was only twenty-eight years of age at the time, quiet but loving support. Brenda was a constant friend. Family members stayed close to her as she started her long road to recovery both physically and emotionally.

Ann had her bouts of crying and yelling out for Dwight and Shawna, while Mrs. Brown supported her and encouraged her to be strong. She spent many days off alone in the corner thinking and crying. Although with each day it may get better, she was overwhelmed with grief and had no where to really turn, to ease the deep pain she was feeling. She did her best to cope. She did her best to help her sons to cope. She did her best to pull what was left of her family together and keep on living, although death had overtaken a part of them.

"Honey, take it one day at a time."

"These days are long. I just want to sleep and never wake up. Why? Just tell me, why us? Why them?"

The Making of a Child of Destiny

"I know sweetie, but you have to keep living. We are here for you."

Brenda got teary-eyed each time she saw Ann and the boys. Yet, it did not stop her from being there and being a best friend. Her husband James was very supportive as well. He lost a dear friend. Between pain medication and nerve pills each day passed slowly. All Ann could do was take it day-by-day and lean on friends and family in that time of need.

Whitehouse offered a cushion. Both the Tillmans and the Browns helped to provide comfort and understanding to Armon and Christopher. The family took a blow. The boys, while yet young, would have to understand that their father and sister were not be coming back and at some point they would have to travel back to Houston and learn how to live without them. Once Armon and Christopher actually realized that their father and sister would not be coming with them, they clinged even more to Ann. It was difficult for them.

"Mommy, I want daddy!"

"I know honey. I want your daddy too."

It broke Ann's heart to hear her son ask for daddy, and not be able to call him and let them hear his voice. All she could do was love on them, hug them and help them as best she could to move past their feelings, all the while she was struggling to move past hers. "Come here baby.

Mommy loves you very much. Daddy loved you very much. God needed daddy and Shawna and so they are with God now. We'll be okay."

"Can we go see daddy and Shawna at God's house?"

"I wish we could, but God wasn't ready for us yet, Christopher."

"But why?"

"Honey, maybe he had something else for us to do here. Maybe he needed you and Armon to stay here with me, and me to stay here with you."

Christopher laid his head on his mother's chest. She just held him tightly, rubbed his head and kissed the side of his head. "Christopher baby, we are going to be fine."

Ann started to tear up. One of the family members took Christopher in an attempt to distract him. Armon went over to console his mother. "Daddy's not gone mommy. He is right here all the time and whenever you feel sad, you talk to him this way." Armon said pointing at his heart. Ann looked at her six year-old son and just hugged him as tight as she could. In that split second she heard Dwight's voice speaking through his eldest son. She knew in her heart, no matter how hard it might be at this moment, it would get better. So, she was finally ready to go back home.

Ann and the boys headed back to Houston. Raymond and Glenda traveled with them to spend some time and to help create some sort of normalcy in their lives. Many cards of sympathy and people's condolences were there waiting. Glenda and Raymond took care to read them first and when Ann was up to it she went through them one-by-one as she was able.

Stepping back into that big home for the first time since the accident gave Ann an eerie feeling. Her dream home had suddenly turned into a big cold empty and lifeless place. As she walked into the house, she glanced at family photos hung about. Chills went through her as she looked upon what used to be simple ordinary family photos. However, now they were bitter-sweet memories of what used to be.

"It's okay, Ann. It is going to be alright."

"I know. It's just so hard. Oh God, it's just so hard."

Ann just shook her head and grasped her chest as she continued to move through the house looking at it much differently than before.

Glenda and Raymond stayed with her to help her and the boys get through the coming days. They stayed as long as they were able, while other family and friends checked on her to see how she was holding up. Both Glenda and Raymond helped Ann to sort out all of the tedious, yet necessary details such as life insurance policies and bills, while also providing a buffer to help the boys cope without their father. With each day Ann became stronger and stronger.

In the accident, Ann had suffered a severe concussion and bruising. Although it was several weeks after, she was still experiencing pain and headaches. The doctor expected it to take some time for Ann's wounds to heal. So during the follow-up check up, the doctor told Ann to continue taking Tylenol, drink plenty of fluids and get as much rest as she could. However, resting was not something that Ann could do easily at all. She was used to snuggling up with her husband, and Shawna running in the middle of the night climbing in the bed between the two of them. Ann missed those precious moments. Most nights after kissing the boys goodnight, she cried herself to sleep and this happened night after night.

Soon Glenda and Raymond traveled back to Tyler, Ann went back to work, and Armon and Christopher got back into their regular routine. She was finally in the house alone with her boys and the house just wasn't the same. There was no Dwight and no Shawna. It was her raising the boys alone, the best she could. Financially speaking she had no worries; emotionally speaking was another matter all together.

Ann accepted that while it may be difficult, she was going to have to get herself together and work hard to raise her boys without their father and accept that life may not be the same without her adorable little girl, but it does and must go on. She was grateful for the wonderful friends and family who helped her to get through that time of her life. It was not an easy time and no matter how much money came from the insurance policy, it didn't necessarily make life easier. It only helped to make her more comfortable in an uncomfortable situation.

Christopher's birthday rolled around and the holidays crept upon Ann. The stress of it all hit her extremely hard. Increasingly, she was experiencing nagging headaches, joint pain, and emotional chaos. What was a fun time of the year for the last several years was now a solemn time. She sunk into a depression around Christmas and New Years as she reflected on the many memories of times of yore. With the help of people around her, she got through those times as well and spent the next several months getting through each moment day-by-day. Ann was determined to stay in Houston, so she kept going, kept praying, and kept living the best she could.

As months continued to come and go, Ann was still having a lot of pain and swelling in her joints. The headaches continued and she was often fatigued. Finally, the doctors who previously had chalked everything up to residual feelings from the accident and depression from losing two family members, decided to explore a little further.

"How are you feeling?"

"I am really tired all the time. The headaches seem to increase. My fingers and toes tingle a lot now."

"Uhm. Well Andretta, with the injuries you sustained in the car accident, it is not uncommon to experience aches and pains. You have been through a lot, and it is expected to be somewhat tired. Your body has been under a significant amount of stress physically and emotionally. You had a severe concussion. Uhm. Yes, it is possible that you could have developed migraines. I can imagine you are also experiencing some depression."

"Okay. I just would have thought that some of this would've subsided."

"Well yes, but everyone is different and perhaps your body is responding this way. However, the tingling…uhm. So that with the other symptoms…Well what I would like to do is run a few tests just to be safe and go from there."

"Okay."

"What I want to do is a complete blood work-up and urine analysis. Let me take a look at that then we will go from there. Are you able to go over to the lab today?"

"Yes."

"Good. It will take a few days to get back. If you haven't heard anything within a week, give me a call back. In the meantime, I will prescribe a muscle relaxer to help alleviate any inflammation in the joints, which can also cause some pain."

"Okay."

"So let's see you back here in two weeks."

"Thanks doctor."

"Stop at the receptionist and she will give you the order for your labs."

"Okay, thanks."

Ann headed over to the lab, then to pick up the boys and on home to prepare dinner and face another day in the house that had yet to turn back into a home. Only two days had passed when she received a call from her doctor's office. She wanted Ann to come back into the office. When Ann went back to her doctor's, she learned that her doctor wanted to run more tests.

"Okay, Andretta, we did get your tests back. It looks like you might be anemic. However, one test came back positive and some showed elevations that I think we should explore closer. The ANA test..."

"The what?"

"Antinuclear Antibody...we call ANA for short, came back positive. With the symptoms you are describing and the fact that this test was positive, it makes me want to test further for lupus. Now, understand that many people who have a positive ANA test, do not have lupus, but often people with lupus usually have a positive ANA test."

"Okay so, what is lupus?"

"Lupus is an inflammatory disease where your body's immune system attacks itself…your own tissues and organs."

"So, how do you get it?"

"Well…you don't necessarily have it… that's what we want to test for. But, if there is a diagnosis of lupus, it is most likely that you have had it for a while, and it was just laying dormant and triggered by the accident."

"So what happens if I have it?"

"Well Andretta, like I said, you may not have it but if you do we would treat it and keep the symptoms under control. Currently there is no cure for it so you would basically learn how to live as normal of life as possible with the disease. But again, just because you have a positive ANA test does not mean you have lupus."

"Okay, so now what?"

"Well, I am going to refer you to a rheumatologist. He will do some further testing. But because lupus can mimic so many other things, it may take some time, so you will have to be a little patient."

"Hell, I have no choice but to be, do I?"

"I understand. You've been through a lot."

Ann left the doctors office and said a prayer. All of this was quite overwhelming and the last time she remembered even going to church was Dwight's and Shawna's funeral. She needed some spiritual edification and she knew it, but Whitehouse was too far away to travel for church especially when she was working hard to stabilize the boys. Armon and Christopher needed Ann more than ever before, and she was determined to get through whatever came her way. What could be more devastating than what had already happened? So her mindset was such that whether she had lupus or not, she would be okay.

Ann and the boys were getting on without Dwight and Shawna. It was difficult, but they were managing. Ann however felt the emptiness. Before when she would get home from work, she had all sorts of things going on to occupy her. Shawna often grabbed her by the leg and clung to her. The boys were constantly going at it, while Dwight whipped them into shape and wrestled around with them on the floor keeping them occupied while she cooked dinner. Shawna would jump on top of the pile yelling, "Daddy, daddy! My daddy!" She would move Armon's and Christopher's hands off of Dwight. Ann would observe them and just shake her head at how Shawna was taking control of all the men in her home. Ann would get tickled as Shawna wrapped Dwight around her little finger.

She could get anything out of her daddy when she flashed him with her big brown eyes. "Hey baby! You know just how to get your daddy, don't you?"

Ann could hear his voice in her mind. She was able to smile for the first time as she thought on the two of them interacting with one another. Whenever she threw a temper tantrum or the terrible two's syndrome kicked in he would playfully say, "See now that's your damn child." They both would laugh watching her little personality rule their world. She would go pop one of the boys and they would call out, "Mama, Shawna's hitting me…Mama, Shawna's biting…Mama, get Shawna…Mama…"

Ann would reply, "Damn, is that the only name ya'll know."

Shawna was a big-little girl and it was funny just watching Christopher trying to pick her up to take her to Ann. "Now come on. She is only two years old and ya'll can't handle her?"

All and all, the boys were equally protective of their little sister, and she knew how to wind both of them up and she would do so every opportunity she got. The house on Strawgrass Drive, no matter how big and beautiful it was, was no longer full of life with the pitter-patter of little feet stirring up trouble and getting into everything. Girls added a different dynamic in the house and Ann was missing that very much. She loved her boys, but girls made things feel very different. All of the little distractions that came up with a house full although at times worked her nerves, were missed greatly. Ann didn't know quite what to do with her time now. There was an indescribable void.

Dinner time was wanting. There was no longer a little finicky female person sitting in the highchair throwing food all over the place. There was no Dwight yelling, "Woman bring Hungry Man Jack his food." Now, it was only Ann, Armon, and Christopher quietly hurrying up to eat so they could get back to whatever they found to occupy their mind and their time. It was not easy.

Speaking of not being easy, Ann's doctor called her into the office again after a battery of tests. It was confirmed, she indeed had lupus. Yet her attitude was very dismissive. "Okay, I have lupus."

Ann blocked that reality out of her mind. She was still struggling with getting stronger from losing her husband and daughter. As Ann left the doctors office alone, she lashed out where no one could hear her. "Lupus, fuck it! Hell. So fucking what! I have lupus. Well shit, I don't have my husband and daughter; I can trade all this fucking shit…Just give me the damn pills or whatever, and let me work to get on with my life!" Ann snapped and really didn't care to hear much about it.

She didn't want to hear about lupus, she didn't want to hear about who died last week, who was in the hospital, who is depressed, or anything else. That was more of a burden to carry on top of the one she was already carrying. She cared, but she was not interested in hearing anything that made it harder for her to just be okay. She already lost her husband and daughter, and her father was recently diagnosed with lung cancer. So at that junction, Ann was like, "I just don't give a damn."

MOVING ON

Growing up Ann loved music, the arts, and nature. She Time went by and it waited for no one. It was already about a year and eight months since the death of Dwight and Shawna. Ann and the boys were getting on quite well. Yet there was still a void. Her life had become somewhat mundane. The same thing happened day in and day out. There was very little emotion or flare. The spark was missing. Sure, she laughed with the boys and with family and friends outwardly, but inside she was still crying. Things might have been going alright and she may have been coping well with her father's illness, yet she still wanted to be close to her husband. She knew her father would be okay.

Ann moved along in her routine getting stronger with each passing day. Things were finally getting better and looking a little brighter until another setback came along. On June twenty-sixth, nineteen eighty-eight, Ann received a call that her dad had passed away. She took it extremely hard and the news sent her into a whirlwind of stress. As a result, her body felt the sting in ways that shocked her and most definitely got her attention.

After a couple of days, Ann started to suffer from a host of symptoms including chest pains and severe fatigue. She broke out in a horrible rash and was knocked on her back sick and hardly able to move for several days at a time. It was the worst she had ever felt physically. She thought she was going to die. Doctors confirmed that she was having an acute lupus crisis brought on by stress. Ann realized then that her condition was serious and not something to push aside or ignore. As she lay in bed recuperating, flashes of Dwight and his dream flashed through her mind. All sorts of thoughts flooded her, and she soon felt the urgency to so something of consequence.

Ann discovered during the crisis that lupus was not something she could minimize and then think that she would be okay. She knew that she had to take her condition seriously and come to understand her triggers to stay alive. Again she felt this nagging sense of urgency to do something. She felt that perhaps time was running out on her. This feeling played a major role in her finally accepting one of the many invitations to attend church. When Ann and her neighbor was chatting one Saturday afternoon as Ann was returning from the grocery store, they were talking about a little bit of this and a little bit of that. Her neighbor invited her to church and this time Ann accepted. The following day she and the boys went to church, and what a service it was. From that moment on,

Ann's life took an unexpected turn. She sat in the pews, closed her eyes and just listened intently to the voice of an angel singing Amazing Grace. As she listened to every note sang in perfect harmony by what had to be at that time one of the most powerful voices she had ever heard, every note sent a chill through her body easing any pain she might have felt.

"Amazing grace, how sweet the sound that saved a wretch like me..."

With tears streaming down her cheeks, Ann bore witness to the goodness of God, and His healing power. The death of her father and the lupus crisis created a major storm in her life. Through this storm, there was a shaking in her spirit. Ann realized that she could actually die from this disease and she was not ready to go. Her soul was stirred that day at church.

"I once was lost, but now I'm found. 'Twas blind, but now I see. 'Twas grace that taught my heart to fear and grace my fears relieved. How precious did that grace appear. The hour I first believed. When we've been there ten thousand years. Bright shining as the sun, We've no less days to sing God's praise. Then when we first begun..."

Ann felt the spirit of God through every word belted out and was filled. "Amazing grace, how sweet the sound, that saved a wretch like me. I once was lost, but now I'm found. Was blind, but now I see."

Ann was thinking, "Who in the hell is this woman with a voice like that?" She was blown away. Ann could feel her voice, her power, and her soul as she sang. She thought of Dwight and Shawna and was blessed that although time was short-lived with them, it was sweet amazing grace that saved her and this day in church started Ann on a real course of healing and soul-searching. After the service, Ann approached the singer.

"My, my, my…you have a voice on you."

"Thank you."

"Have you ever thought to do something more with it?"

"Yeah I have, but I wouldn't know where to start. I would need help on what to do, how to get started…you know."

"Uhm. Okay…Well look, what is your name?"

"Kathy…Kathy Taylor."

"Well look, Kathy, keep singing…start there. Don't stop. I was blessed today. Your voice sent chills through me. Oh my God! Don't stop. I look forward to hearing more."

Ann was amazed at the talent that Ms. Taylor had. Her voice was phenomenal and she would never forget that voice as it was one of the best gospel voices she had heard in a very long time. Ann went home after the church service in deep contemplation and filled with the spirit. A few days later, Tu Tu called her. He was telling her he had this hot group that she should hear. When Tu Tu said that to her, it sparked a thought of Dwight and how he had been working to build his stable of artists. It penetrated her unexpectedly.

"Ann, we're good, I'm tellin' you. Look...right. It's four of us. It's me, Big A.J., Mitch, and Harlon. That ain't their real names but you know...anyway."

"Ya'll have a manager?"

"No see, that's what I'm saying. We can really go places. We need some help though. See Ann, that's where you come in."

"What you talkin' about Tu Tu?"

"Naw see, I figure you know a little something because of what Dwight was tryin' to do. But the truth is, we need somebody to back us."

"What you mean invest?"

"Yeah, but it's bigger than that. We want to really do something Ann...But look here, we need your help."

"Hell, man I know you can sing, but what about those other dudes? I don't know nothing about that...shit, I wouldn't even know where to start."

"Just think about it Ann."

"Alright Tu Tu. Alright. Shit."

Ann hung up from Tu Tu, but the conversation sparked a lot of thoughts about Dwight and his dream to be like Berry Gordy. She was reflecting on the times before he died. She saw how hard he was working to put together his stable of artists and fulfill his dream. As she thought about the few he had on the table she wondered where they are now. Dwight wanted to change the world the same way Berry Gordy changed the world. Tu Tu really got Ann to thinking and she wondered, "Why now? What is this really about?"

Not even a week later, one of Ann's friends she met at Yale Street Baptist Church called her. When they got together or talked on the telephone, Ann and Denise would often talk about the music industry and what Dwight was working on, and about him managing groups and so forth. The conversations weren't really serious, they were typical. So, when Denise called this time, she opened the conversation as usual, and it appeared to be no big deal.

"Hey Ann."

"Hey girl. How are you?"

"I'm good, just been working on trying to pull this group together."

"What group?"

"This girls group. We have some girls, they're pretty good, but it's tough though."

The Making of a Child of Destiny

"Why?"

"Well you know, the music industry ain't easy to break into, and right now you got all these boy groups out there, but there aren't any girls out there. You have a few but, not many."

"Yeah, I noticed that."

"So me and Deena have been working on putting this group of girls together. Our thing is like, it's the girl's time now, so we had some initial auditions to try to put a group of girls together."

"Oh okay. So how's it going?"

"It's going…but the thing is…we really need some help because we got a few people on board and we got some girls, but in truth, we don't have the money it's going to take to really do things…you know, go any further."

"Hell, Denise, that some shit now because my brother just called not even a week ago saying the same damn thing."

"What did he say?"

"Tu Tu told me he had this group of guys that were really good, but they needed some help. Based on what he said, ya'll saying the same thing. Is it that hard?

"Well…see…"

"When Dwight was doing it, I mainly stayed at home with the kids. Hell I didn't really know what the deal was, I just supported him. I listened to some of the artists, but I was not really into it like that. When we drove back to Tyler that night, it was one of the few times I even went with him."

"Wow, Ann that's deep."

"Hell, I don't know a damn thing about the music industry, and you and Tu Tu bringing ya'll ass to me like I'm some damn record producer. I don't know jack-shit about that shit."

"Girl, the truth is, we need some money to take these girls to the next level. I can't say we know a whole lot, but we've gotten this far. I figure with the financial backing we could take them places."

"Okay, so what you saying?"

"I'm asking would you be willing to invest or help?"

"My brother asked me the same thing. Uhm…let me think about it."

"You can also come and check them out to see what they're like. Tell me what you think."

"Alright, let me see."

"Cool."

"Girl, I better get my black ass off this phone. I have laundry and everything to try and get done. Hell, I don't even know what I'm cooking tonight."

"Me neither. I guess I better try and get some stuff done myself."

"Alright then, I'll let you know, girl."

Over the next couple of days, Ann thought about Kathy Taylor, Tu Tu and Denise. She asked herself if this could possibly be a sign. Certainly it must be and Denise just put the icing on the cake and confirmed that possibly, it was for Ann to pick up where Dwight left off. She knew nothing about the music industry, so she understood that if she was going to help, then she must know and understand what she is helping with and how the game was played.

Ann thought, "I have the resources, I have the time, and I have my husband's dream…alright…let me get into this and see."

Ann purchased a book entitled, Music Industry 101. It was helpful in bringing about a better understanding of how to break into the music industry and provided simplistic explanations on everything a person needed to know. It was a comprehensive guide which ultimately became Ann's bible for the music industry.

It took her no time to read the book. Every night when she would usually be overwhelmed with thoughts of Dwight and Shawna, Ann read through the book and in doing so learned about points, distribution, promotions, distribution deals, and a whole list of other things that helped her to understand that this could not only be a great investment, but it could also be an avenue to bring their dream back to life. The book brought new meaning into Ann's life. This helped her to feel closer to Dwight and after reading the book, she knew that this was the right thing to do.

Ann reached a turning point in her life. So when she called Denise back, she shared the good news with her.

"Yes."

"Yes what?"

"Yes Denise. I'll do it."

"You will!"

"Yes, I will. But I want to see what you're working with."

"Yes of course. So, when did you want to come and see them?"

"How soon will you be ready?"

"We can do this Saturday because we're already getting together. We'll make sure everybody's there."

"Alright."

On Saturday, Ann met up with Denise and her partner Deena. There she also met Alonzo Jackson, but they called him Lonnie. He was from the stable of Oakland Bay Area producers. She also met Anthony Moore who they called T-Mo, a songwriter. Denise and Lonnie were also songwriters. Ann met the group of girls that Denise had been talking about. What Ann learned was

The Making of a Child of Destiny

that there were two groups they were trying to blend: The Ultimate Masterpiece and Girls Tyme.

The Ultimate Masterpiece consisted of sisters Nicki and Nina Taylor, ages twelve and ten, who were both background vocalists, dancers and rappers. Then there was Latavia Robertson and Chris Lewis, both nine years old, and also background vocalists, dancers and rappers. Finally, the Ultimate Masterpiece consisted of Millicent Laday, who was eight. She was a D.J., Hypemaster, background vocalist, and rapper. Girls Tyme included Beyonce "BK" Knowles, who was nine; Stacie Latoison, eleven; and Jennifer Young, twelve. All three performed lead and background vocals.

So the idea that D & D Management had was to sculpt these two groups into a harmonious blend to present in one "unique" show that provided hype and entertainment consisting of singing and dancing. The goal was to "provide listening pleasure through radio, video, and live performance."

As Ann sat there watching the girls and observing the dynamics between Lonnie, T-Mo, Denise, and Deena and their approach with the girls, she saw a lot of gaps based on her understanding of Music Industry 101. She realized that she could actually do this, but if she was going to put her money behind something like this, she and Denise had to come to some sort of joint management agreement. Ann learned that no contracts were signed with Girls Tyme, the team wasn't getting paid, and there were no real plans for the girls past what she already saw. It was clear that Denise didn't have the resources to take things to the next level.

Ann gave Denise feedback and she didn't bite her tongue in doing so. Ann's position was, "if I am putting the money on the table, then some things need to be adjusted." So after the rehearsals, Ann and Denise sat down and had a heart-to-heart discussion.

"Okay Denise. I'm willing to help, but I believe there need to be some adjustments that will make things better and help this thing take off."

"Alright, tell me what you are thinking."

"Well first we need to agree on some type of co-management arrangement."

"Oh, no that's cool."

"Okay, then there need to be some contracts in place if you want to do this thing the right way."

"Okay."

"This is the other thing…it's too busy. Ya'll got too many moving pieces…It looks like ya'll trying to create some damn Parliament Funkadelic shit with little girls."

"Ann you are crazy."

"No for real. I see what you are trying to do and I support you on it. But I just think it's too busy and you need some stronger vocals. So what I would suggest is to hold some more auditions and lets pull some things tighter together. What do you think?"

"No problem. Look we need help. We need the money and if you are willing, hey, let's do it. You come in as a manager. I'm not able to do it by myself."

"Okay so if you are cool with that, I will get the paper work together and let's do this thing the right way. I want you to understand that it's gonna happen, and once it does take off, you will always be there. You will always have a place. I don't want you to think because I'm bringing the money to the table that I am just gonna push you aside. That sure in the hell ain't gonna happen. You get me? So our understanding is our understanding. You get me?"

"Girl yeah. The truth is, we need the help, and I'm glad its you."

"Alright, let's do it."

Denise embraced Ann. "Thank you so much Ann. I really appreciate this."

"Hey, the biggest thanks would be to make this successful."

Denise nodded her head in agreement, and they left.

When Ann made it home later that night, she delved even deeper into Music Industry 101. This time it was with much more intention and purpose. She was even more determined to make their dream live. She read Music Industry 101 from front to back and from that moment on, she never put it down. Ann thanked God for the signs and the wonders. She finally heard her husband's voice. He was still present just as Armon said. He was in her heart and so was his dream. With water welled up in her eyes, she looked up to the heavens and said to her husband Dwight, "We are gonna do this."

DO DREAMS COME TRUE

For Ann, "doing this" meant much more than just managing a group. It was something much bigger for her. As she studied Music Industry 101 in great detail, it became the standard operating procedure of how she conducted her business affairs. Her belief was that it was crucial to her success. As she stepped into the role of not only investor, but manager of the process and the group, she went to work to ensure that everyone at the table knew and understood the principles contained between its pages. She wanted her team to know it like the back of their hands. She made it a requirement for anyone that came on board or worked on the team to read it.

Although D & D Management with Denise at the helm started out with eight girls, Ann was fully aware from a business standpoint, that there were some major changes that would need to take place in order to take the girls to the next level. There needed to be stronger lead vocals and more continuity. Some things needed to be tighter and streamlined to help them reach the level of success that she envisioned.

Internally, Ann knew star potential when she saw it, and to be able to maximize on that star potential, some things needed to change and she did not hesitate to make those changes. So, the first thing Ann did was establish a strong team. From a production standpoint, she felt that Lonnie was her guy. It wasn't necessary for her to look past him and go find someone else. She knew Lonnie was the one. However, she also knew that it was hell dealing with him because he was "an arrogant pompous ass" who wanted everything his way.

"Damn it Lonnie, you get on my last got-damned nerves. You might be a good producer, but fuck your raggedy ass. You better piss or get off the got-damned pot. It's my fucking money and if your ass wanna get paid, you gonna do it my fucking way, kapish? You feel me?"

Ann struggled early on dealing with him and there were constant squabbles between the two of them. There were many times Ann had to tell Lonnie off and show him who was running things. He thought when Ann first stepped into the picture that because she was a woman she would back down. She quickly set him straight and went toe-to-toe with him each time he tried to push the envelope. T-Mo came on as a writer. He was Lonnie's yes man and whatever Lonnie said write he wrote. So by checking Lonnie, Ann in essence checked T-Mo too. Once Lonnie realized that Ann was forking over the money, his loyalty shifted. Yet, Ann knew that Lonnie was for Lonnie, so she did not bite her tongue with him.

"Stop being an asshole, man. Sit your ass down! Hell, this is my shit."

Ann knew that Lonnie was a good producer. He had a West Coast flavor with an old school meets real funk sound. But she didn't care about how good he thought he was when she trying to get something done.

"You gonna get your ass in line. I don't give a damn about how good your skills are. Hell if your ass is that damn good then get your ass to work and give me what I asked you for nigga."

Ann was no joke and not someone to take lightly. She had a very clear picture of what she wanted. As she stepped up her game, Denise faded into the background. She was always there in the wings but her role became more silent. She was good about the process and moved aside so that Ann could work her magic. However, Ann's focus was to play off of Dwight's vision of having a Motown type of stable. So every move she made was stable-wise and not act-wise.

When Ann stepped in, she had more of a vision with all the acts and not just the girls. She secured Tayste, which was her brother Tu Tu's group. Then she started working with the girls. The core foundation and grassroots of the stable of Tillman Management was these two acts. The stable later became known as Tillman Management/Girl's Tyme Entertainment, and then from those two acts, Ann built everything else.

Ann paid Lonnie and T-Mo up front for songs they wrote and produced and had an agreement to get points on the back end. She had the skills and an uncanny ability to move people and make them comfortable so that she could get what she wanted. Tayste was showing real promise. With A.J. and Tu Tu doing lead vocals they were just as good if not better than groups out at the time like Jodeci and Boyz II Men. They worked hard to improve their stage presence so they would be a complete package.

Tayste went into the studio and Lonnie and T-Mo started laying down tracks. Tayste was showing outstanding potential for being a top mainstream act. They were tight, had a dynamic sound, and amazing presence. Her vision for them was to be the next hot male group. They had a New Jack feel and after trial and error they came out with the hits songs, Groove Me One More Time and a hot ballad performed melodramatically by Tu Tu entitled, I Wanna Be Loved Just By You.

Around the same time, Ann was molding the girls and getting them ready for the studio. The team worked with both the guys and girls hand-in-hand all the way. With the success that Tayste was having, other groups started looking toward Tillman Management for opportunities. Someone approached Ann about one group in particular called H-Town. Tayste had already produced hits and was going strong. When she took a look at H-Town, Ann felt that Tayste was equally good if not better than H-Town so she was very comfortable in not pursuing them. Although she later regretted the decision because H-Town became a huge success in the music industry releasing great hits such as Knockin' Da Boots and Lick U Up.

While Tayste was already recording, there was still some work that needed to be done with the girls group before they were anywhere near ready to go into the studio. Ann's vision for the girls was to produce a group that was a cross between SWV and EnVogue with an Emotions type harmony. She picked up the dream where she and Dwight left off and moved in the direction of what she and Dwight had discussed. She worked to build a stable of artists that were the best of the best of the entertainment business similar to what Berry Gordy did with Motown. Tillman Management was to become a hit machine just like Motown.

She moved forward with that mindset, and further auditions and house cleaning dwindled down the original eight girls to the best six. Ann was looking for the "best of the best" and to get to that point, she made the necessary adjustments. Mediocrity was not an option.

So from the auditions, two girls were selected, Kelendria Rowland and Ashley Davis. Chris, Millicent, Stacy, and Jennifer were not part of the plan for the girls group being formed at the time. However, the team maintained the idea of possibly circling back after launching other acts. Ann took care to deliver the news to the girls and their parents. Even though the decision to release the young girls was difficult for Ann, the ultimate goal to fulfill the dream weighed more heavily on her mind.

"This may be a difficult situation for some of you, but we are in the business to create the greatest group in the music industry. You will either be a part of it or you can get gone."

As Ann spoke with the girls and their families, she was kind and caring, but very direct as to not mislead anyone.

"The music industry can be a very tough nut to crack. My intentions are to crack it wide open. So this is not personal. It is about business, and no matter how fond I am of any of you, it must be about business because it is only sound business decisions that will help us to achieve what we are after."

Everyone listened as Ann continued to speak frankly.

"Does this mean that I am saying those not moving forward will not make it, no. What I am saying is that

The Making of a Child of Destiny

at this time, Tillman Management will not be moving forward with you. However, when we launch additional acts in the future, we will definitely consider you."

Ann was about the business of creating a successful group that would sell in the industry. She was sensitive to their feelings, but at the end of the day, it was about business and as a new person coming in to help, she had no loyalty to anyone who was already involved. She took the best of what was there. Denise was in agreement and supported her willingly. So the group Girls Tyme was formed and consisted of Beyonce, LaTavia, Nicki and Nina, Kelendria who was called Kelly, and Ashley.

Once Girls Tyme was formed, there was a meeting so that everyone had the opportunity to meet everyone else. This included the management team, the artists, and the parents. Once the formalities were handled, Ann put the girls through a boot camp where she and Lonnie worked to help sharpen them as a group. Lonnie worked on the vocals to make sure they were straight and the harmony tight. Ann also brought in David Brewer as a vocal coach to help them strengthen any areas of weakness.

"Okay, David. What I am looking for is the kind of harmony that the Emotions have. Hell I know they're sisters, but I want these girls to sound like conjoined twins. Every note sang with precision."

"You got it babe!"

The girls rehearsed, rehearsed, then rehearsed some more. They worked on choreography along with Keith from Tayste. Lonnie was Ann's taskmaster keeping them on point with the dancing and the singing. They worked hard.

At a certain point in their development, after rehearsals, the team put the girls in front of people to see what the response would be. They performed at places like Greenspoint Mall and Sharpstown Mall. Ann rented venues such as the Shape Community Center and the Jewish Country Club off Braeswood. Ann also would get the club houses of apartment complexes where the girls lived if the parents had access. Ann's goal was to create a buzz. As the girls continued to develop, they created a following by going around town and performing.

However, Ann had to find something solid for the girls and get them into the studio. The flow of the group at this junction placed Ashley as lead vocalist. Beyonce performed back-up vocals and co-lead. LaTavia was a rapper and hype master. Nicki and Nina were dancers, and Kelly performed background vocals.

"Look girls, I know it's rough and I know it's hard, but I believe in you. We believe in you."

Ann instilled in the girls a deep passion to keep working and by working hard now, they would ultimately become successful. "You are going to be great one day. I promise you that. Just stick with it, be disciplined and things will happen."

Ann became sort of a surrogate mother to the girls. They fell in love with her and started wanting to stay the night at her house. They practiced every day so the parents were able to get to know her. No matter how hard the girls worked, they never wanted to go home. The girls' parents trusted Ann's guidance. Anyone who knew Ann understood that she loved those girls dearly. They were like one big happy family, and Ann's house was their second home.

Ann had a special connection with the girls, even more so than the guys. She gave them extra attention and a little extra of whatever else there was to give. It appeared that the girls began to fill the void of something that was missing in Ann's life. As time went on, and as I came to know Dretta personally, it was very apparent that Girl's Tyme filled the void of Shawna, Ann's beautiful baby girl that had passed away a few years back.

These little girls filled her house and her heart. Everyday she was with them and the more time she spent with them, the more she loved them. Her life soon began to revolve around this new found love affair with not just one little girl, but several. While no one could ever take the place of Shawna, Beyonce, Ashley, LaTavia, Nicki, Nina, and Kelly all became Ann's little girls in another way.

For Ann, this was the first time since their death that she was feeling Shawna's spirit in the house.

"Baby, no one can take your place. Mommy misses you. Tell God I thank him for placing these beautiful six little girls in my life."

Ann observed the girls' musical ability, but she also watched them like a proud mother. Sometimes if you looked at her closely as the girls were singing and dancing, you could see water in her eyes. There were a couple of times that Ann would call Shawna instead of the girl's name and have to quickly correct it.

"Lord Jesus…Hell, I mean Kelly come here."

The girls were used to Ann calling them each other's name, so it really did not register to them. But for Ann, when she hugged them and encouraged them, she was doing so as if it was Shawna, and that is the love that both the parents and the girls could feel. There was nothing fake about Ann's love for them, and at any moment she would have taken any of them into her home as her own. For in spirit, they all represented an aspect of her baby girl and she pushed them as if it was Shawna she was pushing to become better and to hang in there.

Everyone was working really hard. As Ann looked at what was in front of her, she had Lonnie producing, T-Mo writing, and David handling the vocals. Everything was together except someone who knew how to go out and get investors. So a man named Lynn came to the table to complete the inner circle of managers. He seemed to be well connected with corporate people who had money and convinced Ann that he could take the work produced by Tayste and get investors.

When everyone heard the tracks from Tayste, they got really excited. Lynn convinced a group of white businessmen to invest. Unbeknownst to Ann, Lynn formed Encore Records and took the tracks from Tayste and got investments for Encore Records. He continued to go out and hustle for other investments for his company using Ann's artists. He played two ends against the middle. He somehow convinced a group of investors to lease the twenty-fifth floor of the building on Highway Ten to erect a sign saying, "Encore Records" on the outside of the top of the building for all the world to see. It gave the appearance that Encore Records was this big conglomerate.

Aside from not knowing of Lynn unscrupulous antics, Tayste was happy. The girls were happy. Everyone was seeing progress. Most practices took place at Ann's big house on Strawgrass Drive. With all the movement going on breathing life back into her and Dwight's dream, the house was also coming back to life. As Tayste rehearsed, all the other girls would be running around and playing. However, Beyonce would sit quietly in a corner studying the boys carefully while they performed. She loved Tu Tu and the vocal runs that he could do.

"Hey Tu Tu, why this little girl keep staring at us?"

"Man, A.J. she ain't studden you. She just likes what we do."

"No man, look at her, she stealing our stuff."

"Man you crazy."

"I'm tellin' you Tu Tu, man she takin' our stuff. Watch, I'm tellin' you man."

"Come on A.J. pay attention, Bey ain't thinkin' about us."

"Alright, don't say I didn't tell you."

It was evident from early on that Beyonce wanted to hone her skills by studying Tayste and other performers, but A.J. always saw it as her stealing their style.

ALL IN THE FAMILY

It was a whole lot going on in Ann's life, yet a very happy time for her. She was really starting to move and shake and get things going real well. It was okay for me as well, but I, Brian Kenneth Moore, was a little indecisive of what to do with my life. It wasn't a sad time, but it wasn't what I would call a happy time either. My life was just there waiting to be lived. I was feeling like there was something I should be doing.

Wherever the road led me at this junction, I knew music had to be a part of it somehow. Yet, that remained to be seen. Regardless of what I decided to do, I could not imagine life without me exploring those avenues because music was in my heart and was a very big part of me. Then again, for many southern folks, I imagine the same was true. No matter how many opportunities in the military there were, it did not stop me from wondering what I was doing. I wanted to be a star. Then there was another part of me that wanted to help others – give them an opportunity to make it and give to them something that I did not have.

I spent three years telling the guys in the service that I was going to be a star. When I was in the military, I performed as a lead singer in a group called Black Satin. We played across Korea. In an attempt to make things fit better while on active duty, I auditioned for the Air Force's touring band called the "Tops in Blue." I made that move in an effort to try and make the military work for me. I knew in my heart that it was not for me, but I wanted to give it everything I had. When I didn't make the band, once my time was up, I made my exit and did not re-enlist. There was no use trying to kid myself. The military was not for me. There was something bigger and I knew it. It was time for me to go, and I contemplated many options. After leaving the Air Force, I did a lot of soul searching. I had conversations with my elder sister, and I made contact with my trusting friend from old who was always a willing and trusting ear and shoulder if I needed it.

"Kenny Mo, why don't you come to Houston to see how you like things here?"

"You know Cat that might not be a bad idea."

"I cannot imagine you going back to Indianapolis or Greenwood. Honestly, Kenny Mo, what's there for you back in Mississippi? If you don't really know what to do, come here."

Cassey and I were childhood friends. We've known each other since we were about eight years old.

The Making of a Child of Destiny

Cassey was Miss Greenwood High School and a very beautiful young woman. If people today saw picture of her from back then, and could observe her carriage, they would probably say she reminded them of Jackee' Harry from the hit show 227. As she gets more mature, she might remind you of the actress, Jennifer Lewis. Either way it goes, my wife is a superstar and will always be in my book.

Anyway to go back a little, after high school, I went on to play college football at Mississippi College for three years before enlisting into the service. Cassey became a flight attendant and moved from Greenwood, Mississippi to Houston, Texas by way of Orange County California.

When I was a young boy, my mother and father divorced and it turned out to be a back and forth thing between Indianapolis, Indiana and Greenwood. So it was an urban versus rural environment and that had an interesting impact on me growing up. Cassey was a constant friend all the way from childhood to adulthood. We stayed in contact with each other throughout. It didn't matter whether I was in college or in the service, we never lost contact. Little did she know but she helped me to get through some really tough times. When Cassey invited me to Houston, given our history, I had to seriously consider the option.

"Alright Cat, it might not be such a bad idea. I'm really not sure of what direction to take. I keep asking myself, 'Do I want music or do I want football?' You know though either way, Houston may be a good move. I have a friend who plays for the Houston Oilers. I've been getting in shape anyway so…"

"There are a lot more opportunities here. You can stay with me until you find a place. You know it's not a problem Kenny Mo. Hell we go way back man. I gotcha, you know that."

"Alright, Cat, then it's settled."

I headed to Houston. Cassey and I got caught up on the years we had not seen each other. I stayed with her for a while and one thing led to another. We ended up falling in love, she got pregnant and before too long, we ended up getting married. Houston became my home and I must say it was one of the best decisions that I made in my life both personally and professionally.

Later that fall, Troy Peoples, one of Cassey's friends from Dallas called to let us know that he was coming through Houston. Troy played for the Gap Band and his sister Alisa, who we called Lois, was one half of the group Yarbrough and Peoples. They produced such hits as Don't Stop the Music. Troy mentioned that Yarbrough and Peoples, along with Charlie Wilson and the Gap Band would be performing at the club, The Main Event in Houston.

Cat and I made plans to attend the show. Her older sister lived in Dallas and decided to drive down as well to see the show. When she showed up, she had some guy with her by the name of Charles Foley. She and Foley modeled together for Mercedes Benz. Neither of them knew Troy, and we didn't know Foley. They showed up mainly to see the concert.

Everybody was ready for the show. I barbequed that day and we packed some up to take to Troy who had already had my famous barbeque over the summer and loved it, so of course, I couldn't get in the door of The Main Event without his share. It was just understood that whenever we saw Troy, we had to have some of my barbeque with us.

Troy and I had talked on a number of occasions. He had always said to me, "Hey man, if you know of any clubs that the Gap Band or Yarbrough and Peoples can play set it up through Captain, and we'll square you away with a finder's fee."

Captain was Yarbrough and People's manager and when we spoke he mentioned to me to do the leg work for him to get the gigs in this area, so that's what I did. Troy was a cool brother. We got along well; but if I went to that show without some barbeque, we would have had a fallout. When we made it to the venue, I gave him his barbeque.

"Now I know you did not show up here without them ribs."

"Hell, do you think Cat was going to let me forget?"

We went on and watched the show. They killed it that night! We all got to laughing at me bringing barbeque with me, but someone ended up giving Charlie Wilson a taste of it, and that was all it took. Charlie was like, "Hell this is some good shit. Where the hell is the barbeque at?"

"Well you know there is more where that came from."

"Well where is it man? Hell, bring it on."

I invited all of them over for barbeque, and they accepted. So Cat and I went on home to get everything set up and Troy led the crew over after they broke everything down. About an hour later this big tour bus rolled up I-45 to Imperial Valley Drive to the Hollywood Apartment complex. Cat's sister and Foley were outside talking and when the bus doors opened, out popped Troy, Lois, Cavin Yarbrough, members of the Gap Band, and Charlie Wilson. Foley looked at her and was like, "Damn, what in the hell is happening here?"

He was shocked to see the Charlie Wilson's tour bus stop almost in front of the complex. When I saw it pulling up, I came outside, shook Charlie's hand and said, "Come on man, let's go gets some grub." Charlie and I walked inside together talking and laughing. Everyone was having a great time gathered around the complex pool and enjoying the food. The whole time Foley was watching and digging the scene. It was as if he was saying, "Damn, he must be well-connected."

I noticed that Foley was checking out my every move that evening. As soon as an opportunity arose, he came over to where I was and started telling me about his cousin who is in this group and being managed by some woman named Ann.

"You seem like a good person to know."

"Oh yeah? Why is that?"

"My cousin Keith is in this group. You know, they're just getting started. Maybe you can help them."

"You don't say."

"Well, right now, he's being managed by some woman. I want to introduce you to my cousin. I think maybe you can help them. Seeing you know some people and all... you know what I'm saying?"

I did not take Foley that serious. I thought maybe he was talking out the side of his mouth, but I did agree to meet his cousin.

"Set it up. I'll see what I can do."

"Alright, done deal. I'll call my cousin and we'll get a time together."

After the Charlie Wilson's tour bus left and the apartment was cleared, Cat's sister and Foley stayed a little longer before heading back to Dallas. Foley called his cousin Keith later that evening. I spoke with him briefly and learned that he sang in a group called Tayste, they had been in the studio recording, produced a couple of songs, but were interested in setting up a meeting between me and a woman by the name of Andretta Tillman. Keith talked to me about the group in a little more detail and told me to call him Harlon. He also mentioned somebody named Tu Tu and then put him on the telephone. When I spoke with Tu Tu, he told me that Andretta Tillman was his sister and managed his group and another girl's act, but he was interested in working with me.

"If you connected like that, I'm interested in seeing how you can help. Hell, Ann's my sister, man. Let me call her and set up a meeting between the two of you and see what's up."

"Alright Tu Tu. No problem man. You got my details. Give me a call and let me know what's up."

Cat's sister and Foley got on the road and headed back to Dallas. Within an hour of them leaving, Tu Tu called me back and said he had a meeting set up between me and his sister and gave me the details of where to meet.

I hung up the telephone and turned to Cassey and said, "It's on baby!"

And….that was that!

HERE WE COME

The next Saturday I met with Harlon and Tu Tu early afternoon around eleven. When I walked into the place, there were two young men about five feet nine inches tall. One was a brown-skinned dude with what many would refer to as "good hair." The other was dark-skinned and wore a pony-tail. During the introductions I learned that Tu Tu was the dark-skinned one, and Harlon was the one with the "pretty boy" persona.

The three of us sat and talked for awhile. Tu Tu and Harlon discussed what they were looking for while I listened.

"We're happy with Ann, man. I don't want you to get us wrong. Foley told me you had it going on and so I thought it would be a good idea to meet in person and see what was what."

"Well Harlon, here I am, whatcha working with?"

"Kenny, that's your name, right?"

"Yeah."

"Okay, Kenny, Ann's my sister right? And she's a good manager. We're happy with her you know, but we were maybe looking for somebody like yourself to come in and maybe co-manage us… something like that…you know what I'm saying?"

"Alright."

"We've already been in the studio, and recorded some stuff, but we want to go real big. We're looking to get things moving a little faster and stronger. We want a major record deal and we… well…we think maybe you can help us with that."

"Well, Tu Tu, you got the meeting set-up with your sister?"

"Yeah, man. Right after we leave here, we're gonna go over to Ann's house, right. She knows that we're coming by, so…let's do it."

"Alright then, let's go."

We all shook hands and headed over to Ann's. We pulled up into the driveway of this big beautiful house in a really affluent neighborhood. This is the first time I had the opportunity to meet Andretta Tillman. When we arrived, she answered the door and motioned us to come into the living room and sit down.

"Hey, sis, this is Kenny Moore. Kenny, this is my sister Ann. Like I was telling you she manages us. Ann, Kenny here is the one we were telling you about who worked with Charlie Wilson, the Gap Band, and Yarbrough and Peoples."

Ann nodded her head. She showed no emotion. She smiled cordially and I could tell she was receptive. Although, while Tu Tu and Harlon was doing most of the talking, she didn't say much; she mainly listened carefully. As they were speaking, she would occasionally look over at me and she looked me straight in my eyes as if to see right through me. I looked her straight in her eyes too. I was always told by my football coaches to look a man straight in their eyes, no matter who they were or what color they are. Of course Ann was no man, but she was a strong Black woman who you could tell was not on any B.S. She was serious about what she was doing and it was easy to tell that she was sizing me up, but also keeping an open mind to sincerely see how I could assist.

Tu Tu and Harlon pretty much echoed what Foley had told them about my contacts and that they thought I could help them do things on a much larger scale and expand what they were trying to do. The four of us continued to talk for a few minutes and when they saw that Ann and I were comfortable with each other, they left the room so that we could talk it out and see which way to go from this meeting forward.

"Well, Kenny, the way we have to do the deal as managers is, we have to get things on the back end because there's no upfront money to be had right now. Can you work with that?"

"I'm cool with that."

"You know Kenny, you got writers points, producer points, and record label points…you know we can squeeze our way into getting some points if we could do our own productions or split it."

Ann was very clear in terms of what she was doing and what she wanted to happen. I continued to listen as she was laying out a detailed plan for me to understand how she was working. "If we could get access to a recording studio that would allow us to get all the recording done that we needed, and if they would be willing to get their money on the back end, then we could produce final product and take those to the record labels."

"I see what you're saying."

"Yeah. See, Kenny, I'm not looking to just get an individual record deal. I'm more concerned about getting distribution deals and getting my artists signed to major labels. So, how do you think you can help us achieve that objective?"

"Well, I do know some contacts, some football players and people like that. So we may have some means to capital and some people willing to invest."

"Okay. Well, I do have a team in place. What I would like you to do is come over and meet with the team, if that's alright with you. Let's see how you bond and everything. See if you can work with the team in place and see if they feel you and if you all can work together."

During the conversation, Ann reeled me in as we jumped around from subject/to/subject. We talked about a lot of different things. Then out of the blue, she started laughing hysterically. I looked at her and was thinking, "What the hell is wrong with this nigga?"

When she finally got her composure, I was still sitting there looking at her not quite sure what to think. She was finally able to get herself together to talk start talking to me again. "Kenny?"

I looked at her sort of sitting back a little gauging what's going on and answered cautiously. "Yes Ann?"

"You really don't know shit about points do you?"

"What?"

"You really don't know shit about points and how producers and writers get paid do you?"

"I know they get royalty and everything like that. Whatcha trying to say Ann?"

Ann got up and left the room and left me sitting there. I didn't know what to think. I was sitting there in the room alone for about five minutes before she returned with a book in her hand.

"Here, I'm done reading this. Why don't you take it home and start polishing yourself up on how everything works…on how the points system works, so when it's time for us to get paid, we know how we're gonna get paid."

I took the book about the music industry out of her hand, and we just laughed it off. I was cool with it. It wasn't that I didn't know what the hell I was doing, I just needed to learn a little bit more about the music industry for where we were heading. Ann was cool. I wasn't sure what to expect from the meeting, but we did click. While it was a good one, I didn't think it was anything major, but I guess Ann thought maybe I could actually help them.

"Well, Kenny, I think you are the guy to help get us on down the road. What do you think?"

"Uhm. That's cool with me Ann."

"So, can you come back here on Tuesday? We have a weekly management meeting, where the rest of the team will be here and you can get a chance to meet them and see how you blend."

"Sure, see you then."

Tu Tu and Harlon came back in the room. They walked me to the door and I headed on home. Cassey and I chilled the rest of the evening laughing and talking about the activities of the day. The weekend flew by and Monday quickly rolled around. Before I knew it, it was about seven thirty and time for me to head over to Ann's to meet the rest of the management team. I walked up the walkway

The Making of a Child of Destiny

and rang the doorbell. When I walked in, I could see that they were in a heated discussion already. When I walked in I could hear them talking about Girls Tyme and getting them into the studio and the songs they had and if they were good enough.

"Hell Ann, we ready to go. We really need to take the girls out to California, the Bay Area. Let's take them to The Plant. I got the connections…"

Lonnie was still talking when Ann interrupted him to introduce me to the group. "Hey ya'll, I want to introduce the new member of our team. This is Kenny."

Ann could barely get my name out before Lonnie chimed in. "…Who the fuck is he? What the fuck he do? Why we need him? Who the hell is he…"

Lonnie started a barrage of negative reception which was followed by Lynn, then T-Mo.

"What does he do, I'm getting' the investors and everything, Lonnie's producing, T-Mo's writing..."

"Yeah, I'm writing…so what is he a writer…you not happy with my writing?"

"We don't need no fucking body else…This food cut up enough ways already."

Ann kept her cool, although you could see a look on her face like she wanted to say, "If these got-damn niggas don't shut the hell up…embarrassing the hell out of me. Ain't got no damn home training."

However, she was very professional and once they all aired their feelings, she explained to them what my role would be. "Well, Kenny is going to help me with the management."

They all looked at each other, then Lonnie spoke up. "Help you with the management?"

Lonnie turned to me. "Who have you managed?"

"Well…I haven't persay managed anybody. I've worked with Yarbrough and Peoples, Charlie Wilson, the Gap Band…"

"I know Charlie, I ain't never heard of your ass. I know Charlie. I know the Gap Band. I ain't heard of your fuckin' ass."

I sat there listening to them act a fool and talk to me like I was nothing. I turned to Ann and said, "Look Ann, I didn't agree to come here to get abused."

"Ya'll chill out. Chill out. Kenny's part of the team and that's it."

I could see that Ann had her hands full with Lonnie. He was hot-headed and ignorant. The thing is he seemed to always lead the pack on being disrespectful.

"Just stay out of my fuckin' way. Let me do what I do."

Lynn piggy-backed off of what Lonnie said. "I don't think you can do what I do, you know nigga…whatever… I'm the mover and shaker…so…"

I just looked at them and sort of blew them off. "Well okay…cool. I'll get in where I fit in. I'll just sit back here and listen to ya'll."

So we finally went on with meeting, discussing the next steps and the girls getting into the studio and the progress of Tayste songs. There was a lot of back and forth then Ann spoke up.

"Lynn, how are we coming on the investors?"

"Oh…uh…uh…yeah. They just put up…uh…the Encore Records building sign. My thinking is we can sign the girls and the boys to Encore."

"You ain't no fucking record label, Lynn. What the hell you think you can do for us?"

"Well, I'm just saying, if we can sign to them, then we can go and do a distribution deal."

It was a lot going on in the meeting. Lynn was pissing Ann off with his antics. Lonnie was cursing and going back and forth. "Naw, ain't no need for it to be like that."

Then Ann finally reeled everybody back in. "Look, we are gonna do it like this…We're gonna go…we really need to go get the money. I can't keep forking over all this money. We really need to go get access to a studio where we can get the girls and Tayste in there on a regular basis and keep rolling."

Everyone was sitting and listening to Ann as she was handling her business. They dared not interrupt her at this point because she had just slapped the trump card on the table – her dishing out the money. "We need to convince the studio that we'll pay them a little bit up front, but they can recoup their production costs and everything on the back end after we sign the deal."

Ann was working to set up sort of a bartering system. You could tell that the team was not too pleased. The meeting ended with everyone rolling their eyes at me. Lonnie, turned to T-Mo.

"This mother-fucker don't know shit. I tell you now he don't know shit."

He then turned to Ann and started questioning her judgment. "I don't know what you doing Ann, I don't know whatcha doing."

"Lonnie, this is my shit, not yours. So shut the fuck up please. You getting on my got-damned nerves crying like some pissy ass baby."

That meeting was tough but Ann was a safe haven and backed me all the way. She did not allow them to bulldoze or bully me just because they were already a part of the team. They were intimidated and thought that I was coming in to steal their thunder. So, by Ann telling them I would be helping her to manage, they moved out of the way. From that meeting I started attending the meetings every week as a co-manager to Ann. It was a tradition that whenever I would bring my son Brian along with me, Armon, Christopher, or one of the other children who were there rehearsing or playing would come to get Brian while we were having the meeting. At that time Brian was around two or three years of age.

Now, the Saturday following the first meeting I attended with the management team, Ann had everyone over to her house for a rehearsal intertwined with a barbeque and a welcome to the team reception. It gave me the chance to meet all the families and everyone else associated with both Girls Tyme and Tayste. It also gave the groups the opportunity to practice for the show they had scheduled the next day at one of the community centers and the management team to let everyone know what they would be doing before the Sunday.

When Cassey and I arrived at the picnic with Brian, it was a beautiful sight to see. All the families were gathered around and children were running and playing. It was really nice. I was looking forward to becoming a part of the whole process. I didn't doubt for a moment that my family would become a part of Ann's family and the entire music family of Tayste and Girls Tyme.

Ann took me around and introduced me to everyone. It was the first opportunity I had to meet everybody involved with Tillman Management and Girls Tyme Entertainment. The adults were in various groups talking when I came in with my family. The children were doing what children usually do – running around playing and making a lot of noise. Ann took me around to introduce me to the parents first. They were all in little cliques.

Kelly and her mom Doris were standing off to the side. "Hey Doris, this is Kenny he will be joining the team to help manage the girls. So Kelly, you will be seeing a lot of Mr. Kenny because he will be working with you as well. Kenny, this is Doris, Kelly's mom. Kelly sings back-up."

"How ya'll doing? It's nice to meet you. This is my wife Cassey and our son Brian."

"Hi, nice to meet you. Welcome."

"Thanks."

After meeting Kelly and her mother, we walked off to continue the rounds of introductions. As we walked on, Ann was telling me about the type of girl Kelly was. "Now Kelly is quiet, but she's a sweet girl."

"Now Ann, you know sweet ain't gonna get her down the road, right?"

"I know, Kenny. You're right. We got somebody working on that."

Ann led me over to the next group of parents. Tina Knowles was standing with her little girl Solange talking with Carolyn and Nolan Davis. "Hey Tina, Carolyn,

Nolan this is Kenny. He's my partner and will be managing with me. Kenny, this is Tina Knowles, Beyonce's mom, and this is her little sister. Beyonce is sort of like a co-lead."

Before Ann even had the chance to introduce the other two parents standing there, Carolyn interrupted extending her hand forward assertively to shake Kenny's hand. "Hi Kenny, I'm Carolyn Davis, Ashley's mother. This is my husband Nolan. Ashley is the lead singer in the girl's group."

I was taken aback by her abruptness and "everyone needs to know me" attitude. "Okay...uh...well, this is my wife Cassey and son Brian."

Tina spoke up. She was a really sweet person. She and Cassey hit it off immediately. "Welcome aboard Kenny, welcome Cassey. It is really good to meet you. Thanks for helping the girls out and Tayste of course too."

Cassey smiled as she responded to Tina's polite and tactful demeanor. "Thank you Tina, it is very nice to meet you...you as well Carolyn and Nolan."

As we're walking away, Ann rolled her eyes up in her head. I said, "Ooh wee..."

Ann shook her head and said, "Yep, that's Carolyn." We all chuckled as Ann kept talking.

"Now Tina...she's cool. She ain't on that...Her attitude is like she is just here to support her daughter.

She's very helpful…always asking if there is anything I need. She ain't on that other shit. Now that damn Carolyn, that's another story."

I learned as Ann took us around meeting everyone, she was very outspoken and straight forward with me. This was a great quality I found encouraging, since we would be working so closely together. Next Ann took us over to meet, Charlotte, Cheryl, and Yvonne. All three of them are sisters. Charlotte is Nicki and Nina's mom. Cheryl is LaTavia's mother; and Yvonne is Lonnie's special friend. She knew Houston very well so whenever Lonnie was in town, Yvonne took him around. Also standing over with them was LaTavia's step father who was a Houston police officer.

"Hey. How ya'll doing today? This is Kenny. He's going to be working with me managing everybody."

Almost in unison, they greeted us.

"Hi."

"How are you doing? This is my wife Cassey and our son Brian."

LaTavia's step father shook my hand. "Good to meet you, man. Talk to you later."

"Cool."

As Ann was taking me to meet the girls, she yelled for her son. "Armon! He came running over to his mom. "Huh?"

"Take Brian to go play."

"Okay…you wanna come with me?"

Brian went willingly to Armon, while Cassey made her way over to where Tina and Carolyn were talking. Ann took me over to meet the members of Tayste first. As we headed in their direction, Ann was pointing the boys out to me. "You've met Tu Tu and Harlon already. That over there is A.J. and Mitch. Mitch is Harlon's younger brother. Now you know Tu Tu's my brother. His little black ass thinks he's the shit but he can sang his ass off though. Harlon, hell…he thinks he's part of New Edition or something. I think his ass think he's Ralph Tresvant or some damn body."

I laughed as Ann was describing the boys' personalities. She kept a straight face and that made it even funnier.

"A.J., shit. All he wants to do is eat and sang. Now the nigga can sang, but hell I gotta hide my damn food else his ass will eat me out of house and home. Watch him Kenny. You think I'm kidding. Every time you seeing him, his ass gonna be eating on something or talking about his ass is hungry. You watch and see."

Ann had me laughing as she kept going on about the boys. "Nigga you think it's funny, don't you. You gonna see what I'm talking about. It ain't gonna take long either…and shit…that damn Mitch hell…he gonna go wherever Harlon says go and do whatever he says do. The good thing is though, you ain't gonna have a problem with him. Just reel Harlon's little skinny ass in, then you got Mitch. You got me?"

"Hey ya'll, this is Kenny."

They all shook my hand. "Hey, man it's good to see you again."

"Alright Tu Tu, Harlon. Good to see you again too. Am I gonna get to see your moves today?"

Tu Tu spinned around with some dance moves. "And you know it!"

They all laughed as the other boys acknowledged me.

After meeting the rest of Tayste, Ann took me over to meet the rest of the girls. I had already met Kelly when she was standing over by her mom. "Hey girls, this is Mr. Kenny. You gonna be seeing a lot of him. He's my partner and going to be managing you all as well."

Ann started pointing out the girls one-by-one. "Kenny this is Ashley, Beyonce, LaTavia, Nicki and Nina. You've already met Kelly."

"They ain't twins neither Mr. Kenny. I just thought I say that before you asked" LaTavia said in a self-assured manner.

"She older than me." Nina said pointing at her sister with her one hand on her hip and rolling her head. I looked at Ann to keep from laughing. I was thinking to myself, "These little fast tail girls... I bet they can sang their asses off though."

It was easy to observe that Latavia was the most outspoken of the bunch. As we stood there talking with them before they started to practice she was cracking jokes. She was not shy at all. Kelly looked like a little scared mouse. Beyonce laughed, but kept whispering to LaTavia. Ashley was a little "miss diva." She had no problem carrying the jokes on.

As Ann and I were walking off. She started to share with me her take of the girls. "Alright Kenny, those are the girls. They are good girls for the most part, but they each have their own personality as you can see. I'mma let you work that one out on your own...it ain't gonna take you long. You gonna see a lot more when they start performing."

"What do you mean Ann."

"Well look...Ashley, she's the lead singer. You already met her diva ass mama. Like mother like daughter. You better watch out for her mama. She's a Hollywood heffa. She one of them that think Ashley should have her own dressing room and shit. But, hell I don't need to tell you that, you saw that already."

We just laughed. Ann continued to give me the blow-by-blow about the girls. "Now Ashley can sing, but she's stiff as hell on stage. Beyonce...she's background, but we let her do leads some... but Bey...she's a sweetheart. She is always willing to work hard and Tina is just as nice as they come. Her dad Mathew comes from time to time mainly for the shows though."

"Okay."

The groups started dancing and rehearsing. When I glanced over where the girls were, Beyonce stuck out like a sore thumb. "Ann, why that little girl bucking so damn hard?"

Ann fell out laughing when I said that. "Kenny, that's just Bey. I told you she works hard."

"Naw Ann, she just bucking and popping every damn thang. She just wild with it."

She just continued to laugh at me going on about how this little girl was dancing. "Hell, that can become a problem, Ann."

"Why?"

"Well if you got all the other girls standing there and then she's bucking so hard, she kind of upstaging the other girls and the unison don't look right."

"Okay, okay, good eye, Kenny. Yeah, we working on that."

We laughed over Beyonce for a moment, then Ann continued to tell me about the girls. "Now Kelly, like I told you earlier. She's a sweet girl."

"Okay…well…like I said…sweet ain't gonna get you down the road. She needs to have some talent."

"She got it. I just gotta get it out of her."

"Okay."

"I've been working with her. I'mma get it out of her. I got David working especially with her to get her to come out of her shell."

"Okay."

"Now LaTavia…"

"Hell, Ann…that one don't need no damn introduction. She introduced her damn self. She's strong. Her personality is big. That little girl tickles me. I can see she works hard."

"Well you know, LaTavia she is the face and spokesperson for 'Just For Me' hair products. It ain't nothin' to go in the house and see her little ass on the commercial during Soul Train."

"Okay. So she's doing some things then?"

"Now Nicki and Nina, everybody think they are twins. They work hard at the dancing and stuff. They're real. For them it's all about the program. Now, LaTavia is their first cousin. Their mama's is sisters."

"Okay."

"All the families are on board. Everybody get along pretty well. There are no real issues on that front. Of course…"

"Hell you don't even have to say it…As long as everybody stay out of Ashley mama's way…"

"Ashley's too. She just like her damn mama."

I shook my head. "Huhm."

I took everything in that Ann shared and observed the girls. They practiced hard and were ready for the show the next day. Cassey and I went to the show. This was the first time that I saw the acts actually perform on stage and in front of an audience. I saw them practice, but at the show, they rocked it! Tayste was on fire! They sang their butts off. Ann had some great acts, they just needed to be polished around the edges. From what I saw, they had talent and they were bound to go places. It was their destiny.

After the show, the management team met the following Tuesday as usual. They discussed that Girls Tyme needed to go ahead and get into the studio. It was apparent that it was time, and I was surprised that they had not recorded anything yet. The team discussed what they needed. Everyone agreed that Girls Tyme just needed a couple of songs to get them started. Tayste had already produced some tracks and they just needed to get into the right hands.

During the meeting, Ann also raised the issue about investors again. Lynn as usual was he-hawing around, not really giving a concrete response. He always got squeamish whenever Ann brought it up. You could tell she was pissed, but she kept her cool. The more Ann saw how Lynn was operating, the more leery she grew of him. After the meeting, she called me at home.

"Kenny, hey look, I want to start pursuing other investors. I don't want to keep leaving this up to Lynn. I don't trust him."

"Okay..."

"I'm tired of his bullshit. We need to get some investors and stop playing all these damn games. Lynn is full of shit and we need some other investors outside of what he's working on. Do you think you can you reach out to some of your contacts?"

"Yeah, my friend William plays for the Oilers. Some of them are already investing in singing groups. I'll get on it."

"Thanks, Kenny. I ain't fucking around with Lynn, he's too damn shady for my liking. He's on some other shit. But you wait. He gonna fuck up, and I'mma fuck him up."

"I hear you, Ann."

I remained neutral because I could tell that she was really upset. After I hung up from her, I reached out to my boy William. He mentioned that Earnest and some of the other teammates had made some investments in the music industry, and while he was not in the position to invest, some of the others might be willing to explore options of investments or partnerships. William invited me to bring the boys over the next weekend for the gathering they were having.

So that next weekend I took the boys to the party. Everybody was having a good time. Tayste had their tracks with them. Although they didn't perform live for the team, William made sure their tracks were heard. Many of the team members were like, "Man this is hot!"

"Yeah, this is tight."

Haywood, Earnest, and William were really digging the tunes. "Hey man, ya'll got some more songs?"

"We working on some." Tu Tu responded.

"Tell you what, I'm really interested. I mean, this is tight."

"Okay."

"What we want to see is for ya'll to put a little more leg work in, come up with some more songs, then come back and let us see what you come up with."

"Cool."

Tayste was excited. You could tell that Earnest, William and their teammates were serious. "Kenny, man you really got something there."

"I know man, and this is not the half of it."

"Alright… alright. Let's see what ya'll come up with."

The response regarding Tayste was very favorable. So we left the party on a high and ready to kick it up a notch. The guys went to work on the suggestions that the Oilers made to them. Meanwhile, Lonnie and T-Mo was working on some things for the girls. Things were coming together.

Eventually, Lonnie and T-Mo came up with this little bubble gum track about world peace and a few other songs. The girls practiced their new songs until they were seamless, and then went into the Digital Services Recording Studio in Houston to lay down the tracks. With everything going on and a major buzz being created, Ann began to raise the bar in terms of their performances and where they performed. It was about star power and she was out to claim it. She knew she had some hot acts and her goal was to let the world know.

One of the first major performances for Girls Tyme was at the George R. Brown Convention Center during the Houston Black Expo. They rocked three shows that day opening for Jennifer Holliday and Chris Walker. After the girls performed, Ann debriefed them.

"So, how do you all think you did?"

"Well Miss Ann, I could have been a little tighter on my note."

"Okay Bey, what else?"

"Well, I think we need to get sharper with our dance moves. We weren't all on the same beat."

"What about you LaTavia?"

"I think, Ashley needs to loosen up a little bit more. She sounds good but she needs to not be so stiff."

"Okay…anyone else?"

"We just need to work harder."

"Well, Bey…I think you all did great. So, if you feel you need to work on those areas then you know what you need to do. I advise you all to study Jennifer and Chris. See how they work the stage and connect with the audience. Look at how they hold the mic. I want ya'll to study them closely. See how they act on stage. It could be you girls. As a matter of fact, it will be you girls if you keep at it and keep working hard."

Bey immediately went and sat in the audience to watch Chris Walker perform and then Jennifer Holliday. She did exactly what Ann said. Ashley and LaTavia got side-tracked and ended up walking around signing autographs. It was a good show all-in-all.

After that day, the girls worked harder so that they could be more on point for the next show. Nicki and Nina worked with Beyonce and LaTavia to get the steps down and crisp. They had to work with Beyonce so that she could blend her dancing more as to not upstage the other girls. They had a time with Ashley. That child did not have much rhythm at all when it came to dancing. The girls could hardly stop laughing when trying to help Ashley get the moves down. Poor Kelly, everybody yelled at her. That might have had a little to do with her confidence and self-esteem.

The girls took the criticisms from the last show and fine-tuned their program to be ready for the Juneteenth Special at the Brown Convention. This time they opened for rap artist Das Effex. They nailed it and went back to practice fired up and geared up for their appearance at KTRK Channel 13 ABC Affiliate on Good Morning Houston and then Cross Roads, another local show, both Girls Tyme and Tayste were on fire. Tayste had their tunes, but the song that T-Mo wrote, entitled, Sunshine was a crowd favorite for the girls.

"The song we're about to sing…"

Ashley stepped up to the microphone and then all six girls would light up the audience with the words and melody of the song.

"…that all the homeless people across the world. Also the young children at heart…"

"Sunshine, you light up my way
The children of the world reach out to you.
Your light, it's a sunny day
When all the boys and girls can laugh and play

Only chase the clouds away;
Shining through the hearts of people.
Those who think will never heal;
Thinking bout the better ways to read.

Let your wings of golden love shine;
Gather those who live without a home.
Let them know;
They're never truly alone.

"Sunshine, you light up my way
The children of the world reach out to you.
Your light, it's a sunny day;
When all the boys and girl can laugh and play…"

The song hit home in the heart of the people, and to hear it coming from young people made it even more impactful. It was like Girls Tyme's version of We are the World.

So Sunshine consequently, ended up becoming Girls Tyme anthem song. Each time they performed, they sang it. Ashley took the lead and Beyonce had this small piece with the harmony. The song in its own way united the audience just like We Are the World did.

It was a busy summer for Tillman Management and Girls Tyme Entertainment. Things were progressing quickly. With the hype and the response from the people, Ann was having more and more conversations with a woman by the name of Teresa who lived in California. Teresa told Ann that she needed to think about getting the girls in some of the showcases in California where people in the industry could see and hear them.

In addition, Lonnie was continuing to pester Ann about going to one of the big time studios. Ann did not totally dismiss Lonnie, but she knew that what came with the big time studios was also big time money and she believed that before they went that route, there were some other avenues that could be explored.

Ann valued what Teresa had to say. She felt that perhaps Teresa could possibly bring another perspective, another face, and other options to consider. So from her conversations with Teresa, Ann started working on getting the acts in front of some of the big wigs in the industry. The only way that would happen is if she explored taking the groups to California and getting in on some of the action where the real action was happening at that time.

Tayste and Girls Tyme were growing in leaps and bounds and gaining a following. They were working hard for the big time and Ann believed it was time for big things to happen. So, instead of giving in to Lonnie's pressure,

Ann used her own contacts to access the necessary information to place her performers on a much larger stage.

A LOOK INTO THE FUTURE

Ann became ever so focused and aware of the importance of placing the acts on a stage where they could be seen by the right people in the industry. Her contact Teresa became a wealth of information and support in this regard. Teresa worked with Sony Music and also did some work for Columbia records, as well as Epic. "Andretta, many of the talent scouts and A & R people come to the various showcases to discover new and upcoming talent."

"Okay."

"What I'm saying dear is to really get your girls out there, I recommend you bringing them to California and see how they fair in this environment."

"Okay. I hear what you are saying Teresa, how do we make that happen?"

"Let me gather some information, and get back with you. The bottom line is, you really won't know what you have until you first put them among acts in their league, and second, hear what the music execs have to say about it. At the end of the day, we need them to bite."

"I hear you Teresa. I don't want any wasted trips. I want to play smart. The girls are talented. I know I have something here and I want to give them every shot I can to help them gain the success I know they can achieve."

"Well Andretta, the only way to do that is to bring them to compete with the big boys – generally speaking. It can be a tough game. You can have a talent, but until you place that talent side-by-side with other top talent, you are not able to have a realistic perspective. The showcases allow up and coming talent to showcase themselves and have people in the industry seriously take a look at them…"

"Okay…"

"…so, if I were you, I would do whatever I could to get them out here. Let me do some checking to see what is happening, and I will get back with you."

"Thanks Teresa, I appreciate all the help."

"Okay, dear. Let's talk soon."

Ann became very vigilant about creating solid opportunities for the girls and being smarter about doing things. She was not interested in being pressured into making moves that were irresponsible or just to appease someone's ego. So Ann took a hard position against Lonnie and his bullying tactics. Ann played by the book, the Music Industry 101 book that is and empowered herself with information so that she could effectively help her acts break into the business. After all, it was business and she was determined to fulfill her and Dwight's dream. Every move she made, she made with him in mind and she replayed the countless conversations the two of them often had.

"…See baby, there's this man named Gavin right? I think his name is Bill Gavin. He's this old dude…teacher who turned to radio. He plays a lot of music by Black artists and provides opportunities for Blacks to break into the music industry."

"Uhm…okay Dwight…"

"It's like this Ann. This guy produces this report right? It's called the Gavin report or something like that. All the people in the industry…I mean all of them Ann, even these big time record labels…read the report. They swear by it. They listen to what this dude has to say. He's considered the most powerful person in the business. He says who is good to listen to and who is not."

"Huhm, Dwight, that's interesting."

"I know Ann. If Gavin says you are good to listen to, then labels are more apt to pay attention to you."

"Uhm."

Ann was snapped out of her reflective daydream by the ringing of the telephone.

"Hello."

"Andretta?"

"Yes?"

"Hello dear. This is Teresa. I've got some good news for you."

"Great, I could use some."

"Well…there's this showcase coming up here in July. The Gavin Showcase is one of the top showcases here. How soon can your girls be ready?"

"Teresa, we've been ready."

"I know it doesn't give you much time, but I was able to get you a spot in the showcase. I'll send the details. In the meantime, make sure everything on your end is where it needs to be. Here's your chance."

"Thanks!"

"Hey, no problem. Let's do this. If you have what you say you have, then you are where you need to be. Make sure the girls are as polished as they can be. This means their stage presence and personality, costumes, vocals, how they perform as a group…make sure everything is on, because this is the real deal dear. There will be many people watching and listening. When I say many people, I mean the ones who really matter."

"Okay…I hear you, Teresa."

"Talk to you soon, sweetie."

Ann hung up the telephone and yelled out loudly. "Yes! Hell Yes!"

Armon and Christopher ran downstairs like something was wrong. "You okay ma?"

"Yeah, Armon. I was just excited."

"About the group?"

"Yep."

"I'm glad mommy. I like to see you happy."

"Oh Chris…me too."

Ann patted Christopher on the head and shooed them both back upstairs to play. She was extremely excited, and could not wait to share the good news with the girls and the team. As everyone arrived that evening for practice at her house, they noticed something in her countenance, but could not quite put her finger on it. When I arrived, Ann pulled me aside to let me know the news before she shared it with everyone else.

"Before ya'll start practicing tonight, I have some things I want to speak to everyone about."

"Okay Miss Ann, what did we do now?"

"LaTavia, why you think there's a problem? I got some great news guys!"

"Okay then, what is it already. Spill the beans."

"Hold your horses Bey…I spoke with one of my people in California today, and guess what?"

"Come on Miss Ann…stop playin' with us…"

"Okay…Okay." Ann was excited and laughing at the same time. She was really proud of both the boys and the girls, but she was having a little fun with them.

"Okay, great news…Girl Tyme will be performing in the Gavin Showcase in California."

"What's that?"

"Well Bey, the Gavin Showcase is only one of the biggest and most important showcases there is for artists."

The girls started jumping up and down and hugging each other. Everyone was excited. Lonnie was looking like, "How in the hell did she make that happen?"

Tayste was happy for the girls, but they were looking at each other as if to say, "What about us?"

Ann, paying attention to everyone's body language and response to the news, spoke up.

"Now Tayste, there is no need to worry or feel left out. We're working on some things with you too. For this showcase, I was able to get the girls in, but again we are working on setting some things up with you all."

Lonnie spoke up. Ann could feel a little sting in his tone of voice. "When is it Ann?"

"It's in July. So we have a lot to do to make sure the girls are ready. They will have the chance to perform two songs. They need to nail both of them, because there will be some big wigs watching. So Lonnie, T-Mo, David, I am going to need you to step it up."

Lonnie looked at T-Mo, and mumbled under his breath. "Whatcha mean we have to step it up. I got my shit together."

"I heard that Lonnie."

He scratched his head but did not respond because the children were present.

"We gonna be stars!" Ashley said rocking back and forth rhythmically like she was about to jump double dutch or something.

"Being a star will take a lot of hard work girls. And like I said before, the hard work will pay off. Just keep your head on straight, stay humble and hone your craft. So ya'll go on and get to it. Kenny, Lonnie, T-Mo, Lynn, David, I need you to do what you do. Work with the girls, and let's do this."

Both Girls Tyme and Tayste left the room to go start practicing. Ann continued speaking with the team for a few more minutes before they went to watch the practice.

"Okay ya'll. We need to work with Ashley's stiff ass, get her looking better on stage. She has a great voice, but I need her to loosen up a bit. Bey needs to tone down some of that ass-shaking and popping shit. Kelly...she probably needs the most help. David, I really need you to work with her. She has to come out of her shell. No weak links. We need to tighten it all the way up, you got me?

I'm gonna work on getting some outfits for them. I'm thinking of something a little mannish, but girly-girly at the same time."

Ann took the driver seat and started delegating and assigning things for the team to do. She was not shy about it and the closer she got to the goal, the harder she worked, and the more she reflected on Dwight. "Okay, we have barely a month before this showcase. Me and Kenny will work to get the travel details sorted out, and speak with the parents. I need you all to focus on what you do best and let's make it happen!"

The girls had less than a month to get ready for the Gavin Showcase. Ann and I spoke with the parents about the showcase and everyone started preparing for the trip to San Francisco. The closer it got to the date to head out, the more intense things became on the management team. However, the girls were excited mainly about flying and performing in California. I'm not sure what it was, but for them, going to California was a symbol of success. Although the Jackson Five started out in Gary, Indiana as part of the Motown stable, for the young people, California and the Jacksons appeared to be synonymous.

Ann remembered seeing photos of the Jacksons performing in some powdered blue duck-tail suits with sparkles on them. She envisioned the girls wearing something similar but maybe with some leggings to add the feminine touch. Ann went on the hunt to bring her vision alive and rounded up some really neat white tuxedo jackets, blouses with bowties, along with stretch pants. She found them at some pageant place and had them altered with sequins. Ann took the girls to get their nails done, their hair done, facials, on little shopping excursions around Houston, and everything else she could think of to set the tone for them of what to expect in the near future, and also to help build them up.

Word got out that Girls Tyme was performing in San Francisco at the Gavin Convention. That created an even bigger buzz, because anyone in radio or the music industry understood that the Gavin Convention was a really big deal and a great opportunity for any artist that was fortunate enough to be able to perform at such an auspicious event. I often wondered then if the girls or their parents even really knew how big of a deal it was. I wondered that then, and I wonder that today. Even now I ask myself if they realize the wonderful opportunity that Dretta gave them and the mighty door she opened for them back in nineteen ninety-two.

The stage any of those girls stand on today is a foundation that Ann built. She invested in their future as if she was investing in her own daughter's future, and as she did in Armon and Christopher's future. Those boys may have lost a dad and a sister, but over time they gained uncle Kenny and several other "little sisters" who invaded their house almost every day after school and everyday in the summers, helping to turn their house back into a home again and to give them the platform to follow and capture their dreams. It was truly destiny in the making!

    The harder the girls worked, the more Ann pampered them. She wanted them to feel the reward of hard work. She dressed the girls from head to toe, buying them little trinkets and pretty little things as if she were playing dress-up with her Barbie dolls, very similar to how she did with Shawna. Ann's daughter was the most, well-dressed two-year old there was, and there was no doubt about it, Girls Tyme would be too if Ann had anything to do with it. The next few weeks were all about preparation for the performance at the Gavin Showcase.

    The night before everyone was to fly out; Ann had the girls do a dress rehearsal at her house so that the team and the parents could look at everything together. They looked hot, like little stars. "Okay girls, just like you did tonight, do that and then some in San Francisco. Own the stage you got it? Good job Kelly, you lookin' good baby girl, you hear? Don't be afraid to shine. Thanks LaTavia and Bey for helping to get things on point. I'm proud of you. I'm proud of all of you."

Everyone was happy with the entire presentation. Now it was up to the girls to give a solid performance. The families headed home for the night to get ready to fly out in the morning. They all said their, "see ya tomorrows," and "see ya laters."

"We wish you were going Mr. Kenny."

"I know girls, but next time, alright?"

I turned to Ann. "Well, this is it. You got it?"

"Yep, I got it. But we're gonna have to learn more about each other so even when you're not present, I can know what you're thinking and visa versa. I feel you are the only one I can really trust here."

"You'll be alright, Ann. I'm a phone call away."

"I just know Lonnie gonna be on some bullshit. I have to keep his ass close on the leash this trip. I'm supposed to see Teresa when we get there…touch basis with her. I haven't met her face-to-face so I don't want him acting simple and shit."

"Let me know…see you when you get back."

The next day, Ann called me from the airport. All the parents were bright and chipper. The girls were excited to be performing in California, but Ann wanted to make sure they were not tired from the flight and everything. San Francisco is in a different time zone than Houston. So, their little bodies will be two hours ahead for an already long day.

Ann called me periodically during the day to fill me in on what was going on. The day moved quickly and Ann made sure to help me feel as if I was there. It was finally time for the girls to perform at the Gavin Showcase.

"Kenny?"

"Yeah."

"Hey, this is Ann. They're about to perform."

"Okay, you're recording it right?"

"Yeah."

"Good. They need to be able to look back at it to improve. No matter how good they are, they can always get better."

"Alright, I'm going, I will talk to you later."

"Okay, bye."

"Bye."

Several acts performed, and then it was time for Girls Tyme to grace the stage. The girls came out wearing white tuxedo jackets with sequins on them, nice shirts, bow ties and some leggings. Ann found exactly what she was looking for. They all had big hair. They looked like little ladies dressed all in white. They had a Jackson five persona only it was six girls instead of five boys. As Ann took one look at the girls as they were coming out, she knew that they were going to be stars. Just as she was imbibing in the moment, the girls broke the silence in the room.

The Making of a Child of Destiny

"The song we're about to sing…Sunshine, you light up my way. The children of the world reach out to you…"

Ann was more nervous than she had ever been watching them perform. The parents were amazed at how polished the girls looked. The harmonies were on point. "Only chase the clouds away…Shining through the hearts of people…Those who think will never heal…"

Lonnie and T-Mo were fixed on the girls to see if they hit every note on point. Ann was looking around to see if she could gauge the expressions on various people's faces. "Let your wings of golden love shine…Gather those who live without a home…Let them know…They're never truly alone."

Sunshine was their mantra. The audience was mesmerized at the amazing talent of such young girls. They hung onto every note in amazement. It was almost the same expression that Berry Gordy had when he finally listened to the Jackson five demo performance sent to him. When the girls sang that one part of the song where Beyonce came in, she belted the note out and owned it! Girls Tyme turned the place out! They left their signature in California that day. The energy that consumed the room when they sang was captivating. It was too much for their parents to take in all at once. They had seen their children perform before in front of people, but never like this and never on this level. You could tell by the expressions on their faces that the realization of what was happening to their little girls was only beginning to sink in.

Once Girls Tyme finished singing, Beyonce took control of the mic. "We would like to thank our managers Andretta Tillman and Kenny Moore for making this possible. We also want to thank our producer Lonnie Jackson."

The audience cheered. The girls had such a presence and maturity about them; it was as if they were already stars. After they left the stage, the parents went over to their children and hugged them and told them how proud they were of them. Ann talked to the girls. "That's what I'm talking about girls. You killed it!"

When the showcase was over, Teresa and Ann connected. The two of them spoke briefly after the initial "how are you…finally nice to put a face with a voice" tune. Ann introduced Teresa to the girls. "Great performance girls. You should be really proud of yourselves."

The girls shook their heads and smiled. Teresa expressed the thumbs up to Ann. "Okay dear, great job with the girls. I'll put out some feelers and give you a call."

"Thanks Teresa."

No sooner than Teresa walked away, as Lonnie and Ann were standing near the girls and their parents, someone else approached them. "Hello, I'm Arne Frager

The Making of a Child of Destiny

with the Plant Recording Studio. You got one hell of a show there."

"Thanks. I'm Andretta Tillman, their manager, and this is Lonnie, producer…And this is…"

"I know who they are; I won't forget these talented young ladies."

The girls just blushed. Arne handed Ann his business card and invited her to bring the girls to the Plant to do some recording. "Well Andretta, get in touch with me."

It turned out that Arne was the director of the world's famous Plant Recording Studios in Sausalito, California. As the parents were watching the attention the girls were getting from different people in the business, some of them had immediately begun to try to jockey their way to the forefront. Carolyn and Cheryl started asking Ann what they could do to help. Mathew started offering unsolicited advice. Carolyn made it her business to point out that it was her daughter's group. Ann could see already what was coming down the pipes with this crew.

Lonnie was no better. He immediately started pressuring Ann about the Plant. "See, I have a contact who works with him. You know Dwayne Wiggins of Tony! Toni! Toné!" I can use him to set it up."

"Thanks Lonnie, the man just gave me his damn card not even five minutes ago."

She shook her head at how some of them were acting. After the crowd began to die down some, Ann rounded up the girls and motioned for everyone so they could leave the venue and get back to the hotel and get ready to leave out the next morning. Once they got to the hotel, Ann called me.

"Hey Kenny."

"Well?"

"They killed it man! They torn the house down for some little country ass girls from Texas."

"Did anyone approach you after the show?"

"Yeah, actually they did. I finally met up with Teresa in person. She mentioned that she would put out some feelers to see what some of the executives thought about the performance."

"Okay."

"I also met this man named Arne Frager. He is with the Plant studios in Sausalito. He invited us to come and do some recording. Hell no sooner than the man gave me his card, Lonnie's ass got to going."

"What did he say?"

"He mentioned Dwayne Wiggins and how he can set the Plant up through him. I told his ignorant ass, why the hell I need him to set it up when the Got-damned director just gave me his fucking card. Ignorant ass mutha fucka…anyway…"

I just laughed because when Ann got to going, she went there. "…And all of a damn sudden every body want to be Mr. and Mrs. What can I do for you. Hell, go find some damn investors that's what they ass can do."

"What time does your flight leave in the morning?"

"I have to check the exact time, but we'll talk when I get back."

"Alright take care. Don't let them get to you too much."

"Alright, Kenny thanks. I'll talk with you when I get back."

Ann and the rest of the crew flew out that next morning. Everyone arrived back in Houston safe and sound. It was only a matter of a few days when Ann received a call from Teresa. "Andretta?"

"Yes?"

"This is Teresa. How are you dear?"

"I'm good thanks."

"Well, I have gotten some feedback from various people in the industry. The response is favorable. Do your girls have demos?"

"They have done some recording…but not a full demo."

"Well we need to push forward some great demos that can be sent to various executives and have them take a listen. My recommendation is to get on that right away and not to let grass grow under our feet. I think we have something here and I want to help in any way that I can, if you'll let me."

"Of course. Arne Frager gave me his card, and invited us to come to his studio to do some recording."

"Yeah? Okay Arne is with the Plant right?"

"Yes."

"Well my suggestion to you is to get on that right away. Once you get some great recordings, it will be easier to communicate with the big boys."

"I'm on it."

Ann followed Teresa's advice. She pulled out Arne's card and arranged for both Tayste and Girls Tyme to go to the Plant. Arne agreed to work with her on the recording by Ann paying up front for the studio costs, but getting points on the production aspect on the backend. So, no sooner than they returned from one trip, Ann and her team was heading back to California. She shared the news with the team at the next meeting.

"Okay, I got some news and feedback from the Gavin Convention!"

"Ann before you get on to your news, I've got a question."

"Okay Lonnie, go ahead."

"Look, I spoke with Dwayne Wiggins. He said he can make some things happen so we can go to the Plant and do some recording. You ought to let me go ahead and set that up. If we really serious about this thing, then we need to move like we serious."

"What are you sayin' Lonnie?"

"What I'm saying is if we gonna do this thing here, we need to do it right. I was talking to Carolyn and some of the others and…?"

"So whatcha saying? I don't know what the hell I'm doing?"

"Look here Ann, all I'm saying is we need to move a certain kind of way, Ann, and I think if you let me set the Plant up…uh er…handle this you can see some…"

"What T-Mo? I see you over there nodding your head in agreement. What do you have to say?"

"Oh yeah…uh, I agree with Lonnie. We need to move now after Gavin and all. Did you see the response?"

"Okay. Does anyone else have anything to say right now? Lynn? Kenny?"

"Naw Ann, come on let's move forward."

"Thanks Kenny…Okay, Lonnie I hear you about the Plant, but pressuring me is not going to get things done any sooner…"

"But all I'm sayin' Ann is…"

"I don't understand why come I have to keep telling you this is my shit…and I know how to handle my shit. You just make sure you handle your shit. Produce and let me manage. Shit, you making me cuss your Black ass out. I told myself tonight I was gonna be cool. But nigga you keep fuckin' with my shit and I got my shit handled. Just make sure your ass handle yours."

I just shook my head at the whole situation. Lonnie had been pressuring Ann to no end to set up the Plant. Ann already filled me in on the arrangement she made with Arne to go to the Plant. I was simply waiting for Lonnie and the rest to shut up so she could share it with the rest of the team and clue them in on where things were. "Go ahead Ann…continue."

"Okay, Lonnie…I don't need you to set the Plant up with Wiggins, I've got that covered. We have a date for Tayste and Girls Tyme to record at the Plant. I've just been tryin' to tell your Black ass this all damn night…If you can shut the hell up for two damn minutes."

Lonnie and everyone else started looking around at each other surprised. Ann had already scheduled the trip to the Plant and the team had less than two weeks to get things organized. Ann needed to share the pertinent information, so that they could in turn tell the groups and their parents the following day at practice. She wanted to ensure the entire management team was on board and aware of all the pertinent details. So after the management team was informed of the news, the groups and their parents were let in on the excitement.

The Making of a Child of Destiny

"We have some great news for you. Both Tayste and Girls Tyme will be going into the studio to record a full length demo. The major tracks will be laid at the Plant, the others we will do here in Houston, and then mix the two."

"Wow!"

"Yay…"

Everyone in the room was excited about the news. "Girls Tyme turned some heads at the Gavin Showcase. You all did a fantastic job and things are really moving. So you are heading big time and this is real and it's getting serious. I hope you're ready."

"Okay Ann so what will Ashley's group be recording?"

"Well Carolyn, Girls Tyme will of course be recording Sunshine. The rest of the songs, we will get with Lonnie and T-Mo on that…put together a hit list maybe even do a work up on some other songs. That will be determined moving forward."

"Okay so, when does everyone fly out?"

"That's a good question Mathew. Everyone will not be flying out. Only the lead and co-leads of both Tayste and Girls Tyme will be going to California this trip, and then of course the management team."

"Okay."

"So, as much as we would like the parents to be there, it's going to be a hectic schedule. We need to get in and get out as soon as possible and minimize the costs. We don't want any distractions. We want everyone's attention to be on producing a great album all the way around."

Everyone seemed to be cool with what Ann was saying. "Well let me know if there is anything I can do."

"Thanks Mathew, the main thing is support the groups and of course we still are looking to bring additional investors on board. That is always a factor."

"I'll keep that in mind."

"Yes, please do."

The groups practiced for the evening. Armon had already grabbed Brian out of my hands before the night even got started. It was a good parent meeting and rehearsal. Everyone was cooperative, or at least as cooperative as expected. For the most part we all had a great time that evening. All the parents were in attendance as well as Cassey. I was feeling really good about everything and looking forward to working very closely with Ann and the acts.

From the time I came on board as part of the management team, things were moving rather quickly. I hadn't been on the team a good three months and already we were seeing some amazing results and more importantly

The Making of a Child of Destiny

some great relationships being formed. Aside from some of the parents' evident vying for closeness to Ann and to create their own opportunities to be "in the mix," things were going well. Tayste, Girls Tyme, Ann, Armon, and Christopher were becoming a very big part of mine and Cassey's life.

During a break in the rehearsal, Ann ensured everyone had a cup of something to drink in their hands. "So let's celebrate everyone! Tayste and Girls Tyme…Destination - Sausalito, California. Here we come!"

"Cheers!"

"Hear, Hear!"

The next week or so was hectic for everyone involved. However, that did not minimize the excitement of recording at the Plant. When the time came, Tu Tu and A.J. flew out with Lonnie and T-Mo. David was unable to go. The guys left a few days earlier so that Lonnie and T-Mo could do some pre-recording production and tighten up on some of Tayste's recordings. That way when Ann and I arrived with the girls, all their stuff would have been wrapped up and out the way.

The rest of the crew met at the airport. Ann and I arrived first at the airport. Shortly after Mathew, Tina, Carolyn, Nolan, Ashley, and Beyonce arrived, ready to go. Carolyn was making to do all over Ashley, fixing her clothes, sweeping her hair over from her eye. Mathew and

Tina were excited for Beyonce. Tina's disposition was more a support for Beyonce because this is something she wanted to do. "Have fun baby. And…behave don't give Miss Ann or Mr. Kenny a hard time. You hear?"

As we were organizing the tickets and luggage, Cassey and I went over to upgrade the tickets to first class. Ann arranged for a limo to pick us up on the other end when we arrived. She wanted the girls to know what it felt like to be stars. She worked hard so they could experience the whole "kit and caboodle." She wanted to teach them how to handle themselves when they did in fact become famous.

Once the tickets were sorted and the luggage checked, we all headed on to the boarding gate where our flight was scheduled to take off. Beyonce was wide-eyed and bushy-tailed looking around Houston Intercontinental Airport. There were loads of people flying that day and she was captivated by the whole scene. As the airline staff grabbed the speaker to begin to call for boarding, the hugs and kisses goodbye took place. The parents waved and blew kisses at their little pre-teens as they were heading up to the agent to hand them the boarding passes. Back then, there were no security check points to have to go through. So the parents were able to walk clear up to the gates to watch their children board.

"You remember what I told you Bey?"

"Yes, ma'am. Love you daddy."

"Alright now. You know what to do."

Beyonce shook her head in response to Mathew. Ashley hugged her mom and dad and as we were preparing to board the plane, the questions started coming. "Mr. Kenny, why aren't the other people getting on the plane now?"

"Well Bey, the lady only called first class people to board now."

"What does that mean?"

Ashley jumped in and responded to Beyonce's question. "Those are the most important people Bey."

Beyonce scratched her head. "Oh…Well…Mr. Kenny?"

"Yes Bey?"

"Aren't they important too?"

Ann looked at me and smiled, then proceeded to answer Beyonce's question. "See this is what happens when you become famous Bey. Everything is first class and you don't have to wait in long lines and things like that."

Beyonce seemed more concerned about the other people than feeling like a star. Ashley on the other hand was a different story all together. "We gonna be stars Miss Ann?"

"Yep."

"And people are gonna have to wait for us to go first…that's cool. I think I can get used to this!"

"Yes Ashley. And because you are going to be a star, you are gonna have to know how to act."

We headed down the jet way and onto the plane. Beyonce was still taking everything in around her. Ashley sat next to Ann on the plane, while Beyonce ended up sitting next to me. "You wanna sit by the window, Bey?"

"Can I?" She said smiling.

"Of course you can."

"Okay!"

Beyonce hopped over by the window and I moved to the aisle seat. Ann and Ashley were sitting across from us. Ann sat on the aisle seat as well. Beyonce was looking out the window watching everything going on outside the plane. I was getting everything settled so when the plane took off, I could close my eyes and get some much needed shut eye. Beyonce watched the plane take off. She was preoccupied with all the activity from the handlers outside the plane working to the take off.

"Wow! It looks like a map. You see that Mr. Kenny?"

I looked out the window and smiled at Beyonce. I was glad she was excited but I was looking forward to some chill time. Once the announcement came that we no longer had to keep our seats in the upright position, I

The Making of a Child of Destiny

exhaled and leaned back in my chair, closed my eyes, and relaxed. I was comfortable and feeling really good. It was a wonderfully quiet moment. With all the hustle and bustle to get to the airport, getting the luggage checked, getting through security and all the other tasks that had to be handled, I was well ready to sit back and sleep during the flight. Just as I sighed from relief and turned my mind off, this scratchy little ten-year old voice resounded. "Mr. Kenny?"

I opened one eye and looked at her at the corner of my eye, then turned to her. "Yes Bey?"

"How long will it take to get there?"

"About four hours."

"Oh. Okay."

Beyonce went back to looking out the window. I leaned my head back and closed my eyes again.

"Mr. Kenny?"

I opened my eyes back again. "Yes, Bey?"

"What's the studio like?"

"I'm not sure I haven't been there before. But I'm sure it's nice Bey."

"Is it big?"

"I'm sure it is they do a lot of recording there."

"What's the hotel like?"

"It's nice."

"Is it big?"

"I'm sure it is."

"Oh…Okay."

She then turned and started looking back out the window. I closed my eyes again. After about ten minutes when she did not ask me anymore questions. I settled back down to relax. Finally, I was able to get some rest. I took another deep breath in and on the exhale, that little voice sounded again. "Mr. Kenny…"

"Will this damn girl shut the hell up." I was thinking to myself, but then responded politely.

"Yes, Bey?"

She asked me question after question. I thought to myself, "Don't this girl ever shut up?"

That went on for about an hour. Then finally at some point she either drifted off to sleep or was hypnotized from looking out the window. Either way she finally stopped asking all those damn questions and I was finally able to get some shut eye before landing in California. I knew that in about three more hours, things would start to change drastically for these little girls, and I wanted to be well rested.

Ann looked over at me. "I see Bey finally settled down."

"Thank God. I didn't know when she was gonna stop."

We both laughed quietly as to not disturb the girls. "You know Kenny, we will be looking back on this five years from now laughing, don't you?"

"You're probably right, Ann. But for now…hell…I wanna get me some damn rest. I'll see Sausalito when I wake up."

The Plant…here we come!

TAKING THE LEAD

Ann and I landed in San Francisco with the girls. We retrieved our luggage and as we looked in the direction of where passengers were waiting to be picked up, we saw a man fully suited up holding a sign that read, "Tillman Management & Girls Tyme Entertainment." As he assisted with the luggage, we followed him to the doors. When we walked out the door, there parked right in front was a long white stretch limo. The girls yelled almost in unison, "Limo!"

"That's for us, girls."

"For real Miss Ann?"

"Yes Bey, it's for us."

"That's cool."

When Ashley realized that it was for us, she snapped her fingers and tossed her head back. "Now that is what I'm talking 'bout."

Beyonce was excited about the limo ride, but she was more fascinated with the surroundings. She was into what the people were doing and how they were. Ashley on the other hand was more into things and the hype of it all. We got into the limo and headed to the Claremont

Hotel. When we arrived, we walked into the lap of luxury of five-star quality. The girls were wowing all the way up to the door. The hotel was huge; sitting on several acres of land and every square foot of it was beautifully landscaped. It had tennis courts, swimming pools, a hair salon and spa, a full service workout room, and a host of other amenities that if time permitted, we could definitely enjoy.

We finally got checked-in. Our luggage reached the room before we did, but it was nice watching the girls taking it all in. The hotel had plush carpet and was furnished exquisitely. We stayed in a three-bedroom suite. It was very spacious with a full size living room, a dining area with a full size dining table, a kitchenette and separate bedrooms and bathrooms. The room had an amazing balcony that overlooked the San Francisco Bay area. It was just the place to stay and relax for the girls' first real studio experience in the big leagues.

When we opened the doors to the room, Ashley ran throughout the entire suite. "This is fabulous. We even have our own bedroom and beds." She said mimicking the playful voice of a rich lady. Beyonce looked around then plopped down on the couch and started talking about the flight. "Mr. Kenny, you know that picture you took of me on the airplane sitting by the window?"

"Yes, Bey."

"Well, I wanna have it."

The Making of a Child of Destiny

"What do you mean you wanna have it."

"I wanna have it, so I can put it in my scrap book."

"You have a scrap book, Bey?"

"Yeah, don't you? I wanna have the picture to remind me of the airplane ride and of you and how you let me sit by the window. That was nice. When I grow up, I can look back at it…and say, 'Mr. Kenny took this picture and he let me sit by the window.'"

When Beyonce said that to me, it really touched me because here was this little ten year old child who was not even the least bit concerned about all the great things happening to her, but rather very sensitive to the people around her. Even at that age, it was easy to see that she was humble and not at all letting the idea of stardom go to her head.

"Wow, Bey. I'm flattered."

"Ah you just a softy Mr. Kenny."

Beyonce and Ashley continued to sit on the couch. We weren't scheduled to go into the studio until the next day, so it was about getting prepared and resting up for a full day of studio work the following day. Ann's idea was for the girls to relax and enjoy this lesson is first-class living.

"Girls, you know this is just the start of it, right? You're gonna have to work hard."

Both Ashley and Beyonce nodded in agreement to acknowledge that they understood what Ann was saying to them.

"When I become a star, I am gonna live like this every day." Ashley said as matter of fact.

"Miss Ann, how do you think the studio will be?"

"Well Bey, it will be a lot of work but you can do it. I believe in you."

"Has anybody famous ever been in there?"

"Yes."

"Who?"

"Well Bey, let's see…Stevie Wonder,…uh… Let's see who else…Prince, …a lot of famous people have recorded at the Plant. You just have to wait and see."

"Wow!"

"What you mean wow, Bey…Girls Tyme…duh…we are stars too."

"Ashley…"

"Don't Ashley me Beyonce Knowles…we are gonna be stars."

Ann and I just looked at each other observing the girls interaction with one another. I just shook my head. That little Ashley, I was thinking to myself, "That little heifer is already in diva mode. Shit, that one is something else, and a little self-centered too."

Having a son was a whole different experience than dealing with little girls. However, Ann was enjoying every moment of their exchange. She found it to be funny. I looked at Ann and mumbled. "You think this shit is funny, don't you?"

Ann shook her head and smiled.

"Hey girls, you know this is big time right? You already gettin' your shot."

Ashley didn't respond; however Beyonce spoke up. "Yes, Mr. Kenny. Thank you Miss Ann for helping us and making it possible for us to do all of this."

"Honey, the only thing I do is what good managers do. It is up to you to work hard, hone your skills and refine your craft, and prove that you deserve to be where you are. You have a great voice and a beautiful heart. You can do anything you put your mind to. All you have to do is work hard, don't ever forget that."

Beyonce took every one of Ann's words to heart. You could tell that she was listening and thinking about what was said. Ashley was sitting there twirling her hair and seemingly somewhat disinterested in what Ann was saying or distracted by all the material things around her. Either way, she was not fully present in the moment. Finally, Ann spoke up. "Let's go get us something to eat."

After about an hour or so, we went to have an early dinner at one of the fancy restaurants. After dinner we came back to the hotel to relax. As the night was winding down, we were all sitting around watching television. Ann was going through some paperwork and getting things ready for the following day. Beyonce was snuggled up on one of the chairs with a pillow while Ashley was stretched out on the couch with her glass. I decided to steal some quiet time to myself, think about my wife and son, chill for the rest of the evening, and get ready for the next day. "Well Ann, I think I'm gonna have me a glass of scotch and go sit out on the porch."

"No problem, Kenny."

"If you need me, you know where I'll be."

I got my glass of scotch and went and sat outside. I realized that I needed some ice, so I headed back inside to get some ice. As I headed toward the kitchen, Ashley raised up. "Hey you, get me some more ice water!"

"What?"

"You need to get me some ice water."

Now growing up in Mississippi, all I could think about was little kids stayed in little kids place. Don't talk crazy to grown folks or the old folks. Ann looked up at me from her paperwork. I guess she recognized with both of us being from the country, and all, that this was going to pop me off. I had been cool, ain't said nothing to nobody. Ann jumped up as I fixed my mouth to respond to Ashley.

"Little girl what you say?"

"I said get me some water."

"Let me tell your little ass something…"

"Kenny, Kenny, come on…step back outside…"

"Naw…hell naw…"

Ann pushed me outside. She was laughing at me. I snapped. "What the hell wrong with her little ass. Didn't her got damned mama teach her to respect her damn elders." I was on a roll. "Hell Ann, she was already getting' on my last damn nerves. Now her little diva ass think she gonna talk to me like I'm her damn staff or busboy!"

"I know Kenny…"

"Does she know who the fuck I am?"

Ann started laughing harder as I was going off.

"Got dammit! You gonna let that little mutha fucker talk to me that damn way? Who the hell she think she is?"

Ann was still laughing. "I know Kenny…"

"That little pint-size heifer. Think she runnin' something all got damned ready. Who the fuck she think she is?"

Ann was holding her stomach by then.

"I'm Kenny fuckin' Mo. I didn't come out here to be ordered around like some damn lackey ass punk, by a mutha fuckin twelve year old girl!"

Ann was on the floor laughing. I was still going off. She was dying laughing. "Okay, Kenny…Okay!"

"Hell naw! Who that little heifer think she is. I ain't no yes man. Shit! I ain't no busboy!"

Ann was laughing uncontrollably.

"…Never was, never will. Hell if I wanted to be a star I can be a got damned star. But she think her little ass is the shit."

"I know, Kenny, I know…okay, okay, okay. Calm down, just calm down. She's just a little girl."

"I understand, but got dammit she act like a grown woman. She's talkin' to Kenny Mo! Kenny got damned Mo. Don't nobody talk that way to Kenny Mo!"

"Kenny, why are you talking in third person?"

"What the fuck you talkin' about Ann?"

"Why you talkin' in third person?"

"What the hell you mean in third person? How am I talking in third person?"

"…You said… what you talkin' about…fuck don't nobody talk that way to Kenny Mo…"

We both fell out laughing. "Ooh Shit! Whoo…"

"Calm your country ass down!"

So Ann and I sat there for awhile. Ashley and Beyonce saw all the commotion. Ann went back inside to get some ice water. She got me my scotch. We just sat on the balcony drinking and talking. We then went back inside after about an hour of laughing and talking. Ashley spoke up. "Was anybody gonna get me some water?"

"Hell naw, get your little ass up and get your own damn water." Ann said half way laughing.

That little incident put an end to Ashley's thinking that she was going to be a prima donna. The whole time while this is going on, Beyonce's eyes was buck wide open like, "What the hell…I know not to do that…" After Ashley got her water, and we all sat down together. We all realized just how funny it was and started laughing at the situation. Beyonce really thought it was funny. "You see Mr. Kenny? His water head was just moving and everything."

They all were laughing. "What ya'll laughing at?"

"You was out there… Your neck was just rollin' and your head looked like it had water in it."

"Shut up Bey."

"We gonna start calling you Uncle Watermelon Head."

"As long as ya'll do what ya'll supposed to do, and as long as you handle your business…you can call me Uncle Watermelon Head."

We all agreed to that. It was getting late so we all turned in for the night. The next morning, the limo came to pick us up and we headed on to the Plant to start the session. The ride through the hills of South Sausalito was absolutely beautiful. When we arrived at the facility, it was like the "Holy Grail of Music." When we walked in we saw the host of entertainers who have journeyed through. The Stones had been there, Mariah had been there. Stevie Wonder recorded the "Songs in the Keys of Life;" Prince recorded "For You;" Luther Vandross recorded "Songs," Mariah Carey recorded "Music Box;" Aretha Franklin recorded "Who's Zooming Who;" and Kenny G recorded just about all of his stuff at the Plant. Everybody had been there.

This was the first time that I met Arne Frager. Arne was your typical Californian hippie type dude. He was a white gentleman with gray hair, yet a pretty nice guy.

"Hey girls...good to see you again. I've heard a lot of good things about you. I'm excited to have you here."

Arne explained to the girls what they would be doing. As Arne was talking, Lonnie walked in. "Alright girls. Let's get in there."

They went through a barrage of songs. Ashley sang her heart out. They ran Beyonce back and forth in for background vocals as we went along. This happened for about two to three days non-stop. Everything worked out well and they were satisfied at what we had gotten. So we packed up and flew back to Houston.

At the conclusion of the studio visit we left there with two of Tayste's songs being mastered - "Groove Me One More Time" and "Love Just by You." We also ended up getting a couple of tracks done for Girls Tyme as well as leaving with some show ready material and tracks for the girls to use for live performances. That was helpful because it allowed us to better prepare for the live showcases.

The team and parents were excited. The acts were excited as well. Once we arrived back into Houston we arranged a listening party at Ann's house to listen to the tracks. We had a great time. Lynn was glad because it gave him additional material to pursue investments. "This is great. It will help get more investors."

"That's good Lynn, but I wanna say this to everyone on the team. Bringing some solid investors on board is important. So this is something that I want all of us thinking about."

Lynn was uncomfortable with it, but Ann gave him a look like as if to say, "Shut the hell up because if your ass was on the job, you would have done it by now with your shady ass."

The night went on and everyone was feeling pretty good about where things were.

About a week and a half later, Arne called Lonnie and gave him some preliminary feedback from the initial recordings at the Plant. "I just wanted to follow-up on the package that was sent out. I sent it to several record labels. I hadn't heard back from any of the folks I sent it to with the exception of Darryl Simmons. He's over at Atlantic."

"What did he say?"

"He loved it. He passed it on to Sylvia Rhone and Merlin Bob in the New York office. I plan on following up with some of the other folks to get an answer."

"So, what now?"

"Well, Lonnie, I did have a long conversation with Ruth Carson. She is one of the three managing partners at dePasse Entertainment. She was also at the show to see the girls. She was not particularly impressed with Ashley or Kelly's stage persona, and she was not excited at all about Ashley on tape. She feels the real stars are Beyonce and LaTavia. We will discuss that later."

"Yeah, yeah, I see what you're saying."

"I think you need to get the girls back out here. Utilize the background more in the lead and that will help strengthen the sound on tape so the group can break out and obtain a major record deal."

"Okay Arne, let me see what I can do. I'll talk with Ann and see what she says."

Lonnie called Ann and told her what Arne said about the feedback he was getting. He also told Ann that Arne suggested that the the girls go back out to the Plant and tighten a few things up, mainly pulling in some of the background vocals to do more lead as well. "Arne said that there is a lot of interest from industry executives but there were a few things to tighten up on."

"Why didn't Arne call me, Lonnie?"

"I called to see what the deal was and what the feedback was, so he told me. I'm sure he was going to give you a call or something. All I know is he thinks we can get the girls a major record deal but it was suggested by some of the others in the industry who heard the tracks to bring the background vocal to the lead a little more."

Ann received a letter in the mail not too long after that telephone conversation with Lonnie. The letter was addressed to Alonzo Jackson in care of Ann Tillman. When Ann read the letter she was wondering what was going on because based on some of the things in the letter, it was easy to see that Lonnie and Arne had been communicating and there was some other things going on that she was not aware of with respect to Lonnie. After reading the letter, although she was questioning some things, Ann decided to go ahead and take the girls back out to the Plant to re-record some of the songs.

Ann called me to inform me we needed to go back out to the Plant to re-record some things and what some of the music executives were saying. So we packed our bags and in a matter of a few days we were headed back to

Sausalito, California. Mathew and Tina, Carolyn and Nolan, Beyonce, Ashley, Ann and I met at the airport again. Mathew left and came back with flowers in hand for both Beyonce and Ashley.

Tina was standing off to the side talking to Beyonce with tears streaming down her face. "Sweetheart, you know you don't have to do this if you don't want to."

"I'm fine mama."

"Are you sure. You know you don't have to go if you don't want to. I can work harder here."

"I promise, I'm okay."

Cassey comforted Tina to let her know it was going to be okay. "It's alright girl, Bey's gonna be just fine."

"They are just so young to be doing all this traveling and being away like this. I'm not there with her. Her father's not there with her."

"Tina, I promise you, as long as I have anything to say or do with it and as long as I'm alive, I promise I will never let anything happen to Beyonce. Do you hear me?"

"Thanks, Kenny."

"Honey, it's gonna be alright. When my husband says he promise, he means it you hear?"

"Thanks Cassey."

Tina stood there crying. She was having difficulty keeping her composure this time. It was like she was not going to see Beyonce ever again. We talked to her to calm

The Making of a Child of Destiny

her down to let her know that it would be okay. Then we went ahead and boarded the plane. We finally touched down in San Francisco and got checked into a hotel. Ann went the route of saving resources and we checked into a hotel that was more reasonable with respect to cost. Our main focus was on getting the re-recordings done and get out without spending an arm and a leg.

The next morning we arrived at the studio with the girls. When we walked in Lonnie and T-Mo were already there. Ann and I looked at each other because we could feel something in the air but at that time it was not quite clear. As we continued on with the day, we learned that Arne and Lonnie had gotten together and formed A & A Music. They went out to have Girls Tyme sign a production contract with A & A Music. That way, when the girls blew up, Arne and Lonnie would be a part of their production team. The letter that Ann had received at her home addressed to Lonnie was from A & A Music, but Ann had not realized at the time that it was a company formed by Arne and Lonnie.

It was not until the studio that Ann realized what the real situation was and the contracts that were sent to Houston from A & A were from both Arne and Lonnie. The day at the studio, they pulled Ann aside to speak with her about it. Ann conferred with me, and together we went ahead and agreed that it should be okay. However,

Ann was full of questions in terms of how Lonnie was operating. He was not upfront about what was really going on.

When A & A contracts were sent to Houston for signatures, Ann also went ahead and laid out the contracts for Girls Tyme to sign the Tillman Management/Girls Tyme Entertainment contract as well. Ann was making sure to cover all bases. As things were becoming more serious and we were planning major record deals for the girls, Ann had to take into consideration that the girls were minors. Although the parents had been on board, it was necessary to go to the Superior Court of Los Angeles and get authority from the court in the way of a "Right to Work" contract for the girls to be able to work.

We had to get Mathew, Tina, Carolyn, Nolan, Cheryl, and the rest of the parents to sign on the dotted line, and then go back to the Superior Court to get the authority to even sign the girls to a contract. All of this paperwork was handled and sent by the attorneys involved in the process prior to us flying back out to Sausalito to go into the studio again.

After all was said and done, the girls ended up signing a production contract with A & A Music and a management contract with Tillman Management/Girls Tyme

The Making of a Child of Destiny

Entertainment. The Superior Court of Los Angeles approved the contracts and at that point the girls were legally and officially signed with the two entities.

This time at the Plant, we went all out. Although we anticipated on recording a full load of songs the first time around, we ended up only recording a few. However, this time at the Plant, things were much more serious and we actually ended up recording a ten song collection. The interesting thing is, Ann and I learned that T-Mo, who had written all of the songs that the girls recorded, also signed a contract with A & A Music as well. The writer's deal he signed, confused Ann and me because from where we were sitting, they gave the impression that they were all one team. Yet, this trip manifested something very different.

"Ann, why did T-Mo sign a separate contract with them for writers?"

"I thought that was weird too, Kenny."

"It is. It would seem to me that if they have a production deal, Lonnie is the producer, T-Mo is the writer…I would figure that they were collectively a part of A & A."

Ann decided to do some more investigation and pulled T-Mo aside and started asking him some questions. She was feeling something real shady going on. "Boy, let me see what you signed."

T-Mo got the contract for Ann to look at. She started reading through it, and then she turned to me. "Huhm…Kenny, look at this contract."

Ann then handed the contract to me and I looked over it. I read through it and didn't say a word. Ann handed it back to T-Mo and told him thanks. When Ann and I got back to the hotel, I spoke up. "Ann, I think T-Mo sold all his royalties for a dollar. Did you see that?"

"Yeah, that's what I read too, that's why I wanted you to read it."

So after Ann and I talked, we went back to T-Mo. Ann approached him. "Tony, do you realize that you signed all your royalties away for a dollar?"

"Naw, Naw, Lonnie and 'em said we gonna work all that out it was just a standard contract we were signing."

That whole thing raised a red flag for Ann and me. "Damn, Ann that is some fucked up shit!"

"Look, Kenny anything, I mean anything, any contracts or whatever the fuck it is, we both get copies to review it and make sure we are on one accord. We review everything that way we can make sure we are protected. And that way if I miss something or you miss something, we can pull each other's coat tail."

"That is really fucked up! That kind of shit pisses me off."

The Making of a Child of Destiny

"Why are you so upset about it Kenny? Hell T-Mo walked his dumb ass into that shit. He's always going along with Lonnie's shit. I can see why you would be like…well, I guess I just don't understand why you are as upset as you are."

"You know Ann, years ago back in Greenwood, Mississippi, there was this man named Willie Cobbs who owned this barbeque joint on Walthall Street called CC Bar B Q. Anyway, he used to tell everybody that came in who would listen that he wrote this song called CC Rider. He would always say 'that white man stole my song.' He kept saying it over and over again, 'I wrote CC Rider…I'm famous ya'll just don't know it because that white man Perkins stole my damn song.'"

"Wow!"

"Hell yeah. When I think of shit like how David Ruffin died broke…come to think of it a lot of famous people die broke. I'm not with takin' advantage of people. It's just wrong."

"I hear you."

"So, this bull shit with Lonnie and Arne…it ain't cool to me. This is one of the reasons I wanted to be in management so that I could keep people from getting screwed over."

Ann and I continued to talk for hours telling each other stories about how and why we got into the music industry. "Music was in my blood. My whole damn family sang. Not to mention, my husband's dream was to become the next Berry Gordy…Shit! He worked hard at it after he lost his teaching job."

"Hell, music was a part of my upbringing too. I'm a preacher's kid…"

"No way…"

"Yeah I am. Hell I come from a family of preachers. B.T. Moore Jr. and Sr. were both Baptist preachers. Music was a big thing in my family."

"Huhm. I guess this was just meant to happen then. Kenny, I tell you…if Dwight was alive…Shit, I can't imagine what he would be saying right now."

"How did he die?"

"It was a car accident. We were on our way back to Houston from seeing some singers at the church…well he didn't go to the church that day, but I did. We went over to my sister's house for a barbeque…"

"What is this about incidents around barbeque?"

"I know right? Well we had just left my sister's house when it happened."

"Wow! I'm sorry to hear that…"

"Yeah, it was rough for a long time. I had a daughter too, she was two."

"Wow Ann, that's gotta be hard."

The Making of a Child of Destiny

Listening to Ann talk about Dwight and Shawna got me a little teary-eyed. We talked about so many things and we both learned that we had a lot in common. It also gave me insight into why she was so passionate when it came to the girls and the difference that she showed with them and Tayste. Ann motioned her fingers like she was holding a cigarette, she leaned back, and said something totally off beat, yet deep to break the seriousness of the moment.

"Music is my muse."

We both laughed and immediately came out of that conversation. It had gotten really intense for a moment.

"See, you know what I'm gonna start calling you from here on out?"

"No what?"

"I'mma start calling your ass Dretta. Cause you remind me of my older sister. Hell and your ass got drive and you're a dreamer like me…so yep…your ass gonna be Dretta."

"Uhm…Alright."

We both sat there quietly for a moment, and then Ann spoke up.

"Damn, Kenny…I mean this shit is happening right before our eyes. That contract…man that is some real fucked up shit. I can't get over that."

"Yep! We better polish up our game."

"You ain't never lied. This is for real and these guys are out to get it. So let's keep our eyes open."

"Definitely."

"Alright then Kenny, what's your opinion of Lonnie?"

"Lonnie to me is all about Lonnie."

"What about Tony?"

"Ann, shit…T-Mo is too dumb to even know what he's dealing with. But I do believe he is a good-hearted person. He's just a dumb ass."

"…and Arne?"

"Shit, Arne's tryin' to make the hit. He's had all these acts come through the studio, but he's never been a part of the hit."

This is where our friendship really began to flourish and we got to know one another. She asked me about Lynn. I told her I believed that Lynn was a crook. "We really need to keep our eyes on Lynn. Feed him with a long-handled spoon."

Ann and I decided to run it and work together. "Kenny, let's do this thing right. We don't have to do bad business to be successful and to help the girls or any of the acts for that matter get to where they're going."

That day, Ann and I made a commitment to one another to do our best to do things the right way and have each other's back.

The next day Ann and I headed back to the studio. We had been spending on average about ten hours at the studio each day. We had run through Take 'Em to Another Level, Teacher Fried My Brain, 6524287, and about seven other songs. Finally on the third day, Ann and I were watching the recording session. Ashley was in the booth. They were recording this one song when Lonnie kept stopping Ashley and making her start over. "Stop, do it again!"

"They said Jala…"

"Do it again.."

"They said Jala was…"

"Stop! Again!"

"They said Jala was the first girl you…"

Ashley kept starting over and over and over again. Lonnie kept stopping her. Finally after about ten times, everyone got pretty fed up with the process. Lonnie was being hard on Ashley. Beyonce was sitting in the back with me. She was fidgeting and rocking with impatience. As if to say, "Hurry up and get it so we can move on…dang!"

Ann was sitting in the middle. Arne, Lonnie, and T-Mo were up on the board. Because it was so expensive to record, we established a rule that if any of us had any comments, we would make those comment during the breaks or after the sessions. Now the more Ashley kept messing up, the more Beyonce kept fidgeting. "Bey, what's wrong with you girl."

Beyonce gave me this look as if she wanted to say, "What the hell you think is wrong with me?"

"Bey, can you do that?"

"Yes sir."

"Now Bey, you know the rules. If you say you can do it and I stop this session…they gonna cuss my ass out. Now do you hear me little girl? I'mma ask you one more time…can you sang that song?"

"Yes sir."

"Alright then."

I leaned forward to get Ann's attention and we started whispering back and forth.

"Ann…"

"Shut up mutha fucka…"

"Ann…"

"Mutha fucka shut up now…we got this session going on."

"Ann, listen dammit. The girl fuckin up in there, let Bey do it."

"Uh uh."

"Look, Ashley fuckin' up in there; let Bey do it."

"What?"

"Let Beyonce sing it."

Ann turned around and looked at me then looked at Beyonce. "Bey, can you sing that."

"Yes Ma'am Miss Ann."

"Okay, now don't you mess it up."

"I won't."

Ann interrupted the session. "Hey Lonnie…"

"Got dammit didn't I say don't nobody talk during my shit…Shut up!"

"Lonnie…"

"Didn't I say don't be talking during my session?"

"Mutha fucka, look I'm paying you! Listen to what I gotta say!"

"What!"

"Let Beyonce do it."

"Beyonce?"

I then spoke up to back what Ann was saying. "Yeah, Lonnie let…"

"Mutha fucka you shut up!"

Lonnie was not trying to hear what I had to say. He was upset because his session was interrupted. "Man, let Bey do it!"

Lonnie looked over at Beyonce. "Bey, can you do this song?"

"Yes."

Lonnie yelled for Ashley to come out of the recording booth. Ashley came out and came and sat on my right. Beyonce was sitting on my left. So they started talking and giving Beyonce the pitch. Then Lonnie motioned for Beyonce to go into the booth. Beyonce went into the booth and on the first take, she nailed it. "They said Jala was the first girl you kissed and ooh I wish it was I…"

The pitch that Beyonce did that song in reminded us of the ten to eleven year old Michael Jackson. She sounded almost identical to how he sounded back then. Beyonce sang with control and with passion. After Beyonce nailed that song, Lonnie got started. "Hold on…let's go back on this other song."

After that, we went back over and over the songs. On every song where there were parts that he didn't like, he pulled Ashley's voice off and replaced it with Beyonce's voice. We all were excited, but at the same time, the more they pulled Ashley's voice off and put Beyonce's on, I watched Ashley's facial expressions and body language. It was ripping Ashley's heart out bit-by-bit.

"Dretta, that's enough."

"What?"

"That's enough."

I was looking at Ann and then looking and nodding at Ashley to signal Ann to look at Ashley.

The Making of a Child of Destiny

"Dretta, they takin' the girl's voice off of every song...that's enough!"

We called a recess and the team went into the break room without the girls.

"I'm putting her on every fuckin' song."

"Yeah Lonnie, I agree she does sound great."

"I understand Lonnie, I understand Arne...but Dretta...look, you can't take the girl's voice off of every song and have her just do background. Leave her on a couple of tracks and then we can go from there."

The conversation was heated and everyone was putting their thoughts on the table. Arne asserted himself and was all about the business of the matter. "Look here, the people I am hearing from... they like Beyonce."

Lonnie was backing Arne up. "Yeah, there's big people in the industry and hell they ain't fucking interested in Ashley. They want Beyonce and LaTavia. See I tell you... what we need to be doing, we need to get LaTavia's ass out here... get her on tape doing the rap parts."

"Ann, Kenny, this is business and while it may be a hard decision to make, the truth is I've been in this industry for a long time and I have been talking to several executives and you have something, but the something you have has been doing backup. And what they are saying is the back up is really your lead singer and well..."

Ann listened to everyone go back and forth. After hearing what everyone had to say, she finally decided to just stop the session for the day. We went back to the hotel room. Things were pretty quiet. Ashley and Beyonce didn't really say much. It was easy to see that Ashley was totally heartbroken. Beyonce was sensitive to what had happened. I felt sorry for both of them.

Ann started talking to Ashley telling her everything was going to be okay as they pretended to watch TV, while Beyonce and I sat on the patio and watched the sunset. "Bey, you know…you didn't do nothin' wrong. You did what you had to do. It's all good, okay."

"Okay."

"We'll straighten it out."

Beyonce didn't really say anything. She just looked and you could tell that she was feeling sorry for her friend. The truth is, this situation showed the girls the two sides of success. One minute Ashley was leading songs, and Beyonce was singing back-up. The next minute Beyonce was leading and Ashley was doing back-up. It was truly a hard lesson on how the girls handled both situations. "Bey, the truth is baby girl…someone has to do the lead and someone has to do back-up. That's the way it is sometimes and in this case…well that is what happened. But it'll be okay."

What happened was bound to happen at some point, especially the way Lonnie and Arne had been pushing the fact that industry executives wanted to hear more of Beyonce. I thought Lonnie was too tough with Ashley. I don't believe he was sensitive to the situation at all, and for him it appeared to be more about getting the hit and the deal. Ann and I were concerned about the deal, but we were concerned about not breaking anyone's spirit as well.

Ann gathered both Ashley and Beyonce together in the hotel room. "Look girls, you both are still my lead singers. There are going to be some songs you lead on Ashley and there will be some songs you will lead on Bey. We have to do what's best for the team...but you both are the lead singers. One's not more important than the other. You got me?"

Ann worked to get Ashley's spirit back up. Initially when we went to the Plant, it was about getting her album recorded, so we needed to begin prep work for when we got back to deal with the parents. Yet, in us working hard to keep things in perspective, Lonnie was pressuring Ann about LaTavia. He and Arne stressed to Ann the need to get LaTavia out to get her on the tracks. After a heart-to-heart, Ann and I both agreed that from a business perspective it needed to be done.

Ann called Sheryl and arranged for LaTavia to fly out to Sausalito. Toward the end of the week, Latavia arrived and came into the studio to do some rapping on some of the songs. After that, we all packed up and flew back to Houston that Friday. As we were preparing to leave, Ann and I worked on damage control for when we got back. What happened was not expected and we knew that while some parents would be excited, others would be upset. Carolyn was not an easy person to deal with at times, and we knew that she was going to have a real problem with it. In as much as it was tough to deal with her personality, it was going to be equally difficult to keep Mathew in check.

As we were leaving the Plant, the tracks started going out to various labels. Before we even got back to Houston, things were already popping off. The word that kept coming back was "Beyonce... Beyonce... Beyonce..." Ruth Carson agreed to "present" the girls to five major labels that dePasse had connections with and would assist in securing a record deal with a guaranteed two to three hundred thousand dollars per album, three videos per album with budgets of one hundred thousand dollars per video, and guaranteed outside promotion budget.

To package the act the way several of the music executives were suggesting required Girls Tyme to emphasize Beyonce and LaTavia at the forefront and this would give Ann the greatest chance of getting Girls Tyme signed with a major label. It was a delicate situation.

"I know what Ruth is suggesting of course; that's easier for her to say. We don't want to slight anyone or cause any hard feelings. But if we want to have a successful group then we have to approach this from a business point of view and do whatever is necessary for the best of the group."

"I know Arne."

"Good. It's up to you Ann and Lonnie to smooth this over politically so that no one gets upset. After all what we are seeking is in everyone's best interest since it is a six girl group. In essence, the label would be committing to spend over a million dollars to break Girls Tyme into radio and on MTV."

Ann and I discussed the matter in detail on the plane back home. "Okay, Kenny, what are we going to say to the Davis'?

"Shit I don't know...hell..."

Ann and I just shook our head. "Alright Ann, look... let's pretty much tell them what you told the girls. They both are the leads..."

"You know Carolyn is going to be pissed because Ashley isn't on the lead...Also with Beyonce going to the lead, how are we gonna deal with Tina and Mathew?"

"Dretta…listen. It is what it is. You know Carolyn is going to be Carolyn and start tripping and might threaten to take Ashley out the group. With respect to Mathew…well, I'm not really sure, he seems okay."

"Yeah…"

"My suggestion is we should give them as-needed information. In other words, give them information on a need to know basis and be really careful what we say. You don't want to give too much information because you are not sure how they will handle it. On the other hand, you need to tell them something. Just be careful on what you say and how you say it."

"Okay Kenny, but what are we going to tell them?"

"Well I think we should tell the Knowles that there is a lot of excitement about Beyonce and we are going to have her do more lead than before. We should tell Sheryl that we really are gonna need LaTavia to step up to the forefront and that we are going to put more spotlight on her. I think we should tell Carolyn and Nolan that Ashley is still one of our lead singers, but we are going to change things up a bit."

When we got back, we set up the listening party. Ann tried to do some preliminary damage control prior to, but there was just no way around the issue. As we were sitting there at the gathering, everyone was there listening - Ann, Lonnie, T-Mo, David, Lynn, the parents, Tayste, and the girls. All persons were on deck. There was a lot of excitement in the room. However, after about the fourth song, you could see Carolyn's expression start to change. There were just so many songs that Beyonce was singing the lead on. Ann saw it coming and was prepared for it.

Carolyn didn't make a scene but it was obvious that she was not happy. Ann and Carolyn went off to the side. They discussed the situation. It did get a little heated though.

"Carolyn, I promise you Ashley will get back out front."

"You all should have told me. If I had known this would happen…"

"We'll get everything worked out, alright?"

Ann was able to talk with Carolyn and Nolan. Next she went to speak with Mathew and Tina. "The industry feels your daughter will be the next big star."

There was a lot happening at one time. The rumors then started to fly. Either Lonnie or T-Mo put out that the executives didn't want Ashley or Kelly in the group. (Of course Lonnie was cool with the new line-up because of Yvonne). Also Nicki, Nina, and LaTavia were cousins and Yvonne is Sheryl's sister and Lonnie's special friend, so they all were cool with at least one of them making it to the forefront.

However, between the rumors, the attitudes, and the flexing, it was very challenging to handle. Ann was excited about the deal and put everything on the table. She initially did not anticipate that Mathew and Tina would be an issue; but she miscalculated that one. "Ann, I think it was a mistake to tell Mathew and Tina everything. Mathew is gonna be a problem. You watch and see."

We moved the group forward working through the challenges. During several rehearsals and it happened quite often, Lonnie would get upset and talk to Ashley and Kelly very harshly. "Nobody wants yo damn ass in the group no way. So get your shit together."

Ann saw how Lonnie talked to Ashley and Kelly. Ann often had to step in and cover Kelly and help to build her self-esteem.

"The sooner we can get you all on board, the sooner they can become stars…hell most of you are just along for the ride…so hell… ride. But damn ride right."

"Lonnie! Your got-damned ass is along for the ride, nigga. Stop talking to them girls like that."

During that time Ann protected Kelly, so much so it was like Kelly became her daughter. She became extra nurturing to both Ashley and Kelly. All of the girls continued to work hard and we eventually began to push

The Making of a Child of Destiny

through the controversy. As things moved on, the dynamics of everything started to change as well. We worked to get the girls industry polished.

The subject of another California showcase came up. We wanted to avoid it because of the expense, but it was likely in order to close the deal we would have to do another one. To get the girls up to par, we put them before a live audience at least twice per month and they had daily rehearsals. They also performed at the Sammy Awards. This was Beyonce triumphant return and she was very excited about this particular performance because it was the Sammy Awards where her music career first started. Girls Tyme also did a back-to-school concert. They were getting sharper and looking more polished on stage.

Around this time, Kelly's mother decided to move back to Atlanta. This almost put a wrench in things because we were in the middle of negotiations. "Doris, let Kelly stay with me. I'll take care of your daughter. I will look after her like she is my flesh and blood. Things are getting really serious and we are about to close a record deal. Now is not the time to move away."

"I am moving Ann, I don't want Kelly to miss out or ruin her chances, but I'm leaving."

"Leave her with me. Please let her stay. She can live with me. She's gonna make it. I know she will. Your daughter is gonna be a star. Trust me on this. I know one when I see it."

Ann and Doris continued to discuss the possibility of Kelly staying with Ann. They ultimately worked through the situation. Doris agreed to let Kelly move in with Ann. It was a hard decision but Kelly was willing to stay while her mother moved. Regardless of her mousiness, Kelly wanted it just as bad as any of the other girls, and she too was willing to make sacrifices.

At this point everybody wanted it, and was not holding back about it. Every night we were laying the ground work with the music executives. One evening after getting off the line with some of the people from the industry, I was over to Ann's when she got a call from Mathew wanting to set up a meeting.

"Kenny, that was Mathew. He wants to set up a meeting. What do you think that's about?"

"Well, knowing Mathew, you can about guess."

"Uhm."

Ann ended up meeting with Mathew the next day. "You know Ann, Beyonce has now become the focus of the group, I think you should let me help manage."

Ann looked at him as if to say, "Fuck you and get the fuck out of my house."

But she knew she couldn't say that to him no matter how much she wanted to say it.

"Well Mathew… uh…No. We have everything we need. I appreciate everything and you offering, but we don't need a manager."

"Well…uh…Ann…"

"What do you bring to the table?" We have everything set up, everything is ready to go. It would only get things off focus and disrupt everything we are already doing."

"Oh, Uhm…okay. I appreciate you meeting with me."

"No problem."

The conversations with Mathew wanting to become a part of the management team kept surfacing over several weeks. Ann was exerting a lot of energy keeping him at bay. Unbeknownst to Ann, the heavy schedule, the stress, and lack of rest had taken a toll on her physically. As a result she fell into a Lupus crisis and ended up being taken to the hospital where she was admitted. When I found out that Ann was in the hospital, I immediately went up to see her.

"You look like shit! What! You forgot to comb that nappy ass hair. Don't be breaking down on me now."

"Fuck you Kenny!"

We both laughed. "Don't be in here got dammit feeling sorry for your self either… hell. Get your ass up and out of here. You think you on some damn vacation or something."

Ann continued to laugh. "Kenny, stop."

"I'm serious girl. You left me with the fuckin' animals at the zoo. You ain't paying me to deal with that shit. You better get your ass up."

Ann and I laughed and talked over the week while she was in the hospital. We became much closer during that time. Cassey also came to visit her. Ann knew that she had real friends in Cassey and me.

No sooner than Ann was discharged from the hospital, Mathew came calling Ann to meet with her again. This time he threatened Ann to take Beyonce out of the group if she did not make him part of the management team. "Either you let me co-manage, or I will take Beyonce out of the group. It's simple as that."

Ann called me to let me know what was happening.

"That fuckin' bastard. Kenny, I done paid every got damned bill for all this shit. The showcase, the studio, the hotels rooms, the flights…paying to fly Lonnie and T-Mo's black asses back and forth from Houston to California…I paid every got damned thing and this mutha fucka is gonna try and muscle me like that. Lynn's damn ass has his tail between his got damned legs for being found out as the shady ass mutha fucka he is! I cannot even get out the got damned hospital for five fucking minutes before this mutha fucka come calling me with this shit!"

"I told you Dretta, you would have some issues with Mathew. It was a bad move to tell them everything like that."

"You're right Kenny. Shit! And Lynn's ass done stole my checks and writing hot checks! Gotta deal with that shit too!"

"We either have to have some investors or stay on course with this. And we don't have any investors and we can't lose Beyonce."

"Kenny…Mathew wants fifty-fifty management."

"Well, what do you want me to do? I can leave and ya'll just handle it."

"No…No, I need you Kenny. You're the only person I can trust.

"Okay…"

"Would you agree to split my half of management with me like we have with the overall management?"

"Dretta, no that's not fair to you. We did all this damn leg work and got all this shit ready, and his Black ass wanna come in just because he's the child's parent? That doesn't mean he should come in and take half…I tell you what, if you give him half, you just give me ten percent of what you get on Girls Tyme and we will go fifty-fifty like we agreed on Tayste and everybody else."

"...And you are okay with that? Will you have a problem working with him?"

"I won't have a problem working with him. He seems like a nice guy. He might be on some bullshit...but he seems like a nice enough guy...you know I mean...whatever it takes, Dretta. I'm with you. I do understand it is his daughter."

After our conversation, Ann met with Mathew and agreed to let him become a co-manager with her and me as part of the management team with respect to Girls Tyme. So to secure Mathew's point, contracts were drawn up to reflect that Mathew and Andretta were the managers of the group Girls Tyme.

After the other parents saw that Mathew had gotten his way on the management team, they started to attempt to flex their muscles as well. Carolyn and Nolan thought that if they could bring some investors to the table or make some sort of connections that it would help Ashley get more lead time. They had no idea of what the industry executives were saying about Ashley.

"Hey Kenny man, Alexander O'Neal is gonna be having a show here. That's a friend of mine. We grew up together. You know I can make that connection. He got some connections in the industry as well and maybe we can use that avenue to get a deal."

"You know Alexander, Nolan, man?"

"Yeah, we're real tight. He's a friend of mine. Like I said, we been friends since we were young."

Mathew had no problem asserting himself as part of the management team. It was a good mix because he was able to bring that corporate dynamic to the table. He asserted himself with no hesitations.

"That sounds good Nolan."

"Yeah, yeah. I can set that up for us. I got my connections too, you see. Alexander and I go way back."

"Well then hell…word… let's do it."

Lonnie, Mathew, Nolan, and I went to the show. We got to the door and had to pay to get in. Lonnie said, "Shit Nolan man, we got it goin' on. Why we gotta pay to see this nigga?"

"Just come on in man, I got it."

We went in, sat down and had some drinks. We sat there laughing and talking. We were having a great time when Lonnie started to kick off. "Man, that nigga's coked out…look at him. He's coked out. He ain't what he used to be."

Lonnie was steady shooting him down. Mathew was playing the diplomat.

"Hey, ya'll he probably still have the avenues."

I spoke up as things were getting louder. "Well, let's keep it calm. We can't judge a book by its cover. Let's just see what its gonna be."

As we were sitting there, Nolan seemed very nervous. He was trying to get it right. This was his opportunity to show his usefulness. We sat through the whole show. Alexander did okay, nothing really to brag about. After the show, we were waiting on him to come off the stage. Nolan said, "Let me go talk to him."

We were standing right behind Nolan as he approached Alexander O'Neal.

"Alexander…Alexander!"

Alexander looked at Nolan all dazed. "Hey man, what's up."

"It's Nolan man…it's Nolan!"

"What's up homie…good to see ya."

Then Alexander just walked off. We all laughed at the situation. Nolan was humiliated. Lonnie really got to going then. "Oh, man, we came down here for this shit! Hell, he can't do shit!"

We walked on and Nolan was like, "Man, ain't this some shit!"

"Man, we done wasted a fuckin night…let's go!"

"Man, I can't believe that mutha fucka act like he didn't know me!"

I laughed and chimed in. "Nolan, that mutha fucka didn't act like he didn't know you…he didn't know your ass."

We all fell out laughing and teased him about it. Lonnie wouldn't let up. "Man that mutha fucka right there so coked out, that mutha fucka didn't know you from Adam."

"Nolan, didn't you say that was your childhood friend?"

"Mathew man, yeah, he is."

"Well, that mutha fucka right there ain't no childhood friend."

We laughed the rest of the night and on the way home about that night, making the best out of the situation. However, it shot Nolan's credibility all the way down. Although nothing came of it, Ann and I had another plan in place to take the girls to go see William and work with Rob, Troy and Yarbrough and Peoples.

In the meantime, nothing was going to stop Ann from closing the deal. Arne had arranged another showcase, so we worked to get the girls ready.

GOT TO GIVE HIM MORE

Arne insisted that Ann needed to have the girls perform in yet another showcase so that the industry folks could take a look at them again, especially since several adjustments had been made according to the feedback received.

"Andretta, Ruth seems to feel that she can obtain the kind of commitment we're looking for at these labels, but in order to close the deal, she believes the girls should put on a live show in Los Angeles. These folks are concerned with the look and performance and the video isn't strong enough to do it or turn the necessary heads."

"What are you proposing Arne?"

"Well, obviously I would like to obtain the deal we want without going through another expensive showcase and that's still a possibility. But I do believe it's important for us to pursue all available options and help that we can get to reach our goal."

"Arne, I've been the sole upfront investor and I'm spending a lot of damn money. I have foot many of the bills and my thoughts are if we can do it without the showcase that would be ideal."

"I understand Andretta. David and I are exploring the possibility that we can get one of the interested labels to foot the bill to bringing the girls out to L.A."

"Okay."

"In any case, let's talk soon."

Once all was said and done, Arne worked with Ann to schedule the girls to perform as a featured attraction at the BMI Showcase in California. This was a showcase that allowed unsigned talent an opportunity to perform in front of industry heavyweights. It is one of the most powerful music licensing organizations affiliated with the largest groups of songwriters, composers, and publishers that exist. It just so happened that Girls Tyme was the spotlighted act and some of the major players were aware of them as there was already a buzz.

After having opened up for Jennifer Holiday, Chris Walker, Yo Yo and others and performing at events such as the Sammy Davis Jr. Awards, Astroworld, the Black Expo, Juneteenth celebrations, and a beauty pageant, BMI was a natural progression and the preparation for it was similar to other showcases.

As rehearsals continued with a particular emphasis on BMI, Beyonce and LaTavia became more visible, while Ashley, although she continued to sing lead on some songs, was down-played. All of this was to make the deal happen and do what was in the best interest of the group.

The Making of a Child of Destiny

The girls prepared hard to put their best foot forward to get the major record deal. While there was much talk surrounding their talent in the industry, no major deal had been signed yet.

By that time, everyone was getting used to Mathew being a part of the management team. Although he raised a lot of hell in order to get his way onto team, he initially came in as a quiet observer, taking note of how things were managed. Mathew appeared to bring a positive mix to the table because with him came the corporate experience and he was able to assist with additional structuring.

As everyone was preparing and working hard for the BMI Showcase, Lonnie was flying in and out of town, while Mathew and David were placed in charge of the rehearsals. Ann and I continued to work on the business side of things. With Beyonce taking a more prominent role in the group and Mathew and David running the rehearsals, Mathew wanted to move rehearsals to his house. He and David convinced Ann that since most of the other girls lived closer to him on the south side near the Houston Medical Center, and David was living with him as well, it just made sense to move rehearsals to his house. Although LaTavia also lived on the North side, it was no problem for Sheryl to get her daughter there, but Ann had difficulty getting Kelly there because she did not get off work until around five o'clock.

"Come on Ann, you live on the North side, you and Kenny are the only ones that live in that direction. Hell, make it easier for everyone."

"I hope ya'll know you getting on my last fucking nerves. Mathew, all of your damn questions, and needing this or that and wanting this or that, ya'll fucking making me sick. I'mma move the rehearsals to your house since I put your ass in charge of the rehearsals, but I'm gonna be on your asses like white on rice and I don't want no shit. This is an important showcase and we need to close the deal."

"Ann, I need to know everybody you talkin' to and communicating with. Who are the main ones you dealing with?"

"Mathew, you mind the fucking rehearsals and right now just leave the business side to me and Kenny. Get the girls ready to perform. That's your focus right there."

After Ann consented to the rehearsals being moved to Mathew's house, practice beefed up and everyone was buckling down to be in top performance mode. However, that still wasn't enough for Mathew. Next, he and David begin pushing for Kelly to move. They argued that transportation was impacting the rehearsals.

"Look Ann, we need all the girls in one place. With them in one place, we can focus more on the rehearsals, have as much time with them as we need, and vocal training and transportation won't be a factor because all the girls would be there."

"Damn it, I told Doris that I would see after her and that I would treat her like my own daughter. Hell I can't say that I would allow my own daughter to go live with you, Mathew. Is your ass crazy? What the fuck are you trying to do?"

David chimed in to support what Mathew was saying.

"I don't see what's the problem. Mathew and Tina have two other daughters."

"Look Ann, Bey, Solange, and Tina are there. I am surrounded by a bunch of damn women. What could happen to her? Come on now, be reasonable. I think the real concern with Kelly should be here with Armon and Chris."

"What the hell is that supposed to mean?"

"Well shit Ann, it's no secret that there is some physical attraction between Kelly and Armon."

"What the fuck are you trying to imply Mathew? They are kids."

"Yes and kids are kids and when you have males and females in too close corners, it can be an ingredient for disaster."

"Hell, if you take that logic, Mathew, there are just as many men who be messing with little girls, so don't give me that fuckin' shit."

"What are you tryin' to imply, Ann?"

"Just what the fuck I said. Don't be trying to justify Kelly coming to live with you and Tina because of my boys, when there is two got-damned grown ass men over at your house who ain't related to her either. So don't come with that bull-shit. I'm not saying you will, but as a mother, I weigh every got-damned thing. Let me think about it, and I'll let you know."

"Alright."

Ann was getting stressed out over everything going on. Initially she only had to deal with Lonnie's pressure, however now Mathew was also pressuring her. Between Lonnie, Mathew, Lynn and now David, it was wearing her energy down because she felt she always had to look over her shoulder with them. It appeared that since Mathew came on the management team, she was having more Lupus flares.

Ann and I discussed Mathew's questions frequently. "Kenny, why the fuck does this man keep asking me all these got-damned questions all the time?"

The Making of a Child of Destiny

"Who?"

"Mathew! He wants to know who I'm talking with in the industry. He keeps asking me their names, contact information and what they're saying to me. It is beyond him being Bey's father. He keeps hounding me for information that really is not for him to concern himself with… Then the mutha fucka had the nerve to say it would be best if Kelly come and live with him and Tina, and insinuated some bullshit about Kelly and Armon."

"For real?"

"Yeah. On top of that he keeps using Bey as a trump card because he knows that they are interested more in Bey and LaTavia… I told you that he called Teresa and Arne didn't I?"

"No you didn't tell me that Ann. What did he call them for? See, I had a feeling you shouldn't have told him what you did, but that is neither here nor there now. Dretta, it sounds like he is trying to steal the group."

"You know, Kenny, I was thinking that and didn't want to say it. You know he got the girls thinking that he is the manager now and I'm just working with him. I'm trying to make some got damn head waves and this muther fucka is acting like he's making shit happen and he is large and in charge. I don't need this damn shit Kenny. Hell, what does Kenny-Mo have to say about that shit?"

Ann was upset and then we both had to laugh when she started talking about me in third person. "You know I'm sounding like your ass now when…shit Ashley pissed you off in San Francisco."

"You know you're wrong for that!"

"I know. I couldn't help it. Hell, I'm just about as pissed right now as you were then in that hotel room."

"Seriously though Dretta, just be smart, keep an eye on him, and keep on pushing. He seems to have a good business sense, but I'm not sure what his aim is."

"He's gotten wind of them wanting Bey, and since he's the daddy, shit you just don't know what to expect from him."

"Well, let's just keep our pulse on the matter. Keep setting up the gigs and the opportunities and keep it moving."

"I hear you Kenny. You are always the voice of reason. Well, most of the time, anyway. Hell, I don't know about Kenny-Mo though."

We both laughed at a serious situation to stay sane with everything going on at one time.

Right before Girls Tyme headed to California to perform at the BMI showcase, Ann had a major Lupus crisis which caused her to be hospitalized. So, as the girls and their parents were heading to San Francisco to perform at the BMI Showcase on August 26, 1992, Ann was heading to the hospital. I had started a new job and was unable to travel to the showcase so it was up to Mathew and Lonnie to go.

"Kenny, did the girls get off to California?"

"Yes Dretta. I made sure everything was set. Mathew was there and everyone got off okay."

"Okay, good."

"Dretta, what the hell you doing? You better get your ass on up and out of here. Now you know we ain't got time for this shit. You setting up all this shit, and your ass wanna sit back and relax."

"Kenny look…"

Ann showed me where they had to amputate her finger. She tried her best to laugh but she was not as playful as she had been before. You could tell that she was not well. "Kenny don't make me laugh… I, I can't."

"What the fuck you mean I can't. Girl you better get your ass up!"

Ann was laughing as the nurse came in and I was trying to make her laugh even harder.

"Sir, you are going to have to leave. We cannot have her blood pressure going up. She needs to stay calm."

"Okay sorry."

I whispered to Ann, "You know your ass is faking. Ain't nothing wrong with you."

Ann was trying to keep from laughing and getting herself worked up. "Kenny stop it now, shit."

"Sir, you are going to have to leave."

The nurse kicked me out of the room. I called Ann later, but I could tell that she was not her energetic and bubbly self. To start losing fingers was not a good sign of her condition as far as I was concerned. I really started looking at her health as a serious matter at that point.

Ann was recovering, as reports came back from California. The BMI Showcase was a success. Not too long after everyone returned to Houston from the showcase, Ann received a call from Daryl Simmons who contacted her about his interest in the girls. His wife had seen them perform a month earlier at the Black Expo. She told her husband about Girls Tyme and I guess word got around pretty fast because he reached out to Ann. Daryl who was the founder of Silent Partner Productions was also associated with Kenny "Babyface" Edmonds and Antonio "L.A." Reid of LaFace Records. So right after the BMI Showcase is when the first talks with Silent Partner Productions began.

Who would have thought that losing a finger could change Ann's routine around the house as much as it did. However, the fact that one of her fingers was gone created challenges for her. Different friends went over to her house to help out. Charlotte often took Nicki and Nina to go help. Daily rehearsals, conditioning and vocal training had recently been turned over to Mathew and David. Ann and I would go over to the Knowles' house once or twice a week to see the progress. They also at that time started rehearsing at Tina's hair salon and practicing on the customers that came into the salon.

Ann was recuperating pretty well, and Nina was a big help for Ann, spending a lot of time over to her house and then heading to rehearsals. Ann observed Armon and Kelly a little closer since the conversation she had with Mathew. One day Ann walked into the living room and caught Armon and Nina kissing. Ann had thought that he liked Kelly. She did not confront Armon or Nina at the time, but the next morning when Armon was in the bathroom mirror brushing his hair, she raised the issue.

"Armon, I saw you and Nina kissing. What's up with that? I thought you liked Kelly. Which one of the girls do you actually like?"

"I like both of them."

"Well, whichever one you like the most, I will tell you this right now, Kelly is gonna be the rich one."

Armon looked at his mother with embarrassment. Ann just said what she had to say and walked away. Being that Ann saw Armon and Nina kissing, she got to thinking about the conversation with Mathew and reluctantly allowed Kelly to go stay with him and Tina. By this time, conversations between Ann and Silent Partner Productions had progressed to the point where Daryl Simmons was talking about setting up a showcase for the girls to perform for him in Atlanta.

Ann had Silent Partners on the hook. As she was pulling on that line, she received a letter from Arne asking her to call him and that the girls needed her. Inside the envelope was also a check for five hundred dollars reimbursing her for the loan she gave to Lonnie and a copy of the video tape from the BMI Showcase performance. When Ann called Arne back per his letter, she received some great news along with an ear full.

"When you were not able to make the BMI Showcase, I heard you were not feeling well. I asked Mathew to send me the pages and covers for the package. Like I said in the letter to you, I can put together about twenty-five to thirty packages to take along to meetings. Can you follow up with Mathew and make sure that I get them?"

"Yes."

"Also, I need Carolyn Davis' number. Alonzo gave her an airline ticket to use in August. I bought the ticket for him to use, and it was worth a hundred and ten dollars. It may seem like a small thing to the two of them, but it's my money and he had no business giving it to her without consulting me about it first."

"Uhm. I see."

The Making of a Child of Destiny

"I want Carolyn or Alonzo to reimburse me."

"I understand Arne. What's the good news you had?"

"Oh, the good news. The girls got accepted to perform on Star Search! I hope you're going to Florida wth them, because, Ann, they need you."

"I know they do Arne. I'm here and haven't gone anywhere."

"Well the great news is…Girls Tyme has a spot on Star Search. It's next month and will be aired sometime in February."

"That is great news. Shit Arne, why didn't you say that first, instead of giving me all that other bullshit?"

Things were popping and Girls Tyme had very little time to prepare for the Star Search taping which was scheduled for November 4, 1992. In one of the conversations over song choices, Ann, Lonnie, Arne and I ended up in a heated debate on what song the girls should sing for the Star Search appearance.

"I want the girls to sing a song that will display all of their talent. I'm thinking they should do something like Sunshine where you can hear their vocal ability."

"Ann look, Arne and I think we need to feature Beyonce and LaTavia. Hell that's who they want. Everybody else is along for the fuckin' ride."

"Lonnie, that's bullshit and you know it. All of these girls are working hard, and I'm in agreement with Ann, we should feature the girls collectively and build on their harmony."

"Got dammit Kenny, you always agreeing with Ann."

"Fuck you Lonnie, that's because Ann is the only got-damn one who is making any damn sense right now. The girls have great harmony and we should highlight that harmony and feature the girls collectively. Ann's right."

Arne and Ann had strong words over the telephone because Arne was coming from the same perspective as Lonnie, "Bey and LaTavia are the real stars here."

Because Arne said it, Mathew rolled with whatever anyone in the industry said. So he went along with what Arne said. The song that was ultimately selected to perform at Star Search was selected by Lonnie, Arne, and Mathew. Ann and I were in disagreement with the song choice.

Around the time to appear on Star Search, I had to work so I could not go. Ann had another Lupus crisis and ended up back in the hospital. During the last hospital visit when she had the first finger amputated, she was made aware that she would need to have another one removed but they told her they would only take the one at that time. However, as she went into another crisis, it became necessary for a finger and a toe to be removed. It seemed the more Ann became stressed the more she had Lupus bouts. When I went up to the hospital to visit her, she asked me to work more closely with Mathew.

"Kenny, I need you to start working a little closer with Mathew. I told him what to do and he says he feels pretty good about what he's doing, but I want you to work with him. He has a corporate background and I trust he can work well with things.

"I don't know Ann…"

"I trust that Mathew can do that. He says he's okay with things, plus there's this group I want you to take a look at. They are playing at the Sky Bar and they're supposed to be this girls group that is a lot like EnVogue. Hell I'm laid up in this damn hospital and won't be out for about a week, so I need you to do this for me Kenny. We need to continue to look for new talent."

I agreed. This was the first time that Mathew and I went to take a look at groups together. Usually it's just Ann and me. So, I picked Mathew up from his house and I drove to the club.

"You know Kenny, everyone is talking about Beyonce being a future star…"

"Yeah."

"But the truth is…Solange is way more talented than Bey. She will be the real big star."

When Mathew said that to me I was like, "Mutha Fucka, you crazy as hell."

However, instead I responded, "Mathew man that would be great."

Mathew and I clicked well that night. Things were cool. The group we went to go scout out was pretty good, but we didn't approach them that night. Instead, we took note of them with plans to speak with them at a later time. We reported back to Ann. When Ann got out of the hospital, I went over to her house.

"Dretta, the act that we went to go see…"

"Yeah, what about them? What did you think?"

"There's some promise there. I think they have something."

"Well let's deal with them after the Star Search piece, because things are pretty hectic right now."

"Yeah, I know, and this job doesn't allow me the time off to travel as much as I was able to before."

"Hell, this Lupus is kicking my ass. But we're gonna keep pushing. Hell, I go into the hospital with my damn fingers and toes, and it seems like every time I leave something else is cut off and left on the table."

"I know one damn thing, you better keep your ass out of that damn hospital. We ain't got time for that shit. Do that shit when we close this deal."

"I won't be able to make it to the Star Search appearance. I am still in a lot of pain though and I guess they say I'm still in a crisis. But this shit is not going to get the best of me. Hell I might not have any fingers and toes when all is said and done, but I sure in the hell will have my mind and my mouth."

"Hell nigga, I don't think anything can stop that damn mouth of yours."

"You know what…you see this damn tape here where my middle finger used to be…I can still say fuck you nigga."

"I'm glad to see you getting back to yourself."

"When you see this tape go up, just know I'm sayin' fuck you…better yet, when we in our damn meetings and you see this tape go up right here…"

Ann took the part where her middle finger was replaced with surgical tape and stuck it in her nose. "…I'm sayin' fuck you. And when Mathew or Lonnie get to talking they shit…and you see this go up here like this…I'm saying fuck you. That way, you know I ain't agreeing to their bullshit."

We laughed and continued discussing everything that was on our plates, the girls' schedules, as well as how we would work everything out. Girls Tyme had been working hard getting ready for Star Search. Ann and I went to see the rehearsals. Lonnie grew more impatient and Ann and I witnessed more yelling of the girls to get it right. Things were amping up to the next level and the pressure was on to win Star Search. Because Ann was not one hundred percent and I had this new work schedule, Sheryl stepped up to the plate and offered her assistance to help Ann coordinate the girls' schedules, especially since her daughter LaTavia was quickly becoming one of the group's stars.

After pushing to get things perfect, everyone who was scheduled to fly out headed to the Star Search appearance. The girls went up against the champions which were an all white male group by the name of Skeleton Crew. The champions remained the champions with a score of four stars while Girls Tyme, the challengers, received a score of three stars. After the performance, some of the feedback was that it was not a good song choice and three stars were far too generous. Everyone was upset that the girls did not win. They called back to Houston to share the somber news.

"Ann, damn it this is Mathew. These are some racist mutha fuckers out here. The girls didn't win."

"Okay, what happened? How did they do?"

"They did great, they nailed the song. What happened...I tell you what happened. These are some racist bastards that's what happened."

"Okay, I will let Kenny know. Let's talk when you all get back."

"Alright, see you soon."

Ann called me right after she hung up from Mathew.

"Kenny?"

"Yes."

"This is Ann."

"I know who this is nigga. I talk to you every damn day. Don't you think I know your damn voice by now?"

"Shut up Kenny. Look...the girls didn't win."

"What?"

"The girls didn't win. They lost against some man band called Skeleton something. At least that's what Mathew was saying. He's pissed."

"Well, how did he say they did?"

"He said they did good, but honestly, that song was fucked up, but you couldn't tell them mutha fuckas nothing. So I'm not surprised at the outcome."

"That's something."

"The way he was sounding and the way he said the girls were taking it, we are gonna have to do some damage control. I'm not sure if the girls would've chosen that song for themselves if they were given the chance. See what I'm saying?"

"Valid point Ann. When does this shit air?"

"Arne told me it will air in February. We are gonna have to make some headway before it airs. I'm not sure of the impact of this loss."

When the crew arrived back into Houston, everyone was very disappointed at the fact that they lost. This also took a toll on Ann's health and the stress of this played a role in her suffering another minor bout with Lupus. This time Ann managed to stay out of the hospital. It only knocked her down a few days with a lot of pain. When the Lupus became an issue, it was just too hard to tell how long she would be down for. The only thing we could do was not to cause her unnecessary stress and to handle our business so that she would not have to keep cleaning up everyone else's shit. Being that Ann was having more frequent setbacks with Lupus and was in need of a little more support at home, a woman by the name of Ms. Penny came over to Ann's house to help her until she felt much better. In addition, to take some of the burden off of Ann, the team met at her house for meetings.

Ann did not let the fact that she was not feeling well get her down. Although she was not feeling her best, business kept moving and so did she. Ann continued to make things happen. She received a call from a man named Dick Griffy who was the owner of Solar Records. He wanted Tillman Management/Girls Tyme Entertainment to come out and meet with him. Because Ann was not able to go to the meeting as a result of her more recent health crisis and I could not go because of my job, the two of us discussed the situation at great length and with great hesitation, decided to let Mathew go and attend the meeting on his own and talk the deal.

Ann paid for Mathew to fly out to Los Angeles to speak with Griffy. Our thinking was, "If he fucks it up, at least we are still in talks with Silent Partners. It's worth going to see what can come of it."

When Mathew returned from the meeting he and Ann met to discuss what happened. She was not able to really get much out of him other than the meeting went well. After the two of them got together, Ann and I met so that Ann could provide me with the feedback that Mathew had shared.

"Kenny, Mathew said the meeting went well. He did not provide a lot of details. He just said it was a good meeting. Not really sure about where things are with this one."

"What did Mathew say Griffy said?"

"Well, he said that Solar was interested in the girls, but he really didn't give any concrete information. I'm gonna have to follow up to see what is what."

"Huhm…okay."

The interesting thing about the Solar situation was that Mathew went to speak with Griffy, but as things played out, I got the distinct feeling that something wasn't right. Whatever Griffy said or whatever those conversations were, we knew that it changed Mathew. He wasn't the same after that meeting. I started to do some digging and learned that Griffy had a reputation of manipulating and stealing from his artists. Some of his acts included Yarbrough and Peoples, the Gap Band, and Rolls Royce.

When I found out that Griffy worked with Yarbrough and Peoples and the Gap Band, I made a call to Troy to find out as much as I could in order to satisfy my own scepticisms.

"Hey man, we had a meeting with Solar Record. What's up with Dick Griffy? I'm not sure how comfortable you are talking about it but we really need to know what's up with him. How is he…I mean what type of person is he?"

"Kenny man, the guy's a crook. He robbed from us and black-balled Yarbrough and Peoples. He ain't right, man."

Troy and I spoke for some time, he was a reliable source and I was appreciative of how direct and straight-to-the-point he was about his experience with the man. Once Troy shared with me what type of character Griffy was I, called Ann.

"Ann, I just got off the phone with one of my contacts. You remember I was telling you about Troy People's right?"

"Yes. What about him?"

"He told me that this Griffy guy is a character and not someone you can really trust."

"What specifically did he say?"

"Well Dretta, the long and short of it was that he is a crook and he steals from his acts. In other words, if you really want to get ahead, Griffy is not the one to get you to where you are trying to go."

"Well, we need to just move on past that one then. What do you think?"

"I think you might be right."

After a long discussion about it, Ann and I was prepared for nothing to come of the meeting that Mathew had with Griffy. Therefore, we moved forward as if the meeting didn't even happen. As we continued to have our management meetings, I began to notice how Mathew was speaking. Prior to the meeting with Griffy, he was being a parent, a daddy, and a team player. However, what Ann and I started seeing was something very different.

"Shit Ann. You listening to Mathew's ass? What the fuck he mean he is in the business of exploiting people? He wasn't talkin' that shit before LA, what's up with that?"

"I heard that too, Kenny…Huhm."

"I don't know who the fuck this nigga is right here, but he on some shit."

"I wonder what really transpired with the talks with Griffy."

"Takes a lookin' into you figure?"

In one of the meetings involving Ann, Mathew, and me, I confronted Mathew when he got to talking crazy again.

"Look ya'll, I'm in the business of exploiting people. That's what I do now."

"Mathew man, you can't be going around talking about you going to exploit people, man. That's not cool."

"That's all the industry is; it's about exploiting people. And that's what I'm gonna do. I'm gonna exploit people, and do what we gotta do."

Mathew mentioned to Ann and I that Griffy said in order to control the acts, you have to own the name. So we immediately went to file a trademark on the name Girls Tyme. The trademark went under Ann Tillman and

The Making of a Child of Destiny

Mathew Knowles as the owners of the name Girls Tyme. What that did was give management the power if any of the girls got out of line, they could be kicked out of the group because we owned the entity of Girls Tyme. We went on with business and did not think any more about this. We figured, we owned the name and that gave us more control over the girls as well.

After all of this took place, the conversation with Daryl Simmons and Silent Partner Production began to catch fire. Talks were progressing with them even more. At this time, we started to go out and look for more acts. Once again Mathew and I went back to the Sky Bar to follow up with the group we saw before Star Search. Ann and I discussed it and we definitely wanted to sign them as an artist. So that night we went to another one of their performances and approached them afterwards to express interest.

"Hi, my name is Kenny and this is Mathew. We are with Girls Tyme Entertainment and we are interested in signing you and having you to join our stable of artists. Right now we have Girls Tyme, which is an up and coming act. We have Tayste, which is an all-boys group similar to a Boyz II Men, and a few other acts. We are interested in bringing you into the fold."

"We're interested."

"Good, so what we would like to do is talk to each of you to find out a little more about you."

"Cool."

So, we talked to the girls one-by-one. By the time we got to the fourth girl, we learned that she was a model. She was very beautiful. She had a light skinned complexion and beautiful hair. She was gorgeous. Mathew and I sat at the table and spoke with all the previous girls very professionally. We had a couple of drinks. This girl came to sit down and speak with us, and this was the first sign where I saw that Mathew had some issues.

When she sat down, Mathew leaned back in his chair and reached down in his pants.

"I'm just horny as a mug. I just wanna fuck right now. Shit, I'm horny as hell."

I looked at the girl and she looked at me. I was still in professional mode. Mathew was sitting there holding his crotch.

"…huh, I am so sorry ma'am. I am so sorry. He's a little drunk…"

"I'm not fuckin' drunk. I told you! We're in the business of exploiting people, and I'mma exploit you and if you wanna be a star, you gonna have to come on and do something for me. Hell, I know what I can do for you' but what can you do for me?"

The girl looked straight passed me and right into Mathew's eyes.

"Look, I don't know who the fuck you think you are! But, I don't need this shit! I'm a professional model. I do this shit because I sing with my sister, who's one of the singers. This is just a past time for me. I don't need to be no fuckin' singer. I have a kid at home to take care of and this shit here I don't need!"

She got up and stormed off and went straight to the other girls. They all started talking, and looked over at us.

"Mat, what did…what the fuck's wrong with you?"

"Oh man, they gotta understand…my job….everybody gonna be exploited that's what it's about. Hell you wanna get on, you wanna get with what we are about, then you gotta put out."

"Mathew, you can't fuckin' do this type of shit! This is not the kind of fucking business I agreed to do. I don't get down like that mutha fucka! I'm not with this shit! I'm not rollin' this way!"

"Oh, Man, this is just the way it is. If we gonna get some where this is…"

"No Mat…I'm not with that shit!"

We sat and talked for a while. "Man you could've at least leaned over and whispered that shit to her. Hell, don't put me in the middle of your got-damned funky ass shit! I don't roll like that man."

I was outdone when we finally left the Sky Bar. I drove Mathew back home and me being pissed was an understatement. When I pulled up in front of his house to let him out of the car, he tried to talk to me about the situation again.

"What? You think I did something wrong?"

"Hell yeah nigga. You fucked up! That was real fucked up."

"Man that's just the way the business is, you know. Ya'll back-wooded country asses, you and Ann, ya'll gotta understand this business is about exploiting people. That's the way the business is and that's what we're gonna have to do to make this a success. That's what we're gonna do!"

"Man, get your mutha fuckin' drunk ass out of my got-damned car!"

I let him out of my car and he walked on in his house. I wanted to drive over to Ann's house that night, but it was way too late. So when I got home, I called her and told her that we needed to talk. When I hung up from Ann, I shared the situation with Cassey. She was like, "What the hell!"

The next day, I went over to Ann's house so we could talk.

The Making of a Child of Destiny

"Dretta, we gotta got-damned problem on our hands! This mutha fucka's out of control!"

"Damn, Kenny...what happened?"

"That got-damned Mathew's ass. This mutha fucka is a major problem."

I explained to Ann what happened. She was like, "What...what...you kidding me...what?"

She couldn't believe what she was hearing. "Come on Kenny now, Mathew didn't do that."

"Yeah the hell he did, and I don't know what the fuck happened with him and Dick Griffy, but something happened because he's not the same fuckin' guy he was two weeks ago!"

"Kenny look...I need you and we gotta balance this mutha fucka. So please...hang in there with him so he don't fuck us up. I'll keep him working with the girls. We'll handle dealing with the labels."

"Okay."

"If he has to go out again with you, just keep him on a chain."

"Dretta, how in the hell can I stop a grown ass man from doing what he wants to do."

"Hell, tell him you gonna tell Tina or she's gonna find out. Hell I don't know."

When Mathew and I went out, that is exactly what I would say and he would calm himself down at least in my presence. Mathew had issues, and they were not the kind I was really interested in trying to manage in order to get business done. However, for Ann's sake, I tolerated him, but I did not like it. I love my wife, and I just didn't deal like that. I preferred not to associate with someone who did. So it was hard for me every time we had to go out together to see acts.

With the conversations Ann and I had regarding Dick Griffy and what he did with Yarbrough and Peoples, he was out the picture. That thing there was a wrap. We kept communications open with Daryl Simmons. We laid the ground work and discussed how we would handle Simmons. We let Mathew work with the girls and agreed to just carbon copy him on the contracts and things of that nature.

New Years nineteen ninety-three had long passed and the new contracts were signed where Mathew was actually listed for the first time as co-manager on the contracts that Girls Tyme signed. Every year Ann had the team resign contracts to make sure everyone was on lockdown.

With all the mess going on with Mathew, the conversations with Daryl Simmons and getting past the Star Search loss, Ann was hit again with another fire to put out. Carolyn met with her about Ashley.

"Ann, I no longer feel that Girls Tyme is in Ashley's best interest. You are featuring other artists. Ashley needs to be either a solo artist or the lead artist."

"Alright Carolyn, Nolan…Give me a day to talk it over with management."

Ann called me in on what else had taken place.

"Kenny, Carolyn's getting ready to take Ashley out the group."

"Ann, the group is now like Michael Jackson and the Jackson Five. Beyonce is who everybody is talking about…and LaTavia. They're not talking about Ashley. So if Carolyn wants to make that mistake, let her."

"Huhm…"

"…But, I feel you owe Ashley because of the way everything went down. At least still try to get her a solo deal."

So Ann and I agreed that Ann would talk with Carolyn and even if she took Ashley out of the group, Ann was willing to make every effort to sign Ashley to an independent artist deal and continue working with her, because we already had all the contacts. Carolyn agreed. Ashley Davis left Girls Tyme officially and signed a solo artist management deal with Girls Tyme Entertainment. Everyone was shocked that Ashley left the group. So with only five girls left, we started to observe at the rehearsals that

Beyonce had taken on the persona of, "This is my group now."

Beyonce started driving the rehearsals and the girls to work harder. In truth, it had become her group. She and LaTavia had begun to choreograph the moves. Surprisingly, Beyonce's personality did not change in how she would communicate with Ann and me, but her attitude in rehearsals changed and the manner in which she related to the group. David, Lonnie, and Mathew reinforced this new attitude as well. If she had any issues with anyone, LaTavia was her hedge man. In other words, she would pull everyone in line.

When Daryl Simmons' wife saw Girls Tyme perform at the expo she saw six girls. Also, Daryl was aware of a six girl group. At that point, Mathew and Ann auditioned other girls while I was working in order to replace Ashley and deliver six girls. One primary contender was a young girl by the name of Letoya Luckett.

"Alright Kenny, we got a new member, lets go to rehearsal."

"What?"

"Yeah! We gotta new member, Letoya."

"Damn Ann that was quick."

"Hell we ain't got time to waste. You gonna like her though, Kenny."

The Making of a Child of Destiny

At the rehearsal, I met Letoya and her mother Pam. They were very nice people. Letoya was bubbly and a "jokey-jokey" type. However, Ann was right, she fit like a glove. The strength Letoya brought to the group was her ability to move and work the stage. Yet her voice was not as powerful as Ashley's. Therefore we ended up having to put more pressure on David to make Kelly a stronger vocalist. Letoya was a great harmonizer but was not a lead singer.

The way the talks were going with Silent Partners, we knew that an Atlanta showcase was coming up very soon, so the girls had to ramp up things and work even harder than what they had been working before. Plus, Kelly had to bring in more vocals to fill the void of Ashley. On top of that Mathew was really starting to spin even more out of control. He started going over to Ann's house almost everyday attempting to interfere with the meetings Ann and I were having. There started to be a lot of uncalled meetings, where Ann would often have to call me and tell me that Mathew was there at her house and she needed me to drive over immediately.

Mathew was starting to drink a lot more and he would come to Ann's house high as a kite. He threatened Ann yet again to take Beyonce out of the group if she didn't let him co-manage Ashley's solo management deal. All of this was going on when Pam, Letoya's mom, started raising questions about why Letoya couldn't be involved in other things besides Girls Tyme. Ann and I were strategically working to juggle a lot of irons that were on the fire.

While there was no respect for Mathew's crap, Ann and I both respected the fact that Pam was willing to challenge the contract in order to get the best deal for her daughter. Her approach was very different from Mathew's and with much more class, professionalism, and fairness. So we wheeled and dealed and handled things the best we could.

NO TIME TO CRY

Aside from everything going on within and outside the camp, we kept things moving. Although the group dynamics and Ann's health were ongoing issues, we continued to move forward and work hard to bring about tangible results. It was a rollercoaster ride to say the least; but we kept the faith. Girls Tyme, their parents, and the entire management team were doing their best to cope with the disappointment surrounding Star Search. Regardless, there were still labels expressing and interest in signing the girls and so we did not waste time in exploring those options.

Rap-a-Lot, a record label owned by James Prince aka Little James that focused on "gangsta" and southern rap, was very interested in signing the girls to his label. One of the most notorious groups signed to that particular label at the time was Geto Boys led by rapper and performing artist, Willie D who helped both the group and the label reach national acclaim with songs such as "Mind Playing Tricks on Me" and "Scarface." After brief discussions with Little James, Ann and I decided that Rap-a-Lot Records was not the best fit for Girls Tyme. Although the label was known in the rap game, Ann was not interested in positioning Girls Tyme as a rap group. She wanted to secure a much bigger deal for the girls as well as sign with a more established label.

Although Ann did not "get into bed" with Rap-a-Lot, she became good friends with Willie D, who was interested in getting into the management side of things. It was not unusual for me to go by Ann's house and see Willie D. Regardless of the many people doing a whole lot of talking, there was no record deal yet, and mine and Ann's concern was to get a deal – the best deal for the girls.

"Kenny, this is bullshit. We need to get these girls signed."

"I'm with you on that, Dretta. When you think about who we have on the hook, something should close, whatcha think?"

"Hell, I would think so. Who else can you talk to that could maybe walk us through?"

"Let me put in some calls, Dretta."

"Let me know. This shit is getting old, something's gotta give!"

I reached out to a friend of mine named Robert, who was a travel agent for So So Def Records in Atlanta as well as co-manager of the group Whodini along with a guy named Frank, who also managed them. At the time I reached out to Rob, Whodini was on the downslide but they were still a popular group, so it didn't hurt to give him a call.

"Hey Rob, can you guys help us out?"

"Whatcha need B.K.?"

"We are trying to keep this ball rolling and I was wondering if there were some record label execs you all could possibly walk us through?"

"Uhm."

"What about Jermaine Dupri. Can you speak with him?"

Rob went and spoke with Jermaine Dupri's father who was over So So Def at the time and then came back to tell me what he said.

"Okay Kenny man. He thought your girls were interesting, so he said he will talk to a couple of people and see what's up."

"I appreciate that man. It means a lot."

I followed up with Ann regarding my conversations with Rob. There was some talk out there about the group and we didn't want the devastation of the Star Search loss to leave a bad taste in the mouths of some of the people who might otherwise be interested in Girls Tyme or for them to be associated with losing. Consequently, we changed the name of the group from Girls Tyme to Something Fresh. Ann ultimately made the call to change the image and name. At that time, you had groups out there such as Kriss Kross, Da' Brat, and The Boys, who were really jumping.

Ann put out a lot of money to get the name changed and create a new image. She spent a lot of money making sure the girls were on point for the showcases and so forth that she placed her house in jeopardy of foreclosing. Ann was spending money on the girls as opposed to paying some of the bigger bills. Although she had money set aside for her sons, she refused to dip into that. So it was as if she did not have it. After being confronted with the necessity to make some really tough decisions, Ann decided to let her house go and downsize in order to cut her overhead.

"Damn Kenny, this is our dream house. I feel like I've let them down."

"Dretta, you didn't let them down. You did the best you could."

"No I didn't. I know damn well I should have been paying the mortgage. How in the hell could I have been so stupid."

"Dretta, you are not stupid, so stop all that damn beating yourself up."

"Got damn it then Kenny, what the fuck is it…I messed up shit!"

"Ann, you've been running on ten. You have kept a lot of shit together for some time. So stop knocking yourself. Hell, look at what you have put together to make Dwight's dream and your dream and the dreams of others come alive. If Dwight was alive, he would be proud of you."

This was the first time I saw water well up in Ann's eyes. She was really going through it during that time. I spent a lot of energy trying to lift her spirits and assure her that things would be okay.

"You know, Kenny, it just makes me do a lot of soul searching. All these got damned mutha fucking people sending me in all these got damned circles. I just wanna make this shit work. You know what I'm saying…I just want it to work!"

"I know Dretta. We're gonna do this. It's okay…we're gonna do this."

Ann almost whispered, clearing her throat as she attempted to get the words out of her mouth. "Oh, Kenny…"

"What are you going to do?"

"I bought another house."

"What the fuck…!"

"No! Wait. I bought a house down the way that is smaller than this one. It has pretty much the same floor plan. The boys can still have their own room… It's just not this house. This was our house Kenny. This was the house me and Dwight picked out!"

"I understand, but you are gonna be fine, Ann."

"I know Kenny, it's just bullshit! Damn! I ran through a lot of money. Sometimes I wonder if it's all worth it. Do they even understand or appreciate the work that we do?"

It took some talking to Ann to help her get through this period of being confronted with leaving her home. As Ann packed her things to move out of the house, a flood of emotions overwhelmed her. It appeared that all the old feelings of losing her husband and daughter resurfaced. While she had to leave her dream home, Ann stayed in the general vicinity of the same neighborhood so that her boys could continue with the same school and before long got moved into her new dwelling place. She could not yet call it home.

With all of the stress of what was going on in the organization, the foreclosure, and the move, Ann landed back in the hospital from another Lupus crisis. This was the first time that she had to bring home an oxygen machine. However, she would only use it when she was in dire straights. After Ann got out of the hospital, I made my way over to her new residence.

"Hey Blackie! Is your mama as Black as you?...Dretta? Where your Black ass at woman?"

Ann came out from the kitchen. "Hey girl...with your Black ass. Is your mama as Black as you? Is ya mama

Black as the ace of spade like your monkey ass? Black ass mutha fucka! You know your ass is faking and shit! Ain't nothin' wrong with your lying ass!"

Ann just continued walking back into the kitchen with this smirk on her face and chuckling under her breath. I followed right behind her playing the dozens and dancing. I even started singing the dozens and stepping side-to-side. I was loud with it too.

"Hey…I'm a roll tonight girl! Whoop…ten for Kenny Mo!"

I continued playing the dozens and laughing. Ann just kept walking to the kitchen, and I was right behind her clowning.

"Hey Blacky…with your Black ass…" When I got into the kitchen, I stopped dead in my tracks because I had not realized that someone else was at her house. Then Ann turned to me. "Kenny this my mama."

Ann started laughing almost hysterically. My mouth dropped wide open. I was completely stunned. "Uh…how you doing…uh…I'm uh… Kenny."

I reached out my hand to shake her hand. She looked me up and down with a disgusting look on her face, and then said, "Uhm huhm," then she rolled her eyes at me, turned her back and went and sat down with her cup of coffee.

"Now...uh...uh Ms. Brown...uh...you know I was just joking when I said what I said when I came in now..."

Ms. Brown just looked straight through me and had this look on her face as if to say, "You mutha fucka!" However, she just kept looking at me with her nose turned up then said, "Uhm huhm."

Ann just laughed. I was trying to figure out a way to get out of the fools place I put myself, when Ann finally helped me to somewhat get out of the situation by pulling me aside to talk. We walked into the other room where the piano was.

"I got your mutha fuckin' ass this time nigga!" Ann said laughing.

"Ann, you know you wrong for that, you didn't even tell me your mama was here."

"That's what your Black ass get nigga! I fixed your ass this time...Talking all that shit!"

"Seriously though, how you feelin' baby girl?"

"I'm okay. Just a little down. I didn't really want to have to make this change. And getting out of the hospital and coming here...it's just not the same. It feels a little weird for me."

"It's a nice house Ann. It ain't too much different from the one you were in. It's suitable for you and the boys. You can still keep things rolling."

"Yeah, I guess you're right…it's not home yet though, you know what I mean?"

"You gonna be alright girl. You know I'm here for you…me and Cassey, we're here for you."

"I know Kenny."

"Shit don't let them niggas get to you. Hell if I need to kick some ass you know I'll do it!"

Ann's mother heard a lot of what Ann and I were talking about. She walked passed us and the look she gave me let me know very clearly that she was watching me. Her look also communicated to me that she was appreciative of the support that I was offering her daughter, and glad to know that someone else is actually looking out for her.

Although Ann was still recuperating from her most recent Lupus crisis, she was more concerned with Tayste rehearsals and the girls' new image. I explained to her that it would be fine and although she had a detached garage now, Tayste could still rehearse in the garage. I told her the fact that she moved wasn't going to stop things from moving forward.

Ann continued to work on getting the girls a fresh image, which meant a whole new wardrobe as well. As she was paying closer attention to her finances under the circumstances, Ann noticed that things in her bank account were not balancing out. So she went back to the bank.

Ann found out there were a number of checks that had been written on her account made out to Lynn with her name being forged.

"Kenny, this mutha fucka been stealing my money!"

"Whatcha talkin' about Ann?"

"Lynn! That asshole has been writing got damned checks on my bank account, forgin' my got damned name…Shit!"

"What?"

"Got dammit Kenny! What part of what I 'm saying to you don't your ass understand?"

"Wait a minute Dretta, cool down."

"Cool down? I left the bank today. I found out this mutha fucka…it ain't enough that this got damned mutha fucka done bought cars, drugs, and shit on money for the group, but he done gone and started fucking with my got damned money!"

"Are you saying that Lynn wrote hot checks on your account?"

"That is exactly what I'm saying."

"Damn!"

"That mutha fucka gots to go! Ain't no ifs, ands, buts about it. His ass is history!…Mutha fuckin drug addict!…What the fuck!"

"So he'd done burned through the other money and now he done wrote checks on your account?"

"Damn skippy."

"Okay Ann, the first thing we need to do is limit Lynn's access to anything."

"Limit him my ass, cut his fuckin ass the hell off!"

The next meeting that was at Ann's house, she informed Lynn and everyone else of what Lynn had done. They had discussions about it in the meeting. While she was cordial to Lynn, she really had nothing to do with him. He continued to come by the house for a few more meetings after that, but finally Ann just told him he was completely out and no longer a part of the team. The challenge for the team was that Lynn established a friendship with Tayste.

Harlan and Mitch were wooed by Lynn's fancy cars and women. They always invited him to their rehearsals, which was in Ann's garage. They also asked him to find producers for their music. This made for an uncomfortable situation as Ann was managing Tayste. Mitch and Harlan's attitude was that management's focus moved from all of the groups to just the girls. Lynn became Tayste's sounding board for their complaints against the management team. Tu Tu and A.J. were in Ann's corner all the way. This created a rift within the group and thus the ultimate demise of Tayste.

Things were happening in every camp of Girls Tyme Entertainment group. Ann loaned Lonnie money and flew him back and forth from California. She gave T-Mo money. She gave me money to compensate me for my time and efforts since I was spending all that time at her home and really was just getting started on my job. That assisted with me going to buy groceries and take care of other household expenses. She paid the Girls Tyme (Something Fresh) members' parent's bills. Tina and Mathew started having more issues in their household and marital problems. She was being as supportive as she could on that front as well.

In essence, Ann was taking care of all of us. In truth, in terms of intimate comforts and satisfactions, there was no one really looking after her. One guy who came by frequently, attempted to pass himself off as a manager of one of the Clark sisters.

The problem with Tina and Mathew began to manifest itself when Mathew became a part of the management team. It gave him the needed excuse and the opportunity to be gone away from home Often, Mathew was either not at the meetings or he would show up for a minute, then disappear to go be with other women. Whenever Tina called, people answering the phone would tell her that Mathew just left or whatever Mathew told them to tell her. I never lied for Mathew and neither did Ann.

To avoid being placed in an uncompromising situation, whenever there was shadiness going on with him and his habits, Ann nor I would even answer the telephone phone. Mathew's shenanigans didn't sit well with us.

"Ann, that got damned nigga is a dirty mutha fucker, and I ain't lying for his funky ass!"

"Shit, Kenny, I ain't lying for his ass either. Hell let Lonnie's ass get the phone. If Lynn's ass was here he could get it too. All of them are some shady-ass mutha fucka's as far as I'm concerned. So let Lonnie get it, shit. That's two got damned peas-in-a-pod."

"I don't understand what he is doing. He has a beautiful wife at home, I mean gorgeous, and he fuckin' around with some damn, whateva the hell his ass is doing. Shit, I don't want nothing to do with it."

"He gonna keep on and I'mma tell Tina on his ass. I am not down with that Kenny."

"Shit, I'm with you on that Ann."

Although all of this mess was going on with Mathew, we still had to focus on business and not let any of that cause us to lose sight of what we were supposed to be doing at the time. There was this hot singing group called, The Boys, that came to town. They were four brothers out of California. Their names were Khiry, Hakim Tajh, and Bilal Abdulsamad. So Mathew, Lonnie, T-Mo, and I went to go see them perform to compare them to what we had in our stable, specifically with respect to the girls. Their father was their manager. At that time they were on the MCA and Motown label.

They were hot! We were thinking strategically that perhaps we could connect them with the girls to get the girls to open up and perform better and maybe one of the girls would like one of the boys. We were thinking marketing and publicity. Their hit song at that time was, "Dial My Heart."

After the show, we met the father.

"Hey how ya doing? I'm Mathew Knowles, and this is our team. We're part of Girls Tyme Entertainment."

"Hi, how are you? My name is Jabari, I am the Boys Manager and father."

"Well, we are just interested in talking to you about The Boys and your group and any advice that you can give us."

"Well Mathew, I really don't have any advice to give you, I really don't think… you really got nothing. My boys sell millions of records, and little girls buy their songs! Now…who gonna buy your girls' songs?"

"What!"

"Little boys don't buy music."

After Jabari said that to Mathew, he walked away from us like we were nothing. Mathew got mad as hell after that.

The Making of a Child of Destiny

"Who that mutha fucka think he is? He's an arrogant son-of-a-bitch! How in the hell he gonna say my daughter ain't shit! Mutha fuckin cock sucker...I whoop his mutha fuckin' ass!"

Mathew called that man every name but the child of God. He was so mad. He went off so bad that we all just had to laugh. He invented curse words I had never heard and the combination of words had all of us on the floor rollin'.

"Got damned, fuck ass shit hole mutha fuck, fake ass, arrogant shit hole mutha fucka, piss got damned, cock sucka...Hell Mutha fucka! Ass hole... Fuck you, got dammit!"

Mathew flipped the guy the bird while his back was turned, still cursing him out under his breath.

"This mutha fucka don't know what he talkin' about. Who the fuck he think he is? No sanging, fat ass kids, knock-kneed sons-of-bitches, slew-footed mutha fuckas, no dancing ass, skipping like faggety ass, nappy headed punks...Fuck you, and fuck you, and you and you...Shit...You can't sang any damn way! Talking about my got damned daughter like that...Fuck you witcha Black ass!"

Mathew flipped the bird again. The guy was long gone. We laughed so hard, but Mathew took it personally. I guess because his daughter was the one in the group. The rest of us didn't have children in the group, so we were able to let it roll off like "water off a duck's back."

"Mathew, man-to-man, he had a good point. It's something we have to think about."

"Kenny, fuck that mutha fucka, and fuck you too…and fuck you Lonnie, and fuck you T-Mo…!"

We kept laughing while Mathew was going on. "Kenny, your country-ass don't know shit!"

"Mutha fucka you from Alabama how in the fuck you gonna call me country?"

Mathew and I went back and forth until it got so bad that we both just burst out laughing.

"Kenny, I'mma show that mutha fucka!"

The good thing about that whole situation was that for the first time I saw in Mathew a strong sense of, "My daughter's gonna be something" attitude. He let it be known that night that Beyonce was going to be a star. He took on the attitude that, "This is gonna happen!" Mathew wore his passion on his sleeve that night. He demonstrated straight fatherly love that none of us could deny.

That night was the first time I started to respect Mathew. At that moment, I felt that he was in this with us. He was serious about making it happen. I became more open to accepting him as a teammate. Prior to that night, I felt that he just forced himself on the management team because his daughter was a main staple of the group.

However, he demonstrated real passion that evening and I felt that he shared our passion for the group at that point. That was a good time for our relationship.

I shared with Ann what had happened that night, which made for good light-hearted conversation in the midst of her stress. Ann told me that the money was starting to get low. The only thing left was for her to start tapping into Armon and Christopher's inheritance. The deals were taking longer to close than anticipated. Everyone started working extra hard. Tina was pulling more hours at Headliners, which was her salon, to help support her family. Mathew was not working so he was able to support the day-to-day operations more.

I worked more hours on my job. Ann worked overtime on her job. We all did what we could do to take some of the weigh off of Ann. Everybody was pretty much busting their butts while Mathew had free time because he quit his job. He sat all day masterminding stuff and then would bum rush us when we got off work. Mathew showed up everyday at Ann's house asking her questions and complaining about who didn't call him back. This presented an extremely stressful situation for Ann on top of the fact that her resources were getting low. Mathew was overbearing to say the least.

He started calling all of Ann's contacts and telling them that he was now in charge and the primary manager and if they needed to talk to anyone, they needed to speak with him. If they spoke with Andretta, he requested them to carbon copy him on any correspondence. We also found out that he was at the rehearsals telling the girls the same thing.

Ann did not want to dip into her sons' inheritance, so before she had to turn to that she decided to seek assistance from her cousin, Belfred. He was a drug dealer. I personally didn't know he was a drug dealer and neither did Ann. Although, she suspected it, she couldn't prove it at the time because it was not unusual for Blacks from East Texas to come into money from time to time, because of farm and cattle sales. Regardless of how Belfred made his money, he was very supportive of Ann. He and his girlfriend Sha Sha started coming to Houston frequently and visiting her. Belfred probably had an ideal that something was about to break and I am sure in the back of his mind, he was trying to find a way of getting in on the action.

"Ann, instead of you stressin' out and everything, why don't I just loan you a couple of dollars."

"I don't know Bel...I gotta think about that one."

"Whatcha mean you gotta think about it? Let me help out."

"I'll let you know."

After hesitating and much thought, Ann decided to go ahead and borrow $25,000 from Belfred to tie us over and keep her from going into the boys' money that was set aside for them. He agreed to give the money to Ann in three installments. She agreed that once we got a deal, she would give him the money back. Belfred was making so much money at the time that he really didn't care about loaning the money. He was more concerned about helping his cousin out, but Ann had a lot of pride, and didn't want anybody giving her anything in that sense.

After Ann accepted the money from her cousin, Silent Partner also stepped up their game. Finally after all of the discussions and time passed, we finally were at the point of signing the agreement with Silent Partners. As we were working on finalizing the terms for the deal, squabbles crept up prior to signing because Silent Partners were not interested in signing dancers to a label. Their attitude was that they can get dancers anywhere.

Simmons attitude was, "Here today, gone tomorrow, I'm not signing!" Simmons and his partner, Sylvia Rhone, were both of the belief that there was no need to sign dancers. They also felt that some of the background vocals could be stronger. Their goal was to get more control of the girls because at that point, Tillman Management and Girls Tyme Entertainment had complete control. His move was to kick the dancers out and replace one of the singers with a better singer.

The first target was LaTavia. They then reconsidered her because they felt that if the group went down, then LaTavia could be their, "Left Eye." Instead they wanted to groom her to learn to sing. At that point, LaTavia went from being a rapper to a singer. After they decided to keep LaTavia, the target then became Kelly. Ann shot that idea down immediately. Silent Partner management started to complain that Kelly was a little stiff; she had not blossomed, and had an attitude of "we can accept one dark girl, but not two."

Ann challenged that mindset.

"Regardless of what you wanna do, there will be dark-skinned girls in this damn group!"

They felt that they could get a lighter-skinned singer who was a stronger vocalist to come in and be part of the group. So there were consistent talks of getting rid of Kelly.

There were rumors that Silent Partners were pursuing Ke Ke Wyatt to be one of the replacements. The deal hit a snag because Andretta Tillman had an ecliptic fit when they tried to kick Kelly out of the group. I had never seen Ann so irate in my time of working with her. The way Ann fought for Kelly was as if she was fighting for her daughter, Shawna.

The Making of a Child of Destiny

"They are not kicking my baby out of the group! Hell to the naw! They can fuck all this shit. Kelly stays and Mathew's fuckin' has jumped on board with that shit!"

"What?"

"Look Kenny, his ass just wants to get a deal. If Kelly goes, ain't no fuckin' deal, I call the whole got damned thing off! And... if his Black ass fuck with me on this one, I'll sue his got damned ass and fuck up all his shit...and he knows what the fuck I mean!"

"So what are you gonna do, Ann?"

"Ain't no deal unless Kelly is a part of it, that's what the fuck I'mma do. They can take that shit or leave it. I will fire Mathew's ass and make his got-damned life a living hell! He can take that shit to the bank and he best not fuck with me on this. He best not attempt to write checks his ass can't cash!"

"Okay, Dretta, I support you on this!"

"Damn skippy! Aint no other way around this one. Now as much as I want them in the group, they can dismiss Nikki and Nina, but they asses ain't getting rid Kelly. Aint no price right for that shit!"

There was nothing that Lonnie or Mathew could say. They insisted that Ann was messing up the deal. Ann's position "was fuck the deal, you ain't taking my girl out the group! I promised her mother, and ya'll ain't taking my baby out the group! That's all to it!"

After Ann took such a strong opposition about letting go of Kelly, Silent Partners, whose arguments fell on deaf ears, conceded on getting rid of Kelly. The battle lasted all but a week. Kelly stayed, but Nikki and Nina was let go. At that point Something Fresh formerly Girls Tyme consisted of four girls: Letoya, Beyonce, LaTavia, and Kelly. Looking back at how passionately Ann fought to keep the girls in the group, I know inside she was fighting for them as if she was fighting for her daughter Shawna.

Silent Partners, Inc. at One Capital City Plaza, 3350 Peach Tree Road - Suite 1500, Atlanta, Georgia finalized the deal including Kelly Rowland and they signed the agreement on June 11, 1993. To that point, as far as Ann was concerned with girls being replaced, Silent Partner could "Shut the fuck up!"

Although Nikki and Nina went to Atlanta along with the others to do the showcase for Simmons under the auspices of Something Fresh, with the hopes and dreams of being part of a record label deal, they returned only to learn later that those particular dreams at that time were shattered. Ann continued to allow them to come to rehearsals for awhile and she pampered them as long as she could. Ultimately things got more hectic and she did not see them as often as she would have hope to.

After the fire was put out, Silent Partner Productions took over the production of the girls. That meant that Lonnie was pushed to the side and Arne was completely out of the picture. Lonnie was not happy, but Ann kept Lonnie around in case anything fell through. Her thoughts were if something happened, at least she would still have her producer. After all the delegating and acting as drill sergeant in preparing the girls, he was relegated to only being able to submit material to the girls through Ann. Ultimately that satisfied Lonnie as he was still able to have some involvement, no matter how minimal. However, overall A & A Productions was not too happy with the situation.

Silent Partner Productions handled their business and had an established track record. Lonnie was not a part of that. They didn't need a Lonnie because they had Baby Face and L.A. Reid. Consequently, T-Mo lost his voice as well. He fell with Lonnie. So things moved along with some adjustments. Ann noticed that things were lagging. Although they signed with Silent Partner Productions and were working on some things, almost four months had passed and nothing was really happening. Ann wanted to keep things moving.

"Okay Kenny, I need you. I need you to help me balance Lonnie, and keep an eye on Mathew's ass."

"Ann you know I gotcha."

"Hell, I need you to help pacify Lonnie. There's no need for him to fly back and forth from California.

Also, we need to keep Mathew's fuckin' ass at bay, before he fuck some shit up!"

"Okay so what is Lonnie gonna do?"

"Well his ass is staying with me right now. Instead of flying back and forth, he will just be here for now. I need you to help with that."

"Oh okay...damn."

"Also, Silent Partner is dragging their feet. I don't want to take a chance on them not being able to get everything done in a timely manner."

"Okay, so whatcha ya thinking?"

"Kenny, this is taking too long. They seem like they are dragging their feet. Every got damned time we take one step ahead, they seem to be coming back wanting to change something else or saying some shit like 'there's a snag'. I don't know what the hell to think!"

"Uhm...what are they saying?"

"The question is not what are they saying, it's what is Mathew's ass up to? He is steady kissin' Daryl Simmons' ass. That's why I need to watch his ass and keep him on tight reigns."

"Hell, that mutha fucka just can't be trusted. He blows like the wind!"

"And...Kenny...get this...Letoya damn mama is playin' up telling me some shit like we still haven't given

The Making of a Child of Destiny

them a clear answer as to why Letoya cannot do other things other than singing."

"She is still on that shit, Dretta?"

"Hell yeah!"

"Damn, these are some ungrateful mutha fuckas. I don't get it!"

"It be different if someone was putting up some damn money."

Pamela Luckett, Letoya's mother, and Mathew started going back and forth. She ended up hiring the law firm of Warren M. Fitzgerald, Jr. to represent her and do her talking for her. Mathew took an aggressive position with her and sent a letter on Ann's letterhead without Ann's knowledge stating "…if you cannot abide by what management has said and the agreement in place, while it has been a pleasure working with you, I will inform Mr. Simmons that we are having issues with you, and that Letoya is no longer a part of Something Fresh. He sent this letter to both Letoya's mother and her attorney.

The Luckett's attorney fired back stating that they did not agree with the contract and felt that the requests were unreasonable. Mathew responded and said they would find a new singer. At the same time all of this was going on, Simmons was trying to get another singer in the group anyway, so for him this was not a problem. After Mathew was willing to eliminate Letoya out of the group and there was no resistance from Simmons, the Lucketts pulled back and decided to drop the issue for the moment.

What Pam didn't understand at the time was that when she made the move she did on challenging the contract, it gave Mathew the opportunity to give Simmons what he wanted and that was for one girl to leave the group so he could put his girl in. What I do not think she anticipated was them threatening and willing to follow through with kicking Letoya out of the group with no regrets. So when she realized that it was not going to go the way she thought, she settled down. Mathew was quick to send the letter because he knew that Simmons had someone (that someone being Ke Ke Wyatt) in the wings to step in, but Pam had no idea of the politics going on behind the management scenes.

Andretta was dealing with all this madness while working her tail off to get a real deal for the girls. She was complaining that things were not happening fast enough and that is when we decided to go get the money.

"Alright Kenny, it's time for us to make a move. This shit ain't rolling like it's supposed to be."

"Okay, Ann so whatcha you want me to do?"

"I want you to go get the money. We're burning through capital too fast and nigga's aint bringin' in shit!"

"Let's do it then, I can go back to my boy William. The truth is Ann, we are producing hits, and we just need to be able to get them pressed."

"So see what he says."

"Alright."

I reached out to William again. I spoke with him to see if there was any interest. William pretty much just shot me down. He wasn't willing to invest in a studio. Lynn resurfaced. When he did, he came back in a new Porsche.

"Hey, I got the money for a studio and ever' thang, you know… I can help ya'll out, you know."

Lynn was tried to get back into saving grace. Ann and I were not interested in dealing with Lynn. With Lynn came too much other baggage that was not worth carrying.

"Man, it's sounds all good, but we ain't interested…"

"Come on Kenny man, let me help ya'll out. We got something here."

"Lynn, you ain't right and Ann is not interested in dealing with you. She doesn't trust you and you got too much goin' on that ain't good for these girls."

Once we turned Lynn down, he blew the money and went right back to doing what he had been doing before. He was messing around with drugs, women, and planting seed in Tayste until they had disdain for the management team. He divided Tayste. Ann and I got together and said we could not deal with Lynn at all and didn't want him coming around under no circumstances, Tayste or otherwise.

While this is happening, Mathew got wind that Lynn had gotten some money and blew it on cars, drugs, and women. He was livid! Mathew started hounding Ann after that.

"Andretta, you let this dude blow all this money! He had the money that we needed and you let him blow it on bullshit!"

"Mathew, get the fuck back, I ain't let nobody blow shit. Lynn is his own got dammed man and we pushed him back some time ago, so how the fuck you gonna put that shit on me?"

"You didn't get the money. You let him take it and blow it!"

"I didn't let Lynn's ass take shit. Hell your ass know he stole money from my account, so whatever he went out their and got in my damn name is his crooked ass shit…so don't be sweatin' me with that bullshit, Mathew!"

"Well it's like this…this record deal is getting' ready to come, and when we get this advance, I'm handling the shit. This ain't gonna be happening on my watch! I'mma be in charge of the money from the record deal.

I'm gonna pay out who needs to get paid, and if you don't like it, then I'll take Beyonce…shit and go somewhere else!"

"Mathew, get out of my got damned house. I just got home from work. I don't need your bullshit. Go get a fuckin' job and stop makin' it your job to fuck with me…please."

"I ain't playing, Andretta…I'mma be in charge of the money…"

After Mathew left, Ann called me. I went over to her house to help lift her spirits. We sat at her baby grand piano like we always do when she was feeling low.

"Look Dretta, don't let Mathew's crooked ass get you down. I know it's a tough situation, but it's gonna be alright. No matter what you do, hold on to Beyonce, because she is gonna be a big star."

"Shit Kenny, Mathew's ass is just simple! I can't stand him. He get on my last fuckin' nerve…and he always threatening with takin' Beyonce if I don't do what he says."

"We all know he's a dirty mutha fucka…that's a given, but we will get through this."

Ann was stressed. Lynn blew money that should have been used for the girls and to pay her cousin back. Feeling that her back was against the wall, she agreed to let Mathew control the funds from the advance whenever the record deal came through without my knowledge. I found out after the deal was done.

"Look Dretta, I know you are stressed, but maybe this will help. I got this friend in Atlanta. I will contact him and see what he can do."

"Who is he?"

"My friend? His name is Al. He comes into town frequently because he is working on opening a Sally's hair supply place here in Houston...I can get with him and see what we can make happen."

"Okay. Will he do it?"

"Well, every time he comes, Cassey and I work with him helping him to find good locations. I can see what his thoughts are. We're good friends though, so..."

"Well call him then."

I called Al. he already knew that we were dealing with the girls group, and that they were a pretty hot group. When I asked him about investing, he didn't hesitate.

"How much money ya'll need, man?"

"Al man, we need about a hundred and fifty thousand dollars."

"Okay, okay...let me know...did you wanna come and get it? You know...meet with my attorney...we can talk about it."

I flew out to Atlanta to meet with Al Clark. I stayed at his big ole house up in Stone Mountain, Georgia.

We did it up had a great time. When I got there, Al scheduled the meeting for the next day with his attorney. We were getting ready for bed that night when Al called me.

"Hey Kenny, come here man. Do you know what I do?"

"Al man, I figured out what you do man. Don't forget man, I've run around with you."

Al was a number's runner. Right before the Georgia lottery came in, he was running all the numbers.

"Yeah, yeah…okay," he chuckled.

"Okay so lookie here Kenny. Got something to show you in my bedroom."

"Nigga, I ain't no funny shit now."

"Man shut your ass up. Come here."

Al pointed at this bag. So when I saw it I said, "What? It's just a bag."

Al just laughed, then dumped the paper bag out on the bed. It was nothing but money.

"There's your money right there. How much do you think that is?"

"A hundred and fifty thousand I guess. Shit I don't know."

"That's a million dollars boy! Obviously you ain't seen a million dollars before."

"Obviously not, because I wouldn't swear that was a million dollars."

All broke it down and counted it. We counted stack/after/stack. Then tallied them up, and it was a million dollars indeed. He put the money back in the bag.

"Come on, let's go down here."

I followed Al outside. There was this switch by these big Rottweilers in a big pen. Al hit the switch and the dog house lifted up hydraulically. Under the dog house was a cement bin. He went over to the bin where there was a safe and he put the bag of money in the safe, locked it, and then came back out of the gate. We went back into the house, wound down for the night and went to bed.

Al woke up the next morning mad as hell. He was slamming cabinets and things downstairs. When I heard the commotion, I went downstairs where he was.

"Al, what the fuck wrong with you man?"

"Come on Kenny man, let's go walking."

As we were walking, he was huffing and puffing. He was mad.

"Kenny, what kinda mutha fucka are you?"

"What man?"

"I ain't never met no nigga like you!"

"What do you mean, Al?"

"Nigga, I showed you a million dollars, and you didn't get your got dammed ass up nil one time last night…"

The Making of a Child of Destiny

"Al, man I came here to get a loan from you, not rob you man. What the hell wrong with you?"

"I ain't never met no nigga like you. The average nigga would've got up…walk past my door or something." Then he started laughing.

"Nigga, what the fuck you laughin' at?"

"Shit, Kenny. I'm glad you didn't because I had my gun and every thang…Shit I was sayin' this big mutha fucka here, I'mma have some problems with him if he decided to try and take my money."

Al had three of his guys stay outside of the gate by the dog pin all night.

"Shit Kenny man, my whole thing was, if your mutha fuckin ass get me in bed, these niggas be out here, and if you got past the Rottweilers, I told them no matter what happened, don't let that mutha fucka get my money!"

Al was laughing his ass off. I was in disbelief this nigga went through all that shit just in case I tried to steal his money.

"Man, Al, you crazy as hell! You went through all that shit? Just for me?"

"Kenny, you's a big mutha fucka shit, I didn't know! I didn't know."

"Man, you mutha fuckin' touched in got damned head, that's what you are."

Al and I just laughed. By then we were back at the house from the walk. Al then turned to me and said, "Come on, let's go see the attorney."

We went to the attorney's office. I thought we were going to a regular criminal attorney's office. I thought he would be a typical guy in Atlanta. Since Al ran numbers, it had to be someone who could get his ass out of trouble. When we walked into the attorney's office, I notice all of these pictures of records on the wall of TLC, La Face Records artists, and others. There was several of TLC more than anyone else. TLC was like "The Group" to the girls. As I witnessed this I was like, "Oh my God to myself, this guy must be in the music industry too."

As Al and I were talking to Darryl, I realized that this dude really did know what he was doing. So I gave him my whole pitch. Attorney Darryl said, "I like you and I like your girls." He turned to Al and said, "Al, I assume you are going to give them the money, right?"

"Yeah."

"Okay then, well, if we are gonna do it, we gotta do it right."

"Okay."

"Now, Kenny, you are one of the managers, right?"

"Yes I am."

"Well, I tell you what…you go back and you bring them here and we'll get it done, we'll get it done right."

When Al and I got back into his car, I called Ann from his brick phone.

"Hey Dretta, Dretta…"

"What!"

"Baby girl…shit! I got something to tell you."

"Kenny, I got something to tell you too."

"What…what?"

"Naw, naw you go first."

"Got dammit, I done got here, I done got the money baby for the studio."

"What?"

"Yeah, and you know this attorney, his name is Darryl…he got TLC and all their pictures on the wall…"

"That's great."

The next day, Ann called me back.

"Kenny…let's keep them in our pocket…but…you might as well come on home, we just got a deal."

"Got a deal with who?"

"We just got a deal with Elektra! Now Kenny, who did you say that attorney was?

"Attorney Darryl…why?"

"That's interesting because we just got a deal from Elektra and either he knew someone or someone knew you got to him… That's odd because as soon as I spoke with you, then the next day, we get the news that Elektra wants to sign the girls."

"Somebody in the Simmons camp must have gotten wind that I got to Attorney Darryl. Since they were dragging their feet…"

Ann and I was always under the impression that perhaps Attorney Darryl might have called and said hey, "he was sittin' in my office and he got someone who is willing to put up the money and he is one of my clients…" Consequently that perhaps that made Silent Partner speed up the process and secure a deal. Now if we had signed with Attorney Darryl, we most likely would have signed directly with La Face records and side stepped Silent Partner Productions all together. However, we went ahead and agreed to sign with Elektra.

LET'S MAKE IT HAPPEN

I packed it up and returned to Houston. Everyone kicked into high gear knowing that the talks were much more serious regarding a record deal with Elektra. It was unfortunate because a lot of disrespect was starting to happen. With Nikki and Nina being gone, Charlotte was out of the loop in terms of rehearsals and details with respect to the group, but she still maintained a good friendship with Ann. Her presence was more to check on Ann to see how she was doing.

Since there was a growing focus on Latavia as the "second star" of the group, a kinship began to evolve between Cheryl and Mathew. As a result, there was also a growing trend where Cheryl started assisting Mathew instead of going through Ann which would have been the appropriate thing to do. The talks about Mathew taking the lead in terms of managing the group could have been some of the motivation behind her disrespect.

The girls traveled back to Atlanta to start recording with Silent Partners. Many things were happening at one time. Ann was having daily bouts with Lupus. She was more jittery and not quite as strong as she had been in the past. Belfry and his girlfriend Sha Sha came down and started hanging around a lot more. Whenever Belfry had to leave and go to work, Sha Sha stayed with Ann to help out around the house and provided support to Ann wherever she needed it. Mathew started coming around more causing unrest. He started to change drastically and became more aggressive in his demeanor. Mathew often went in Ann's garage to do cocaine or other drugs, then would come back in ranting and raving. He often called Darryl Simmons, then afterwards would come back to Ann yelling and carrying on.

"We gotta get this fucking shit going! Shit Ann you ain't makin' it happen fast enough!"

"Look Mathew, we are doing what we can. There are a lot of people involved and you just have to be patient. Things are moving."

"Shit, they ain't moving got damned fast enough! Make some mutha fuckin shit happen, Andretta!"

Mathew consistently harassed Ann, telling her she needed to get a deal done, while telling others and giving them the impression that he was in charge. Mathew became more aggressive. He was also hard to get in contact with so the record executives felt more comfortable contacting Ann and talking with her when it came to handling the business. These antics caused unnecessary stress and pressure on Ann. The way Mathew had started overtly behaving and telling the girls that he was their primary manager and leading others to believe the same, it gave rise to additional disrespect toward Ann. All the while, he had to "kowtow" to Ann to get things moving. However instead of talking with her and asking her questions, he had tirades, shouted, and threatened her to get answers or his way.

Mathew's drug use was becoming a major problem. In addition to his constant criticisms of Ann and accusations, he also kept demanding money for various things. He started to identify a host of bills or other items that needed to be paid and insisted that Ann write checks so he could take care of the things he outlined. The excuses Mathew presented to get money from Ann ranged from mailings to photos to producing new tracks with no name producers. Mathew saw how Lynn stole checks and manipulated money, and he too began to take on an air that he would get money from Ann and do whatever the hell he wanted to do. Although Ann knew that some of the reasons Mathew gave for needing money were not legitimate reasons, he pressured her to no end to give him money and if she didn't, he threatened to take Beyonce out of the group.

During that time, Ann became fearful that Mathew would take Beyonce, because word had gotten back to her that Beyonce was the key. I had heard that Beyonce was the key to the success of the group as well, so I kept reiterating to Ann that whatever we did, we could not lose Beyonce. I encouraged Ann to stick it out. So many times Ann often gave into Mathews ridiculous requests just to keep from losing Beyonce.

Sha Sha witnessed a lot of Mathew's behavior and became very upset with how he kept showing up every day at Ann's house causing her even more stress than what she was already dealing with. Sha Sha was a light-skinned, very attractive young girl around nineteen years of age. She was accustomed to being at the house and Mathew showing up unannounced, often in a tirade. There were times that Sha Sha would be on the couch sleep with short pants on, and would feel Mathew staring over her. For awhile she would get spooked.

"Look Ann, I don't know what's wrong with him, but somethin' wrong with that mutha fucka, and I don't trust him."

"What he do?"

"He keeps standing over me, staring at me like he is undressing me with his eyes. He's weird."

"Huhm."

"Ann, he got some problems, and shit the way he be acting trying to look under my clothes and shit, hell I'm afraid that mutha fucka gonna try something with me."

"I'll keep an eye on that Sha Sha and I will also talk to Kenny about it as well."

"I'm tired of that mutha fucka looking at me like that!"

It became almost a routine that when Mathew came over, he would stare her down. She got to the point where she would ask him, "May I help you?"

Instead of responding, Mathew, who was almost always high on something, would just walk off. It became so excessive that Sha Sha started speaking up more assertively to try and encourage a behavior change on his part.

"Mutha Fucka what's wrong with you! Stop staring at me all the got damned time! Ann, this mutha fucka is perverted! He got some got damned issues! Get the fuck out of my face you fuckin pervert!...Shit, before I get someone to whoop your ass!"

Ann had to take Sha Sha aside and talk to her.

"Sha, I know something is wrong with him, but we gotta get it done."

Once Ann talked to Sha Sha to give her a better understanding of what was going on, she tolerated Mathew's behavior.

While Mathew's erratic behavior was going on and he was adding additional pressure on Ann, another Atlanta showcase came up for the girls to perform as Something Fresh. At this point it was officially – Beyonce, Latavia,

Letoya, and Kelly. All four girls had been recording in Atlanta with Darryl Simmons already. Right before the Atlanta showcase, Ann had a Lupus episode where she needed to be hospitalized again and another finger removed. She ended up going into surgery two days before the Atlanta show.

Ann insisted on going to the showcase. She wanted to demonstrate that she was okay and still in charge. Ann had the itinerary for the show and as far as she was concerned everything was set and ready to go. As I was unable to go to Atlanta this time, I asked Sha Sha to escort Andretta due to her recent operation. Once Ann and Sha Sha arrived in Atlanta and checked into the hotel, Simmons had a meeting with everyone. When Ann was at the meeting, she felt that Darryl and Mathew made some type of pack because of the way that the two of them were talking to her. It was as if she did not have control when in fact she did because the contract was between her and Silent Partners as the lead manager.

"Well Ann, we made a few changes and we want you to take a look at them."

"Okay, Darryl, that's cool!"

Ann didn't think too much about it, nor was she alarmed. Ann had confidence in Darryl's ability being that he had been in the industry for awhile, and figured he just wanted to do something just a little differently. She never suspected that anything was wrong. Before the showcase they all went over to Darryl Simmons' house to hang out before the showcase. When they arrived, Sha Sha felt that the girls were acting funny, and she was not really she was not digging how things were going on.

"Ann, what the fuck is wrong with these niggas? I mean these little bitches got some damn nerve acting simple and shit! What's up with that?"

"Sha, it's alright."

"Naw the fuck it ain't alright! How you gonna let them disrespect you and shit! What? Did they forgot who the fuck you are or something?"

"Be cool Sha, it's alright."

"Uhm...what...shit! Can't their asses even come and show you some love or something? Hell, at least say hello. They act like they got sticks up their asses! You ask me, Ann, something is very wrong here, and I ain't diggin' this shit at all!"

"Sha, I see what's going on. Someone has been saying something."

"Damn straight! I bet anything that mutha fucking coke head mutha fucka is behind this shit!"

"Who, Mathew?"

"Ann...who the fuck you think I mean? You know he's a weird ass mutha fucka and anytime there's some shit, I bet you it has his name written all over it! Perverted ass mutha fucka! And his ass is tryin to pimp his daughter…asshole!"

"Sha!"

"Fuck all that nice shit Ann! He's a got damned trick!"

"Apparently this shit is true, Sha. I had been hearing that he was saying he was in charge and shit. The girls are acting really strange…and that damn Kelly…hell, if anyone should be showing some love over here it would be her."

"Black ass bitch! All of them can kiss my ass Ann, you too nice to them ungrateful wenches! You're better than me. Hell, I go get me another got damned group of girls and they all could kiss my high yellow ass!"

"We can't do that Sha. We've come too far. I've invested too much in these girls to throw my hands up and walk away or be moved to one side."

"I guess you're right, but something's gonna have to give, 'cause this shit ain't right Ann, and you know it!"

Ann got up and walked out and called me to talk on the telephone.

"Hey Kenny, this is Ann…are you busy?"

"What's up?"

"You know, we had been hearing about this mutha fucka saying all kind of shit."

"Yeah…what about it?"

The Making of a Child of Destiny

"Everybody's acting a little strange."

"Whatcha mean, Dretta?"

"The girls are walking around here, half-ass speaking and shit. Others looking at me like what the fuck am I doing here and shit…"

"What?"

"Yeah Kenny, I'mma ask what's up because even the girls are acting all funny. If I hear that this mutha fucka has said some shit, I'm jumping all in his ass."

While Ann was on the phone talking to me, Sha Sha went around the house talking to the girls one/on/one. Latavia was the one who actually spoke up and told Sha Sha that Mathew said he was taking control of managing the girls and that Ann was going to work with him. Once Ann got off the telephone with me, Sha Sha told her what Latavia had said. Ann was livid!

"Ann, this mutha fucka is crazy! That girl…Tavi, Latavia…hell whatever the fuck her name is said that that mutha fucka done said some shit!"

"What she say?"

"She said that Mathew told them that he was in charge and you were now pretty much answering to him."

"What the fuck! I had been hearing a bunch of shit, but this takes the cake!"

"No wonder they ignoring your ass…he's an ignorant ass mutha fucka you ask me!"

"Let me handle this shit, Sha!"

Ann went up to Mathew while he was standing talking to Darryl Simmons.

"Mathew, why the hell you runnin' around telling the girls and everybody you are in charge when you know I'm the damn manager and your ass is working with me?"

Darryl was taken aback at the abruptness and straight forwardness of Ann in her confrontation of Mathew. He seemed surprised at the whole situation.

"Hey…whoa…whoa…whoa…What ya'll gonna do?"

"Darry, what do you mean what we gonna do? Mathew knows damn well what the deal is."

"Andretta, I ain't got time for this shit right now, we here at the man's house chillin out and this ain't the time for this bullshit!"

"It's just the time for this mutha fuckin shit Mathew!"

"Look we can talk about this shit later, we got a damn showcase!"

"Fine, but we gonna talk about it!"

After that, Ann and Sha Sha headed back to the hotel, as did Mathew and the girls to get ready for the showcase. Somewhere between Darryl's house and the showcase, something was said to the girls. As Ann and Sha Sha walked into the venue for the showcase, she heard

The Making of a Child of Destiny

the new music. However, the ultimate disrespect followed.

When Ann walked into the room, there was no acknowledgement of her presence.

The girls were all sitting with their parents, and there was a separate table for Ann. The centerpiece on all the tables had "Baby Dolls" on it. Ann soon found out that Darryl Simmons and Mathew had gotten together without consulting her and changed the name of the group from "Something Fresh" to "The Dolls."

She was mad as hell, but kept her cool because there was a room full of executives and more arriving as the night went on. All she could really do without causing a scene was whisper to Sha Sha to observe.

"Sha, look at this bullshit. They have changed the girls' names. Haven't consulted me or said shit to me about it."

"That's bullshit Ann."

"You just wait, I'mma get in Mathew's ass."

When it came time for the girls to perform, they were introduced as "The Dolls." As the night moved on, Ann became so upset that her fingers started to bleed through the bandage and for the first time she was about to cry.

"Andretta…don't you cry. Don't you dare cry!"

Ann was tearing up, but fighting the tears back.

"Don't you let these mutha fuckas see you cry!"

Ann was working on getting her composure, while Sha Sha continued to offer support.

"Don't you let them see you cry. You can cry all you want back at the hotel, but don't let these mutha fuckas see you cry! They ain't worth it!"

Ann was able to get herself together and keep it together. However, what was extremely hurtful that hit to the core of her soul was seeing Beyonce, Latavia, Letoya, and Kelly over in the corner pointing looking at her hand and laughing. She heard them say, "Look she got her fingers cut off…"

Words could not express the profound pain that Ann felt at that moment seeing young girls, especially three of them that she had mentored and cared for, for years behave in such a manner. The very deal which made it possible for them to even be at this night was because of her hard work. Being young and lacking understanding in some areas is natural. Yet, the ignorance and level of insensitivity these girls showed at that moment was beyond comprehension. Ann was devastated, but her love still allowed her to look beyond their cruelness to believe that behind it all was the manipulations from adults. Yet, that belief still did not change the fact that Ann was extremely hurt and almost broken from the girls making fun of her.

Ann made it through the show. Afterwards the girls came over to her asking if she was okay. It was more two-faced than anything. Ann showed very little emotion toward them to protect her heart. Sha Sha looked at them as if to say, "Get your mutha fucking, black and high yella asses out of my got damned cousin's face! Hell fuck-ass naw she ain't okay…Bitches! Go back to that got damned pimp daddy ass coke head mutha fucka…bounce, before I put my foot up your ass!"

However, Sha Sha only rolled her eyes while the words stayed in her mind and on the tip of her tongue. By the girls' actions, they had been prepped on what to say and do. Ann had no idea that their names had been changed to "The Dolls" and in her observation, they knew that she didn't know, but pretended otherwise.

"You know Sha, Darryl Simmons know what the fuck he's doing. I believe his ass is guiding Mathew and he's souping Mathew's head up talking about how Beyonce's the star and shit!"

"Mathew's a fuckin' perverted asshole Ann, and Simmons…well, this is bullshit!"

"They think they got the group, but it's not that easy, Sha!"

Ann ultimately made it through that trip to Atlanta; however, the disrespect continued because Mathew increased his trips to Ann's house and well as his drug use.

It was getting out of control. He started lying even more to Tina and giving her the impression that there were meetings going on at Ann's house when, there was not. When there really were meetings going on, they usually lasted between three to four hours. Mathew used them as a cover for extramarital affairs with different women. Mathew might show up at the start of a meeting and then leave; or he would come at the end of one after screwing around and getting high. There were many times that he would be so high that he ended up sleeping on Ann's floor or couch because he couldn't drive home for being so high.

Ann knew one of the girls that Mathew was having an affair with, and when she first found out about it, she was very angry at both the girl and Mathew because she knowingly was messing around with a married man. Even worse, the girl knew Tina. While she knew Mathew better, she knew damn well that Mathew was married to Tina. They spent so much time together she was damn near living with the man. Ann would often say, "That's a dirty mutha fucka, and mark my word…his shit gonna come back on him!"

Ann felt so bad for Tina, who started calling excessively looking for Mathew. Ann got to the point she would not even answer her own phone because she was not going to lie to Tina. Lonnie was still living with Ann,

T-Mo came around because of Lonnie, and some of the others who was coming in and out, really didn't know what the hell was going on. When any of them would grab the phone, they would say whatever Lonnie or T-Mo yelled in the background.

"He ran to the store…he's out back in the garage…we had been meeting he fell asleep on Ann's couch and too tired to drive home…"

The excuses were numerous. After a while when even the clueless became clued in on Mathews behavior, he convinced them to stick with him because he would take them places. They believed him because Beyonce was the key focus of the group. Mathew played that trump card as far as he could take it. Beyonce, being a young girl, was almost completely oblivious to all this background mess going on around her.

When Mathew did stay the night at Ann's, he would be walking around when everyone else was sleeping. Sha Sha was very uncomfortable, so she started sleeping in Ann's room. What made her most uncomfortable was that Mathew was always looking at her and undressing her with his eyes. She was afraid that he might try to do something.

Mathew was completely out of control as if someone had given him some gas and he was pushing the "metal-to-the-peddle." Mathew was not stable and Ann was not feeling the best about how things were going. I was still communicating back and forth with my friend Al. So knowing this, Ann wanted to make a shift.

"Kenny, let's go back and talk to Al, and back door this shit."

"I'm with you on that Ann."

When I called Al back, he agreed to put up the funds. Attorney Darryl was waiting on us to come back with the girls to sign the agreement. It was a catch twenty-two because we needed the girls, and we could not figure out how to get the girls to go back to Atlanta to sign a new contract without Simmons and Mathew knowing. While Ann and I could sign as the managers, Attorney Darryl's position was that he could not go to one of the major labels and by-pass this deal that we were in with Silent Partner if he could not be sure we had the girls.

Ann and I did not want to "stir the pot" to alert them that we were after a side deal. Although were in the deal with Silent Partner, we could have gotten the money from Al for the studio and kept working. With the dynamics of the deal and the sensitivity around the matter, that put a hold on Al giving the funds. However, he continued to come over to see how things were progressing. His position was that the girls were hot and he was ready to go, but we just couldn't pull the strings without Mathew and Simmons knowing. Around the same time, the girls were also performing another showcase in New York for Elektra.

Even though the behind the scenes conversations were taking place, apparently the meetings with the attorney Darryl helped the Elektra deal get expedited. While we had agreed to sign with Elektra a while back, Elektra still had not come forward with the paperwork to sign. The reality was there was an agreement for a deal, but the deal had not closed. The conversations we were having on the side with Al and Attorney Darryl changed that reality because Elektra finally came to the table to sign us.

We finally signed with Elektra. We had a signing party and it was a much lighter time because finally we had a record deal and Ann felt that some of the stress had come off because she had accomplished what she was after. She got the deal and now she could really get the girls out there in a much bigger way. Getting this deal was a big accomplishment because we had a stable of artists and it was not just "The Dolls." Our position was all we needed was one deal and then we could get the other artists in the stable going.

The advance from Elektra came through, and as Ann had agreed, the advance went to Mathew to manage the distribution of funds. This advance was to cover the budget for the recording of the album. The girls moved to Atlanta to record. The advance that Elektra gave was to cover all production costs with mainstream producers to end up with a high-quality product.

"Look, I ain't gonna pay all these mutha fuckas that kind of money."

"Mathew, naturally the main stream producers are gonna cost more, but they are the best and you have name recognition which is going to make our shit better."

"Nigga, why in the fuck should I pay these got damned producers to do the same shit we can go get a no name mutha fucka who's just as good? Why should I when I can get people like Lonnie and all these other cats who can do it? I can pay them five thousand dollars and get the shit done and keep all this other advance money!"

"Mathew, you can't do this. You have to use the money what it is for."

"Look Ann, I ain't paying these mutha fuckas all this money to produce these songs. We got people who can do this!"

"We have to get the people they said get. We have to show the label that we used their money properly, Mathew."

"Shit, I got the advance, I'mma say how the shit gonna get spent, and I told you, Ann got damn it, I ain't payin' them mutha fuckas all that got damn money to do what Lonnie and 'em can do!"

The Making of a Child of Destiny

Mathew would not listen to reason, he ranted and raved and insisted on doing it his way. There was nothing that I or Ann could say to get him to cooperate. Lonnie was like a hungry gremlin so there was no way he would turn it down and even if he did, Mathew was still gonna find a way to short cut and short change the process.

Mathew went and got some local producers and some people around Lonnie that had songs that the girls recorded. While "The Dolls" were in Atlanta recording the album, Mathew spent a lot of time traveling back and forth. His marriage started to suffer drastically from the travel, the drug use and the rumors that Mathew was having affairs with a couple of women in Atlanta. While we were trying to manage all that was going on as best we could, things on Mathew's home front started to get completely out of hand. Although the girls were making progress on the album, the songs they were recording were "so/so." Ann knew that it was going to fail.

"Mathew, we must use this money to record using these other mainstream producers, so that they will help to push the album and their names would be on the album."

"Got damn it Ann what's your fuckin problem? I got this shit!"

"Mathew, you cannot mess over Elektra's money, you got to do it their way."

"Look mutha fucka, I got this shit! I'm controlling the money, and this is how we gonna do this shit!"

That fight with Ann and Mathew went on and on. Ann kept insisting that Mathew use the money for what it was intended, and Mathew kept threatening Ann and insisting on doing it his way. It was not too hard to see from where I was standing that Mathew was doing exactly what Lynn was doing whenever he got money.

While the songs were being produced, after about a year and a half of working on the recording of the album and getting polished as young artists with a major record label, the product was completed and finally turned over to Elektra. We listened to it, and Ann and I felt that it was no where near what a major label would expect. However, it was turned over to the label as requested. They reviewed it and after doing so decided that they could not push the album and consequently, dropped the girls. That album was completed but never released.

Ann had known that it would be a failure. Yet Mathew's habitual drug use, extramarital affairs, and ego hindered him from listening to reason. He and Ann stayed in constant conflict that entire time. While she knew that the record would need to be tightened up, she had no idea that the label would drop the girls. Everyone was devastated and extremely disappointed.

The Making of a Child of Destiny

When Elektra dropped the group, Mathew had no other avenues and thus crawled back to Ann with his "tail between his legs." So on top of messing up his marriage and his relationship with Ann and the management team, he also messed up with Silent Partners.

"Damn Ann, we are back to square one!"

"That mutha fuck is a fuck up! Now let me see his got damn ass try to threaten me over Beyonce's ass. At this point, we be lucky if anyone in the industry even gives us a second look."

"Damn! That mutha fucka!"

"Kenny, what we gonna do?"

So Ann, Mathew, and I had to have a pow-wow.

"Ann we need to get another deal…we have to…"

"Mutha fucka you messed up the last got damned deal!"

"Fuck you Kenny."

"Fuck you mutha fucka! You low down dirty stank ass mutha fucka!"

I was so pissed off watching Mathew back begging her to go make something happen, when he was the reason why everything was in the state it was in. I mumbled under my breath, "Punk ass mutha fucka…"

I needed a breather because I was very angry at the situation. Here we worked our butts off to make something happen, and had to tolerate his mess to make it happen, then he went and screwed the whole think up with his shit! I walked in the kitchen to take a pause from the meeting. Sha Sha was standing in the kitchen.

"What's up Kenny?"

"That punk ass mutha fucka…"

"You ain't gotta tell me shit…If you only knew how I felt about is stank ass."

"Baby girl you ain't never lied."

"I feel sorry for Tina. That mutha fucka is special. I can't stand that nigga. If you only knew how many times I wished someone would take his ass in alley somewhere and beat the shit out of him."

"Hell, I came real close to it…"

"I wanted to fuck him up myself. I was thinking about all sorts of diabolic shit. Why don't he just go the fuck away! Damn, do ya'll need Beyonce that damn bad that ya'll have to deal with his bullshit? Hell it don't seem worth it Kenny."

"Hell…sometimes I wonder Sha Sha."

I finally walked back in the room where Mathew and Ann were still talking. Ann was explaining that some major changes had to take place for us to continue.

"Tillman Management and Girls Tyme Entertainment cannot go any further, because people are already associating us with messing up the advance from Elektra."

The Making of a Child of Destiny

"That's true Ann. It's like the Star Search piece."

I looked at Mathew, rolled my eyes, and then said, "Association is a mutha fucka!"

"That's right Kenny," Ann said shaking her head.

"Hell, no major label is gonna give us any money, and regardless as to who fucked up, we are the management team and no major label is gonna give us the money."

Mathew sat there looking pitiful. I was completely pissed off I mumbled under my breath, "This mutha fucka come with a bogus ass album…"

Although Mathew completely messed up, we all re-grouped and formed a three-way partnership between Ann, Mathew and me. Mathew took fifty percent, while Ann and I each took twenty-five percent. Mathew's argument was that I was Ann's boy so it would give him a level playing field. Hence, this was the birth of Music World Entertainment. Ann kept Tillman Management for all the other acts. The girls however transferred to Music World.

Belfry stepped in again and provided more funding for Ann to keep things moving and to keep her from tapping into the boy's trust fund. We got back on the horse to make things happen again. Ann got back on the telephone with some of the former players, and Teresa resurfaced giving advice again. Things started to pop! The girls started coming around again and spending more time at Ann's house, but Sha Sha was not thrilled.

"Kenny, what the fuck...they trifling asses want to start coming back around talking about hey Aunt Sha. Fuck them bitches!"

"Girl you know you crazy."

"I can't stand no fake ass niggas Kenny. You know I am as real as they come, and this shit..."

"Girl, be cool. We tryin' to handle some business."

"Yeah, Kenny...I'mma handle some fuckin' business alright. They plastic! And that mutha fuckin Mathew...after all that bullshit, I hope Ann set that nigga straight!"

"Things are gonna roll alright Sha Sha."

"Alright Kenny, I am not on no bullshit. I've been here for Ann and my sentiments is that now that all they shit done fell through now they need her again and they wanna be all fake and shit. They are a bunch of got damned users!"

"You right."

"You damn right I'm right. That's right mutha fuckas...kiss her ass. Lick all up in her Black ass...I can't stand their asses Kenny."

"I know Sha Sha, but it's all good, girl."

Although things were starting to look up with the girls, it looks like things were moving forward again, along with that also came more stress. Ann ended up back at the hospital with another Lupus crisis. Sha Sha called me to let me know that Ann had been taken to the hospital. I rushed up to the hospital. We could see Ann's health deteriorating so it wasn't a total surprise that she had another crisis. Me being the cheerful support that I was, walked into her hospital room with the normal banter.

"Hey Blackie! Where your Black ass at? Your mama so Black, I bet when she get out the car, the oil light come on…"

I was loud as hell in the hospital cracking all kind of Black jokes. This was the first time that I came to see her up at the hospital and she wasn't really laughing. She gave some half shallow laugh, but not the from the gut laughter that she usually gave. "Kenny don't make me laugh. Please don't."

When I looked at her this time, it really hit me that this was very serious. I was taken aback and a little afraid.

"Kenny, I really wanna talk to you about something."

"What Dretta? What?"

"If something was to happen to me…"

"Ann, I don't wanna hear this shit! I'm not finna listen to this…Ain't a got damned thing gonna happen to you so I don't wanna hear that shit! We gonna get this shit done and we finna roll!"

"Kenny…"

"No Ann, you can't start thinkin' negative because we hit a bump in the road…and that's all it is…a bump in the road. We are where we need to be. We got it back in hand. We back in charge, they learned their lesson and ain't none of them runnin' shit and it all gotta come through you if they want this shit to happen. Let's just make sure we emphasize that a little more and I'll step up and handle the meetings and dealings with Mathew and kind of keep the pressure off."

"I know…I know…but if something was to happen to me…"

"Dretta, I really don't wanna hear this but…what?"

"Kenny, if something was to happen to me, I want you to raise my boys."

"Huh?"

"Yes, I want you to raise my boys. I want them to have a stable environment…and uh…I just want you to raise my boys. They love you. You like a dad to them anyway. I want you to rais the boys and then that way…You'll already know what percentages and my contract…so if something happens to me…you would run the estate and…you'll already know my percentage of…uh…with the new management company."

I sighed and said, "Yeah Ann."

The Making of a Child of Destiny

"I know you will take care of my boys and you'll give them their inheritance and all of that."

"Ann, why would you want me to do that? Why would you want me to raise your boys? You know…it would seem to me that your sisters and brothers…you know would be better."

"They would be but…a lot of times people be all about money, and…it don't necessarily be out of love…you know when something happens. I'm just sayin'…I'm not saying somebody's bad and wouldn't give my kids their money and all of that but…I do know folks act funny, especially your family. They will feed your children and everything else. When they turn eighteen they put them out and keep the inheritance and the kids ain't got shit."

"Well Ann, put it in a trust and…"

"I already have."

"Okay, I am not going to keep this conversation going. Quit talking like this and get your Black ass up and out of here, and cut all this other shit out."

This was a very touchy time and while I was attempting to make it a laughter situation, Ann was very serious.

"You finna have this conversation Kenny…"

"Alright Ann, we'll have it another time.

Ann spent a couple of days in the hospital. When she finally got home she rebounded a little faster this time. I was at her house when we went to the piano to talk.

"Dretta, you remember all that shit you were telling me when you had all those drugs in your system at the hospital?"

"I meant what I said. As a matter of fact, I'll tell your ass exactly what I said."

"Dretta, you are not gonna have to do this. I'm telling you with my gut, Bey, is gonna be on that some Michael Jackson shit! I'm telling you. When the Commodores sang Machine Gun, I say Lionel Ritchie was a star, so your ass ain't going no damn where. This is finna happen! It's gonna happen, we just gotta ride it out Dretta."

"Yeah."

"It's always darkest right before the sun comes out. I'm telling you. We are going to ride this thing out. Something good is gonna happen. Trust me on that. So let's just hang on in here…and keep rollin'."

"I'm tired of carrying all these folks. Mathew and Tina done broke up. They don't live together anymore. Now I'm having to send money and stuff over to Tina to kind of help her out so she can buy food to feed Beyonce and Solange."

"huhm."

"Shit Kenny, Tina footin' everything and having to work all these hours while his lazy and trifling ass done went and started living with this other damn woman."

"That's some shit."

"Yeah Kenny, and my ass is caught in the middle because I know who it is, I know where his Black ass is, and his ass still running here trying to have management meetings and shit. He needs to handle his got damned business. Now his family is in an apartment some damn where."

"Damn, Ann you shittin' me."

"No, and it pisses me off because while his ass is laying up with some got damn woman, I'm sending money over so Tina can feed the girls."

Ann recuperated and was getting her strength back. The girls were still coming around and appeared to be getting back to themselves. Ann felt like things were getting back to normal. Beyonce and Kelly were getting back to being Bey and Kelly. Just as Ann was feeling like things were getting back to a reasonable environment, all of a sudden a shocker hits the whole camp.

Not only were Mathew and Tina having problems, Cheryl and her husband were also breaking up. During this time every thing was extremely tense.

I called Dretta because it was so bad but nobody was saying anything.

"Dretta, what the fuck is going on?"

"Kenny, come by the house tonight."

"What's goin' on?"

"Just bring your ass by the house. I'll talk to you when you get here."

"Alright, I'll be by in a few."

"Talk to you then."

When I arrived at Ann's everybody was just quiet, too quiet.

"Dretta, why you so fuckin' quiet? Why you and Sha Sha all tight-lipped and shit? What the fuck is goin' on?"

"Kenny, you know that mutha fucka has been molesting LaTavia…"

"What! The police dude?"

"Yeah."

"You're lying, Ann."

"No, he's been molesting her for years."

"What in the fuck…"

All of this was just coming out. We just sat there.

"How in the hell could Cheryl not seen that this mutha fucka be messing with my baby?"

"Wow."

"I don't understand these hoes for mothers and…"

Ann went off. She was beyond upset.

"How can you be so fuckin in love with a man that you can't see he's fuckin' you and you can't see he's fuckin' with your baby?"

"Shit."

"How can you be that damn blind to this?"

Ann was so mad that she started planning things for LaTavia and then called Charlotte.

"Charlotte tell Cheryl to just go ahead and let LaTavia come and stay with me."

Charlotte replied.

"No Ann, she can come and stay with us."

Ann's goal was to make sure she got out the house and everything. While Cheryl and Charlotte was dealing with the family issue, Ann and I was like, "What the fuck!"

Then while me and Ann was sitting there, she had an "ah-ha" moment.

"Kenny, damn…I should have seen it. I should have seen it."

"What?"

"I should have seen it."

"What, Dretta?"

"Out of all the time we've been rehearsing, or they've been performing, LaTavia has always appeared to be more sensual than the other girls. Bey butt be buck wild. Kelly was stiff, Letoya had her funny way on stage, but LaTavia was always sensual with hers. I should have seen it. I should have seen something."

"Ann you can't see shit like that. You wouldn't expect a damn Houston police officer to go and be molesting his step-daughter, especially as public a persona as she's had. Hell she's been a model for a national product line and she's been in Girls Tyme and now The Dolls. She's been in Something Fresh. Hell Ann, she's been in all these groups for all this time. You can't expect no shit like that."

Cheryl kicked him out and the family worked to get LaTavia some counseling. The whole situation sent shockwaves through the entire camp. We asked all the questions. How do we deal with this? How do the girls deal with her? Will they treat her differently? These were the questions and concerns from all the parents and adults. The blessing was though that Beyonce had a way about her that when she really realized that LaTavia had been damaged, she was very compassionate.

Beyonce seemed as if she felt LaTavia's hurt. One of the reasons why I even love her today is because of this special way about her. She and LaTavia were already close, but Beyonce drew closer and more protective of her after learning about what had happened to her. I believe it was this situation that caused Beyonce to become like the mother hen of the group. It was like Beyonce said, "How dare them. How dare they hurt one of us?

After this, Beyonce started to develop thick skin. She was still sweet but she was more edgy and protective.

You could see Beyonce sort of grow up with LaTavia and the realization that this has happened. That buck wild personality that LaTavia had was still there, but you could see that the innocence had been stolen. She was no longer like a young girl with her innocence. People had come to know what had happened. So she was somewhat forced to be a young lady instead of a little girl. She was robbed of her virtue. She was forced to be a little more mature.

After it had come to light what had been happening to LaTavia, I really did not hear too much else about the case of LaTavia's step-father or what happened to him. The group didn't talk about it because we did not want LaTavia to be treated differently or for her to feel like something was wrong with her because of what happened to her. We actively worked to overcome this major issue and did our best to help LaTavia and the girls to overcome it as well.

HARD TO GET, EASY TO GO

The bad news about LaTavia left things somewhat gloomy and added to the extreme disappointment of being dropped by Elektra. Mathew was driven by his greed and worldly vices, mishandling money and spending it for frivolous pursuits of women, and drugs, and as a result costed us what we had worked so hard to achieve. He lost favor with Elektra executives. They were embarrassed by the whole situation and made sure everyone knew about the bogus album production. As a result, word ran through the industry like a brush fire and no one wanted anything to do with Girl's Tyme Entertainment because of Mathew's actions.

We were in a tough situation. As Mathew had worked tirelessly to usurp Ann's position as lead manager and when she gave him a little leeway, he screwed things up for everyone.

He forced his way into every conversation or negotiation that he could and used Beyonce as a pawn and bargaining tool. He was messy and this was one of the biggest messes so far. If there was one bright spot during that time, it was that this one messup he was unable to clean up, so it forced everyone to run back to Ann for guidance.

At the end of the day, Ann was the one making it happen and if the crew would have just followed her guidance without trying to compete to be the HNIC, then we would have undoubtedly been a lot further and would not have lost the first major deal we signed. Some people had their own agendas and were dead set on getting their agenda across regardless as to what the cost and believe me, it cost us big. It was apparent by the attitudes that they were not prepared to face the consequences, but as the saying goes – "It costs to be the boss!" Unfortunately, no one at the table was prepared to put out. So once again they expected Ann to come to the rescue. They wanted to know what she was going to do.

As Sha Sha said, "Now their Black asses wanna come and lick all up Ann's ass, sticking to Ann like flies to shit and begging like dogs for a bone. They act like some got-damned crying punk ass babies. What we gonna do Ann…How can we make it right Ann…Fuck You! Do it your damn self…Punk ass bitch!"

Sha Sha was upset because she saw first hand what was going on and how they handled Ann nearly bringing her to tears in Atlanta. That was enough for Sha Sha to tell them all where to go.

"See Kenny, those mutha fuckas can eat shit and die treating her like that. They get what the fuck they get. Mathew's ass is out for what Mathew can get and he don't give a damn about nobody but his got damned self or who get hurts in the process!"

"I want to make sure that Ann's stress level stays down because whenever this bullshit with Mathew is going on it stresses her out more."

"I know. And the thing is Kenny, since the Elektra thing went down; his ass has started lurking around even more. Somebody need to pull his crooked ass in an alley and whoop his mutha…fuckin'…ass!...Coke-head bastard!"

"Sha Sha, just keep helping Ann and doing what you can to minimize some of the stress off of her."

"Oh you don't have to worry about that. I'm just not sure how much longer I can stay, but I'll be here as long as I can! Bank on that!"

"Well I hope you have some time."

"Kenny to be honest, my major concern is Ann. Belfry left me here to help with his cousin and I don't give a shit about the group if it means Ann's health. And I sure in the hell don't give a flyin' fuck about Mathew and his bullshit."

"You don't like Mathew's ass very much I can see."

"What the fuck?...Boy...I throw this got-damned pan of hot water on your ass."

I laughed at Sha Sha's response to that statement. I knew that would wind her up more than she already was. I allowed her the room to vent. I realized that Sha Sha was young and although she was strong, what was going on got to her too. So I offered as much support as I could.

"Hell fuck ass naw! And your ass don't like him either, Kenny, and you know it!"

"Shit...He's a dirty mutha fucka, I give you that."

Sha Sha and I continued talking in Ann's kitchen while she was cooking. Ann was in her bedroom resting.

"You know he's on some bullshit and I ain't as forgiving as Ann's Black ass. Personally I think he's a user, and those girls are ungrateful as hell. I believe that cokehead bastard would sell Beyonce's little yellow ass on the got-damned street corner if he thought he could get away with it. And Kelly's Black ass got some damned nerve being all simple and shit for everything I hear Ann did for her nappy-headed ass."

"Oh yeah! Shit Mathew didn't hesitate to get rid of her when Darryl Simmons and 'em was closing the deal."

"All his ass is interested in is making a dollar, and he don't give a damn about how he does it either. Kenny, you should see how he be pushing up on Ann and pressuring her."

The Making of a Child of Destiny

"Damn, Sha. I see him in the meetings and how he is when I'm here, but you mean to tell me that mutha fucka comes around on other times with that bullshit."

"I ain't lying, you should see him. He's a creepy ass mutha fucka, and the way he be looking at her sometimes…ugh…It's creepy man."

"What?"

"Ann is too damn trusting and forgiving. She should have cut his ass off a long ago. She loves those girls though Kenny and I don't get it."

"Yeah Sha Sha, there's something to that though. She know they are gonna be stars and they keep saying to her that Beyonce is key. So she works hard to not let that slip through her fingers so she has to put up with his sorry ass."

"Mathew's ass is getting over on some trick ass shit Kenny, dangling Beyonce like a piece of meat, and he's willing to sell everyone else's ass down the river if it means more money for his dope-head ass! I tell you…I don't get it."

I sat there for a moment, thinking back on the intimate details Ann shared with me about her husband Dwight's death. I sighed and realized that Sha Sha had no clue about much of what was driving Ann.

"Yeah, you're right, Sha Sha."

"Hell Kenny, I might only be nineteen, but damn it doesn't take a rocket scientist to figure this shit is bullshit no matter how you sling it! This house is a revolving door. Do you know how many damn people come in and out of here? She's too nice to people and they don't deserve it. They fuck up her shit, then they go fuck up theirs, and then like some bad ass kids who got their ass kicked out on the street they wanna come running back to Ann to make it all better."

"Uhm."

"She buy them clothes, she pay their bills, she pay their got-damned mama and daddies' bills, she pay for them mutha fucka's bullshit while they flying all over the damn country like they got something…and for what? So those little bitches can stand over in a mutha fuckin' corner in Atlanta and laugh at her hand bleeding and shit! So those punk ass mutha fuckas can go behind her got damn back and try to cut her every chance they get and take her shit like she owe it to them?"

I just shook my head while Sha Sha was going off.

"Shit! Like I said, now that the Electra deal unraveled Mathew's ass been kissing all up in Ann's ass."

That day, Sha Sha and I ended up talking a while. It just goes to show that one person on a team can impact the entire team. When Mathew thought things were on

The Making of a Child of Destiny

the up with Elektra and was dealing with the no name producers, he had gone out and got a couple of acts that he intended to manage on his own and put them out there. However, when the situation crumbled, he was forced to look to Ann again for help.

Things were tighter in Ann's house. She started getting calls from Tina telling her the electricity was off at the apartment or she didn't have food for Beyonce and Solange. Ann was in a catch twenty-two because Mathew was at her house excessively, while Tina was busting her butt to make ends meet. So Ann shelled out money to help Mathew's family. Tina didn't get any money from him for support and whatever he got from Ann or stole; he spent it on women and drugs.

Given LaTavia's situation, Charlotte started coming around the house more to help Ann more. It was just in time because Sha Sha ended up having to move back to Tyler. Since Ann was by herself more again, Charlotte and her girls ended up spending more time at Ann's. Ann was working on regrouping with everything that went down. She reached out to me and Lonnie to see what the next move was. She asked me if I thought we should go back to Al in Atlanta to try to get the money for the studio.

When I reached out to Al, his attorney advised him against it and had turned a cold ear to the idea of giving us the money because of what happened with the Elektra advance. Al's attorney's position was that we did not know how to manage money. Mathew's dumb move, although we insisted against it, had killed the Elektra contract and shot down any funding through Al. Now with all these doors closing, creating Music World really became a smart move given what we were facing. With these conditions, no one was going to talk with us. We had to present a new brand and image as we did when the girls lost on Star Search.

As we were working to reorganize and pick up the pieces of what was left, Mathew started talking about taking Beyonce solo.

"You're gonna fuck the girl's life up Mathew. Leave her alone. She has the talent, we all know she has the talent. Leave got damn well alone mutha fucka. You done already fucked up her first major deal. Leave her tha fuck alone!"

"I know she got the talent, Ann, that's why she should go solo."

"You already fucked shit up, you done fucked up the money, don't fuck up her life too. Let me fix it. Let me think about it and I'll get back with you on how we need to move forward."

"Well, yo' ass need to hurry up and fix it."

"Mutha fucka, you broke it. Like I said, give me a got damn minute and let me see how to clean up your shit! Let me do what I need to do!"

"We need to make it happen now. People are talking bad about us and everything."

"Mutha fucka, they are talking bad about your gotdamned ass."

Ann still had a lot of support in the industry. Teresa began advising Ann again as she was loyal when everyone else had shied away. Willie D started coming by again helping Ann to chop it up. Ann had quite a few people at her beckon call that she could call to use as sounding boards in terms of how to regroup and how to go about rebuilding.

Willie D, Rob, and Dwayne Wiggins all pretty much said the same thing. "No fuckin' body gonna give you money anymore!" They said we would have to get a surrogate to basically take us back in. This gave us some leverage because no one wanted to put their name out there in terms of dealing with Mathew when they knew that he was the one who blew the last deal. Unfortunately we were branded too, but everyone knew we were under the situation of a parent with a star child.

"Okay Kenny, this is the word. We have a lot of people still on our side. They know Mathew's dumb ass don't know what the hell he is doing. They are still willing to work with us, but they don't want to touch Mathew."

"So what are we gonna do Ann?"

"Well the good thing is although we are in a partnership with this asshole, in the contract I am the Manager, so I still have control and the industry is back in my corner. They will not deal with him at all."

"Okay so what you saying?"

"Well, what I am saying, Kenny is that it is our game again now."

"Shit then Ann, what we waitin' on?"

"Lonnie mentioned to me that Dwayne is still interested in the girls and thought that we should go through his company."

I started laughing at how things were playing out, and then said to Ann, "Lonnie's slick ass is something. Mathew threw his ass under the bus so this is his way of getting back in charge I guess."

"Lonnie's ass is gonna be who he gonna be, Kenny, but, if this is the way we need to get back into the game, so be it!"

"Shit, Ann, I'm with you on that. Lonnie ain't been no issue with me. I know how to handle that mutha fucka. He ain't a problem. It's Mathew who is the real dirty-ass mutha fucka we gotta worry about and watch."

The Making of a Child of Destiny

"Lonnie ain't fuckin' on Mathew's ass. I think with the A & A shit and now this Elektra thing…hell I wouldn't be surprised at what Lonnie would do. He might be wishy-washy, but he ain't fooolin' with Mathew's ass, mark my word. Hell he know Mathew would sell him to a pack of wolves if it meant getting what he wanted."

"Girl, you ain't never lied. That mutha fucka ain't got a damn loyal bone in his body."

"I know we need to keep his ass at bay so he can't mess up another got-damned thing. I mean that shit!"

The group's name was changed again and they signed a contract individually as LaTavia, Beyonce, Kelly, and Letoya and collectively as Destiny under our newly-formed entity – Music World Management. We started meeting with Dwayne Wiggins of Tony, Toni, Tone. After hashing things out with Dwayne and his company, Grassroots Entertainment, Inc., located in Beverly Hills, California, and Music World Management entered into an agreement in the spring of nineteen ninety-four for them to be a surrogate and work with the girls. Grassroots Entertainment, Inc. were represented by the law firm of Bloom, Deckham, Hergog, and Cook. This was about six months after we were dropped by Elektra. LaTavia, Beyonce, Kelly, and Letoya were all around thirteen years of age at the time.

Lonnie and Ann met with Dwayne to iron out the production details and start production. They discussed who they would pitch to once the recording was done. The girls started flying back and forth to and from Oakland, California to work with Dwayne and Lonnie.

"Kenny we got things moving again. Teresa is on board and said that she would be willing to follow the deal."

"That's great Ann, but do you trust her? I mean, how are you feeling about that?"

"Kenny, shit Teresa is cool. It's Mathew's fucking ass and that got-damned Darryl Simmons and Sylvia Rhone that I don't trust. All three of those mutha fuckas stabbed me in my got-damned back! Hell Mathew wants to take over and since Beyonce is his daughter and Darryl and Sylvia feels she is the key, hell…"

"Alright, as long as you know."

"It's fine Kenny. As a matter of fact, Teresa advised me to take the deal to Tommy Mottola."

"He's the one at Columbia or rather Sony right?"

"Yeah. They are one and the same."

"Oh I remember that."

"Teresa has been helpful through all of this bullshit. She knew how I was embarrassed at the showcase."

"Wow, I didn't know that."

"Hell yeah, Kenny. She's been there."

The Making of a Child of Destiny

"Okay."

Although Teresa was not tied into the Elektra deal, she was consulting with Ann and remained loyal to her even when others bailed on her.

"I really believe that Simmons' ass was coaxing Mathew along. Hell TLC was crying about their shit as well."

"You know something was going on Ann, because Attorney Darryl was ready to do the deal from under their asses. He must know how they operate."

"All of them were probably some crooked ass mutha fuckas anyway. That's probably why they were so damn comfortable with Mathew's stankin ass."

"I hear you."

"Hell Kenny, all Mathew's ass-kissing and sweet talking ain't doing a got-damned thing! Do you know that mutha fucka still have the nerve to threaten about taking Beyonce out the group talking about going solo and shit!"

"What?"

"I told that no good dirty mutha fucka he don't scare me with that shit because ain't nobody foolin' with his greedy ass…bastard! Just pisses me off to even think about this shit. He don't listen to no got damned body. He wanna be the big man…ain't got a got-damned thing."

"He's still clowing Ann?"

"Hell yeah"

"Sha Sha mentioned he was coming by a whole lot more."

"That mutha fucka is here so got-damned much that you would think he lived here. Tina has called him numerous of times. That mutha fucka out fuckin' around and snorting shit that he can't even help his got-damned wife and kids keep the damn lights on or food on the damn table. And he has the nerve to threaten me…trifling ass mutha fucka."

"What…he tryin' to fuck up Beyonce's chances?"

"I told his ass to leave her alone; he is going to fuck up her shit to. That threatening shit ain't working with me no got-damned more. Everybody knows what he's about, and they don't want shit to do with him. He knows it too."

"That's why his ass harassing you with his bullshit. You need to stop him from coming over so much Ann."

"If I knew how to move his ass back, I would do it in a heartbeat, Kenny."

Ann was on a lot more medication around this time than before. While Charlotte and the girls came by more frequently, Cassey and I would stop through often. If Cassey couldn't make it, I would still pop over to her house. However, Ann was still alone quite a bit. So there were many times that Mathew was there and no one else was there with her.

I started to notice Ann acting a little funny and out of character.

"What the hell's wrong with you girl?"

"Oh no Kenny, I'm fine. I'm just handling a few things that's all."

"What the hell is going on? You haven't called me in a couple of days?"

"Kenny, I just really need to talk to you."

"Okay, your ass gonna have to do something because this shit ain't cool now."

Ann came over to the house. She kept trying to talk to me.

"Kenny, I need to talk to you about something."

"I figured that's why your Black ass was here girl."

"No seriously Kenny, we need to talk. We need to revisit that conversation from the hospital."

"Now Dretta, you're doing fine. We don't need to revisit this."

"Shut the hell up Kenny, I really do have something I need to tell you. I just really need somebody to talk to."

"Dretta, I really don't wanna have the conversation with you…"

"Ann, you know Kenny don't wanna talk about if something happened to you." Cassey said who was sitting there listening. "He can't handle it, that's just him."

Cassey motioned Ann into the kitchen. As they started to talk I was listening through a little opening to the kitchen.

"Cassey, if something was to happen to me...uh...I want you and Kenny to raise the boys."

"Ann, we're praying ain't nothing gonna happen to you. Honey things are gonna be fine. You're looking stronger, things are going better."

"I know Cass but I need to know that if something did happen that you and Kenny would do that for me. Every now and then I get sick. Nobody's there at the house with me and if something happened to me who gonna know. Hell if I wake up dead...I'm just saying if something happen."

Cassey was very comforting to Ann rubbin her back and stroking her lovingly. For the first time I listened intently, but neither Cassey nor Ann knew it. It was a tough situation because Ann was almost pleading Cassey to promise her that we would take care of the boys. As I continued to listen, they talked about the boys, the insurance.

"Cassey, the boys would financially be fine. I have their money in a trust for them. If something were to happen, Armon and Christopher will not be a financial burden on you and Kenny. I know you have Brian and they can be like big brothers to Brian."

"What about your family, Ann?...One of your sisters?"

"I know how families can be, Cassey. They'll get the boys and get the insurance and when they turn eighteen throw them out on the streets. I'm not saying that's what my family would do, but I know how people get to arguing and fighting and I just don't want that for my boys."

"Okay."

"I know you and Kenny will provide a stable environment for them. I know ya'll love the boys and the boys love ya'll. I know you won't throw them out on the streets or misuse their trust fund. Plus they will be in the general area where they can stay in the same school."

Cassey just continued to listen to Ann talk.

"That's all you would have to do is use some of the insurance money and buy a car for Armon and he can drive them back and forth to school from here."

"Ann, we don't need to talk about this, but whatever you need us to do you know we will do it."

"Thank you Cassey."

"Ann...why is this such an issue all of sudden...I mean, what is going on?"

Cassey started to seriously probe Ann's mind because she was sensing something else.

"Do you need me to start coming and staying at the house with you or Kenny to come over? What is it?"

"Well I need somebody."

"Why…"

"Cassey I've been having the weirdest dreams."

"What?"

"Well I would take my medicine and I would wake up as if I had been having sex."

Cassey started laughing. Then they both started laughing.

"Got damn it Ann, shit can't you tell if you been having sex?"

"Well hell Cassey, its been so damn long, shit I don't remember. I don't know if I'm having flashbacks and dreaming about Dwight or what the fuck is going on."

"Ann you know you crazy as hell, don't you?"

"No for real the other night…I realized someone was in the bed with me."

"What? Who?"

"I don't know…but…when I took my medicine, Mathew had came over and I told him that I was sleepy and too tired to even talk about business and that I had just taken my medicine."

"So what happened then?"

"Well he said he was just gonna lay on the couch. And I went back to my bedroom to lie down. As I was drifting, I saw a silhouette of someone walking toward me as I was nodding off."

"So…what happened, Ann?"

"Well this time I realized that I had had sex…"

"Ann, are you telling me you were taken advantage of?…Cause you know if you are sedated because of your medicine and someone had sex with you without your consent, you know what that is don't you?"

"What I'm saying is that…when I woke up, I realized I had sex, and I did not consent to having sex with anyone…but because I had my medicine I don't remember…and that the only person who was at my house at that time was Mathew, and I sure in the fuck did not give him my damn permission."

"Damn Ann why didn't you say something before?"

"Cassey, my medication puts me completely out of it when I take it. That is the only way that I can get some sleep. I really thought I had been dreaming those other times, until the other night. When I woke up I knew without a doubt that I had sexual intercourse because of what was going on down there."

I came into the kitchen after hearing that.

"What the fuck! Ann are you saying that Mathew took advantage of you?"

"I don't know Kenny because I don't remember. But I know my body and I do know that I had sex that night the way my body felt and the way my private parts felt."

"Shit!"

"Kenny, hell…when I take my medicine, I can't do anything. I can't move my muscles, I can't fight back. I can't do anything. I just don't know."

Ann was very upset.

"Well Dretta, that fuckin' explains why the last couple of times when I have been over to the house, this mutha fucka was walking through the house like he owns the got damned place…going into the refrigerator and all kinds of shit like that. Hell, nobody every did that before."

Cassey nodded her head in agreement.

"Hell, he's fuckin' comfortable and probably thinking, 'I'm sleeping with her or I did this for her, I can have my way.'"

"You don't think…"

I didn't even let Ann get her comment out before I started back up.

"That's what the mutha fucka act like! He act like he got a fuckin' run over the house and shit."

I was livid. At that point, all bets were off for me. Here my friend is on about thirty pills a day and busting her butt to make everybody successful and I hear this? All bets were off. I started pacing and drinking, walking back and forth into the kitchen where Ann and Cassey continued to talking. I said to myself, "I gotta do something. I gotta figure out a way to protect my friend. Okay this shit is happening...she can't control herself. I gotta put something in place."

At that time Cassey's younger brother Chauncey and his partner were staying with us. They were up and coming producers. Whoosy was also a choreographer. They were working with some local acts down in Acres Homes. When they came home that night, I had a conversation with them.

"Hey Chauncey man...Whoosy...I know ya'll lookin' for a place to stay. I need ya'll to get ya'll shit and I'mma take ya'll to a place where ya'll gonna stay."

Chauncey had already met Ann. He said, "What?"

"Get ya'll shit. Ya'll finna go over and stay with Ann, and I'll fill ya'll in on the ride over."

On the ride over, I explained to them that I had good reason to believe that Mathew is taking advantage of Ann when she is sedated from her medicine and to help run her day-to-day operations. I told them I needed them to spend the night there; make sure ain't no shit happening.

"I'll make sure Ann give you one of her cars to get around in. But if anyone of you has to be in the studio, at least one of you have to be here to help take care of the boys."

"No problem, ma'am. We got it."

"Thanks Chauncey."

"You cool with that Whoosy."

"You know me man."

Whoosy was from Mississipi and was country as hell, but he is good people.

"You gotta make sure Armon and Chris gets to school and all that."

"Alright."

We finally made it over to Ann's house and busted up in there like the police.

"Kenny, what the hell ya'll doing here?"

"Ann, you remember Chauncey, you remember Whoosy?"

"Yeah."

"Well, they need a place to stay and since you got an extra bedroom upstairs, I think that would be the perfect place for them to stay."

"Huh?"

"I think this will be the perfect damn place for them to stay!"

"Well Kenny you know…"

"Ann, I said they are gonna be staying here!"

"Uh…okay."

Ann just looked at me.

"Chauncey and Whoosy your bedroom is up there on the left. That's where ya'll be staying. Go put your shit down and then come on back down here so I can show you through here."

When they came back down, I walked them through the house and pointed out everything they needed to know.

"This is the refrigerator. This is the stove. This is Ann's bedroom. No fucking body but Armon and Chris goes in Ann's bedroom. Are we clear?"

They nodded.

"If there is anything ya'll need to say to Ann or if Ann needs your help, stand at the door and she'll invite you in. Are we clear?"

I went through the whole routine with them and basically took over the house.

"Here are the car keys. One of you is to be here at all times. Are we good?"

Chauncey was cool with it.

"Oh yeah Mo…yeah, yeah…"

Whoosy was fine as well. So Ann and I went to the piano. She was sitting and playing with the two fingers she had.

"What are you doing Kenny?"

"Dretta, I heard what you told Cat. Now…I'm been telling you all these fuckin' years just stick it out, just stick it out. But the shit done got out of hand. So…I'm just gonna put some things in place to make sure that you are okay."

"Okay."

"You already said that you can't take care of yourself when you're on the medicine. Sha Sha's gone and I don't wanna call her back up here. Hell, Chauncey and Whoosy ain't doin' shit. We can talk to Sha Sha about comin' back up at a later date. They gonna be here for six months or just until you get to feeling better."

Ann looked at me.

"Ann, are you sure?"

"Yeah."

"What I'm asking is are you sure he did this to you?"

She said, "Yeah."

I looked at her as if to motion the question again.

She said, "Yeah, I'm sure."

"Okay."

Belfry came back into town. I had heard from reliable sources that he was in fact a reputable drug dealer. He was driving through with some friends.

"Hey Belfry, let me talk to you."

"Yeah man, what's up."

"You ever give Mathew some cocaine or something?"

"No man, I ain't give that nigga shit! He ask me all the time but I never gave him none."

"I ain't gonna tell you what to do, but I'mma tell you this. If that mutha fucka ain't off balance, he gonna kill your cousin. I'm tellin' you point blank. I ain't telling you to give him drugs or what to do. If you ever around this mutha fucka and he acting funny, do what you gotta do. But keep that mutha fucka off balanced."

Belfry listened.

"I see his game now. It's at any cost now; he's out to get her. He's a crook. He wanna be close to her and have access to her to see what's going on. This mutha fucka's on some different shit."

"You really think so man?"

"That's what I think."

I didn't tell Belfry that Ann said that Mathew raped her. I just told him to keep him off balance if he is ever around.

Chauncey and Whoosy were set up at the house. They were cooking and taking the boys to school. Any studio time that needed to be coordinated, Chauncey would do it. He also handled the books and anything that dealt with Lonnie and Dwayne Wiggins. He became like Ann's secretary. Pretty much anything that needed to be done was handled the two of them were right there and they were good at it. Ann was so appreciative she gave them a shot on one of the girl's songs.

The first night that Chauncey and Whoosy were at the house after I went home, Mathew showed up. He bammed on the door and busted all in and saw Chauncey and Whoosy in there.

"Hey, who the hell are ya'll?"

"I'm Chauncey."

"I'm Whoosy."

"I'm Kenny's brother. We just moved in with Ann."

"What the hell ya'll just move in?"

"We helping Ann. Kenny asked us to come over and help out."

"What? Kenny!"

"Uh…uh…How the fuck he gonna tell ya'll you can come and stay over here?

"He told us we can come and stay and Andretta agreed so we are staying here."

"Oh…oh…so, what do ya'll do."

"Chauncey said, "I'mma producer."

Whoosy followed with, "I'm a choreographer and I write."

"That's good shit, let me hear something…you know maybe I can do some good things for you."

The Making of a Child of Destiny

Mathew got ready to try to walk into Ann's bedroom.

"He, Kenny said can't nobody go in the bedroom. Ann's sleep."

"I gotta talk to her fuckin' ass."

Whoosy said, "No man, naw man. Mo said naw!"

"What?"

"Mo said hell naw man! Can't nobody go in the damn room, so can't nobody go in the damn room man."

"You a country ass backwoods ass mutha fucka ain't you?"

"It's just like that. I gave Mo my word! And I don;'t need Mo and the boys comin' down on my ass. So you can't go in the room man. Yousa gonna have to talk to her when she wake up."

"Yeah, yeah…whatever. Tell her ass I'll be back to talk to her in the morning."

Everytime Mathew came over, they called me. I told them not to let him near her. It got to the point that I would pop up just as much as Mathew did. He would come by and see me or he would be there and I show up.

"What's up Mat whats going on?"

"Nothing. What the fuck you doing here man, ain't no meeting."

"What the fuck you doing here, since we ain't got no fuckin' meeting?"

"I…I…just came here to talk to Andretta!"

"I was too. That's funny ain't it?"

He wasn't feeling me and I wasn't feeling him, but we got his ass under control. It got so funny over time that Ann started laughing at the situation. Her health started to come back and she was regaining her strength. She wasn't trying to cook or anything, she mainly rested and kept the stress level low, while Chauncey and Whoosy blocked Mathew's access to her. She recuperated tremendously to the point of going back to work. Although, I was acting out of anger, the way we were handling the situation, helped to bring my friend back to a healthier state of being.

We kept working with Grassroots Entertainment. Soon, we started to hear from Sony. The girls had basically moved out to Oakland with Dwayne for a brief while to keep things moving forward in the most cost-effective way. Teresa was helping Ann to get things set up to keep them moving on. Finally a couple of nice tracks came about including No, No, No and Killing Time. When Ann called me to come over to listen to the tracks, I thought they were on point.

Dwayne along with Taura Stinson wrote the song Killing Time and Dwayne ended up negotiating to get it placed on the soundtrack for Men in Black. Everyone was getting excited. For a moment Ann had began to lose faith, but once her health returned, she too was back to herself. We started to get a lot of calls to get the girls to be in their videos and sing hooks on their projects. Things finally started to happen again but in a much bigger way. We were gaining momentum and Ann regained her health.

"Come on Kenny, let's go get this big record deal. I have a master. Now it's time to go get a deal."

"Well come on then, shit!"

"I've been talking with Teresa and I started talking with an executive at Columbia/Sony Records."

Ann was excited that the executive loved what he heard. He liked the girls, and he thought that we had something. He said to Ann, "I am not about to give you all a four hundred thousand dollar advance for nothing when one of the girl's daddy already blew the money from the Elektra deal. I'm not going to do it!"

Ann asked the executive, "What do I need to do?"

"I don't know Ann, you have to go figure that one out."

After the call with the executive, Ann then called me.

"Kenny, what we gonna do? I got four hundred fuckin' thousand dollars, a major record deal, he loves everything, but I can't get the damn deal signed."

"What?"

"Teresa banging her head up against a wall trying to figure out what we gonna do."

"Dretta, uh…well…they ain't gonna give us the money. That mutha fucka fucked that money up! We know that for a fact."

"Yeah."

"Now, what would we do if we were going to buy a car, and the mutha fucka told us that we didn't have the credit to get the car, Dretta? What do we do? Come on Dretta…we Black folks, what do we do?…What we do Dretta?"

"We go get a co-signer."

"There's your answer."

"Huh?"

I looked at her until she got it. Then it hit her.

"You Black mutha fucka, you're right!"

Ann called Teresa and she thought it sounded like a great idea. Teresa said, "But Ann, it gotta be somebody we trust because it's going to be advanced to that particular person that we get to co-sign with us."

Her thing was she could go get some artist like R. Kelly to sign and he could come give us some bullshit music and we're right back where we were like with the other deal. The conversation went all the way round. Ann pitched the idea to Lonnie then to Dwayne. There was already a partnership agreement in place, so who better to

The Making of a Child of Destiny

do it than Dwayne Wiggins. So we took the deal under the Grassroots banner and said, "Okay ladies and gentleman, here's Destiny."

Ann went and got the deal, and because we got with Dwayne Wiggins, Columbia/Sony awarded us the contract for Destiny as well as the advance of four hundred thousand dollars.

She told Dwayne, "Okay, Dwayne, you have the advance. Now you know we have to get the album recorded with reputable people, and give some of the advance to the girls."

Ann continued on with the ground rules for the agreement.

"I want the master for every recording to make sure things go the way they are supposed to go and you do what needs to be done. This way, I can make sure you don't give me no bullshit!"

Dwayne agreed.

"I'll have the master recordings to show Columbia/Sony executives that I either approved or disapproved of the recordings, and I can go sound the alarm if you start bull-shitting."

Ann was not tripping about the money. She wanted to make sure that everything went the way it was supposed to go. Immediately after this happened, Mathew stepped back into the picture.

"I need the advance for the girls. I need to make sure they are okay and that they are compensated."

Ann and Mathew fought over how the advance should go. Mathew continued pressuring, Ann until she agreed to give him the fifty thousand dollars to distribute equally among the girls. She was not concerned because she knew that Dwayne understood that she was due her portion from the deal as well as future royalties from Destiny and the album sales. Mathew was steady trying to get his hands on the advance.

"I need that damn money."

"No you're not getting it. We're going through the proper channels."

It was a constant battle with Mathew once money was seen. Ann was more focused on getting the other acts now built up. Her whole thing was to solidify everything and get the girls out there. Her conversations with me were about the business and making it stick now that we had signed with Columbia/Sony.

"Kenny, let's get the videos done, and everything else done that need to get done."

"Okay."

"We can take the money from that and I need you to be my road manager and be my eyes while the girls are on tour."

"Alright. Shit I'm feeling you. Hell we rollin'."

The Making of a Child of Destiny

We started to build and map out the plans. We were still waiting on the money. Then Dwayne was said, "Well Ann, I got to send fifty thousand dollars your way, what do you want me to do with it? Do you want me to send it to you?"

"No, the girls have waited, let's get it to them. Give it to Mathew to let them split it."

"I will send the other part after this second wave when I send the next recordings."

"Dwayne, I'm okay for now, I'll get mine my money then. I can wait. You know. Everbody still a little hungry."

Ann was still financially okay. Her position was to take the first advance and give it to the girls, they earned it. She wanted to put a couple of dollars in their pocket. Mathew wanted to be all big and everything so she handed the money over to him and instructed him on how to distribute it. He didn't like that too well. He wanted complete control. Although Chauncey and Whoosy were still at the house, there were times where neither of them could be there. Since Ann had her strength back, it wasn't too much of a concern.

Mathew would be hiding behind trees and things to try to catch her by herself. He started fighting and pressuring Ann again over the money now that he knew money was coming.

"Ann you got any more got damned money from old boy?"

"Mathew, I put the fucking deal together. You ain't did shit. You need to get the fuck on before you fuck up this deal like you did the last one. Be the fuck quiet and let me handle it."

"I got a deal and I've been talking to people and I'mma take Beyonce out the group. In fact, I have guardianship over all the girls."

"Mathew, you know I just got out the hospital, I'm not for your shit today!"

"I don't give a fuck about you just gettin' out the hospital."

Unbeknownst to Ann, Mathew had been demanding the parents turn over guardianship. Mind you, he still had been telling them that he was in charge and he wasn't telling them what Ann had been doing to secure the deals. So, the parents were thinking everything going on was because of him. They were only going to rehearsals and hearing from Mathew and David. Mathew brought some paperwork over to show Ann. Kelly's mother had given him guardianship. Of course he already had guardianship of Beyonce, and he had two contracts pending where he was trying to get Pam and Cheryl to sign. The contracts were already documented and legally drawn up.

The Making of a Child of Destiny

"This is what I have and I will have full guardianship of all the girls by the weekend. They are still minors and I'm taking the group from you right now and I'll kill this deal and go get it myself."

Mathew came with all sorts of threats. This went on for about a week. He was making demand-after-demand, particularly as it pertained to money. I am not sure what all happened with that situation, but what I do know is that Ann eventually conceded. Her health began to deteriorate again. As Chauncey and Whoosey's production company picked up steam, they weren't at the house as much. Consequently, Mathew's visits increased.

Because of the guardianship papers, Ann agreed to partner with him again, and give him the lead on management of the girls creating a fifteen/five split of the management partnership for the lifetime of Destiny Child. In other words, Ann would receive five percent of the management royalties for the lifetime of the girls, while Mathew received fifteen.

"Kenny, I'mma let this mutha fucka think he's in charge, but we get fifty percent of the management royalties for the lifetime of the group. But I'mma show his ass one last time. When the final album is done, then it's will be turned over to Tommy Motolla. I'mma show his ass who he gotta go through to get it turned over to finalize the deal."

Ann had worked the deal where she knew she was going to have to turn the masters over to the label once all the songs were complete.

"This mutha fucka is runnin' around like he's the got-damned shit. I'mma have one last laugh on his ass!"

OUR SECOND CHANCE

Over the course of two years we were working very hard on getting the ball rolling and the recordings done so that Ann could have something to turn over to Columbia/Sony after signing with Grassroots. While Mathew was still being Mathew Ann knew at the end of the day that she would get the masters for each of the songs from Grassroots because that was the arrangement. During that two-year period, things were stagnant off and on and it wasn't as easy a sailing as one might have hoped it to be. There were many conversations with Columbia/Sony and Grassroots in putting things in order.

We had to iron out many details including the travel back and forth to Oakland, how we would structure things so that it could work for everyone involved, and take Ann's health into consideration. Things were not as peachy as it appeared to those who were not behind the scenes. It was hard work. For Ann it truly was a labor of love and things did not move nearly as fast as we wanted.

Because things moved slower with the deal, the advance took a little longer to come through. One of Ann's worst nightmares came upon her – to go into the boys' inheritance. More monies were needed to get the girls back and forth to Oakland and for other expenses. So, with the deal not coming in a timely manner forced Ann to use some of the boy's money from their trust; but things changed fast. Everyone was excited and looking forward to what was to come. Ann started talking seriously to Tommy Motolla and working the deal, hashing things out in terms of the type of deal it would be. Tommy liked what was recorded by Dwayne. Tommy and Ann worked everything out. By this time we were rolling into nineteen ninety-seven. The album Destiny was being recorded and the girls were floating on "cloud nine." Everyone was chanting "Destiny, Destiny, Destiny…" Because there was already an R & B disco type all girls group from the seventies named Destiny, there was a discrepancy when it came time to signing the record deal with Columbia/Sony. The label felt that there could be some confusion on the name and confusion in terms of which group was which. The other group was Alton McClain and Destiny.

    As we discussed the matter, we decided that we could not just use the name Destiny. As we threw it around, Tina came up with Destiny Child from the bible. So, Ann took the name to Columbia/Sony and we ended up signing the contract with Columbia/Sony under the name of Destiny's Child.

Once the contract was signed, Mathew started back up with that same mess about being in charge. This time Ann was not as hot around the collar as before. She knew it was coming. She knew he was going to react and do the same shit that he did with the Elektra deal. She laughed as if it were a joke to her.

"Kenny, here this mutha fucka come again. Here he comes again."

"What?"

"I done got the fuckin' deal, now he wanna step back to the front like he doing all this shit. He's a fuckin' fuck up but wanna act like he's Mr. Big Shit and running shit."

"Uhm."

"...But I got something for his ass this time!"

"What?"

"Well, he's talkin' all that shit but when the time comes for the album to go back to Columbia/Sony, guess who got the fuckin' master?"

"Who?"

"I do!"

"What?"

"I got the fuckin' masters and when the shit is done, we gonna have a listening party...me and you. Fuck all those other mutha fuckas, just me and you gonna have our own got damn party to hear it."

"Well shit, cool! I'll come on over to hear the tracks."

"Yeah, I have the masters."

When the payment from the first advance came, Ann wanted others to get their money first since so much time had passed. Although Ann was upon hard times herself, she was still willing to wait until another allotment came through because she knew that push/came/to/shove she had access to resources in an emergency situation. She let the first advance money go to the girls and others to tie them over, while she used the boys' money to tie her and her family over.

Although this was going on and her health was not one hundred percent, she was still upbeat. After going into the boys' inheritance, Ann was confronted with her own bills piling up. One Saturday evening when I was cooking at home, I got a call from Ann.

"Hey Kenny, whatcha doing?"

"Dretta, you know I'm over here barbequing."

"Oh okay."

"What's up baby girl?"

"Well, I'm waiting on my money to come on Monday. You know, me and the boys over here hungry."

"Shit Ann, how in the hell you hungry and you ain't got money and you done paid all these other fuckers' bills…What did you do with the advance?"

The Making of a Child of Destiny

"I gave Mathew the advance and…well he was gonna divy it up and make sure everyone got something."

"You trust that son of bitch again? What the hell is wrong with you?"

"No, no Kenny listen…there was only so much… and I broke everything down exactly how it should be split and Mathew would only get part of it."

Ann gave me all the details of how it was broken down and once she explained to me it made sense.

"Kenny, I will get mine on the next wave. I am cool with that. I only took a loan out of my boys' money to tie me over until the next payout came from Dwayne, and then I was going to pay it back."

"Girl, I got so much food over here, why don't ya'll just come on over?"

"Okay, then we on our way."

At that time I was financially doing okay. Things were flowing pretty well for Cassey and me. When Ann and the boys came over, we had a good time. After that weekend of having Ann and the boys over to eat with us, it developed into a routine almost every weekend. It became like our family ritual. I would buy the food and Ann and the boys came by. This drew our families even closer together. Brian, Armon, and Christopher were like brothers. Ann and Cassey got along well. We all became a close knit family.

"Shit, I had to go into the boys' savings to keep things moving until I get my money from the deal."

"Ann I don't see how you do it."

"I sometimes wonder myself Cass."

"Dretta you know if you need something me and Kenny got it!"

"Naw we good…but his ass can keep this barbeque going."

Ann and Cassey laughed. Then Cassey said, "Shit, you ain't never lied."

They both continued to laugh as they were eating ribs. I continued over at the grill listening to them and making jokes.

Time passed and when it came time for the next payment to come from Dwayne, Ann was anticipating getting her portion from that allotment. However, for whatever reason, the monies did not come. That placed Ann in a situation again where she had to go back into the boys' inheritance a second time. Ann was postponing bills and buying time with bill collectors waiting on this payment and it didn't come. Ann was so upset and got irate. She started cursing everybody out at that point.

"Ya'll mutha fuckas fucking around, now ya'll fuckin' with my boys' money. What's the got damn problem Dwayne? Now I gotta go back and get some money from my children to deal with this shit, cause ya'll asses fuckin' me around!"

Ann was getting agitated and the stress was getting to her. She came over during our weekly barbeque night and she was still livid.

"Dretta, what are you so pissed about?"

"Kenny, them mutha fuckas messing with my got damn money."

"Whatcha mean?"

"You know them tired ass mutha fuckas still haven't given me the advance?"

"What?"

"They are on some bullshit Kenny and now I had to go right back into my boys' money."

"Dretta, you know I told you that me and Cass got you and the boys."

"No Kenny! I know you mean well. But hell, I still have money to pay you from the advance as well."

"Ann you know I ain't worried about that. When it comes, it comes. I know you will handle your business. Hell your Black ass won't take it from me, what about Belfry?"

"No he is tapped out, and ain't trying to give me no more money. I went ahead and took out another loan. So I'mma give them a chance to get this thing right."

Ann was able to keep things moving a little longer with the second loan from the boys inheritance. She calmed herself down and kept moving forward. Then one day she got a call from one of the team members who happened to stop by Mathew's house. Ann called me extremely upset.

"Kenny, get your ass over here right now!"

"What's wrong?"

"Just come over."

"Alright, alright, I'm on my way. Hell give me about fifteen minutes."

When I arrived at Ann's she was pacing the floor and very upset.

"Kenny, one the team members just called me about thirty minutes ago with some fuckin' bullshit!"

"What Dretta? Calm down shit so I can hear your Black ass."

"Kenny this ain't no got damn play time."

"What's his name called me and said he happened to stop by Mathew's house and when he walked in he saw Mathew in his underwear and Kelly was in the bathroom. It looked inappropriate."

Ann was talking so fast in giving the details of what was said to her that I had to tell her to slow down.

"Dretta, slow your ass down…now what you say about something inappropriate going on?

"I don't know what the fuck is going on over at the Knowles' house. One minute Tina is kicking Mathew's trifling ass out, the next minute she is taking his ass back."

"Dretta, calm your ass down so I can get what you are saying."

"Shit Kenny, the word from one of the team members is that there's some inappropriate shit going on between Mathew and Kelly and we need to watch his ass with these damn girls. He said he popped up and walked into something going on that didn't look right."

"Where was Tina and the other two girls?"

"Hell I don't know! He just called and told me what he saw and said it didn't look right to him. I now that son of a bitch is crazy, but I know he better not be messing with that little girl!"

"I know that mutha fucka has done some low-down shit, and even given your situation on what may have happened to you, Ann, but that mutha fucka is not that damn crazy!...I know he ain't that fuckin' crazy!"

"Kelly is really timid, man, and she…"

"…yeah but, Dretta, no…if you look back…Tavia had some tell-tale signs that you could kind have looked for. She was a little more seductive and everything. You don't get that from Kelly."

"Kenny, I sure hope not."

Ann and I held that information close to the chest. Ann spoke discretely with the other adult members outside of Mathew and asked them to be very observant and watchful to see if there was any sign of inappropriate behavior going.

Ann said, "Look, the last thing we want to get out is that we have some internal bullshit like this going on here in our camp from someone on the management team."

None of us were sure as to what really happened, but we were going to make sure as far as within our scope of control and power of what wasn't going to happen if we could help it. However, we could not control what happened behind close doors at the Knowles' house.

As Ann and I examined what may have been going on, we saw a disparity in the treatment of Kelly compared to the other girls. Mathew appeared to be extremely hard on Kelly. He was verbally and emotionally abusive to her. It seemed that he was always mad at her, telling her things like, "You can never do nothing right!"

I felt that if he was messing with her, it would seem like he would let her "have her way," but he was very hard on her. I personally felt he was aggressive with Kelly and treated her differently in that he was dominant toward her especially. It could have been because her mother was not present. Who knows, but we were keeping a look out and it was a hard signal to see. What many of us saw and discussed was that he was extra mean to Kelly. We talked amongst ourselves in private meetings to see who saw what.

"That son of a bitch is overly mean to her for whatever reason. But hell, I don't see no touchy-feely."

"Well, I think there's an anger there that can be taken either way if you ask me."

"Well shit, if he's fuckin' with her, this is his dominance over her."

"What do you think Kenny?"

"Ann, to me, a lot of times that Mathew's screaming at Kelly, she's not even messing up, so I don't know. His ass is mean as hell to her in my opinion."

As we listened to everyone's take on the situation, Ann and I always had our one-to-one conversations about it. We thought that if something inappropriate was going on when no one was looking, that maybe this was his way of humiliating in the public and showing her that he was in charge, with the thoughts of something like, "no one's gonna listen to you anyway."

It was really hard to discern the truth in that particular situation. Andretta was going to confront Mathew, but my concern was not knowing what sort of sparks might fly as a result of the confrontation.

"Ann, we are in the thick of the music deal and we don't need no extra shit with Mathew's name associated with it!"

"Why you say that?"

"If word gets out that something like this is going on and Mathew is tied to it, there's no way they're gonna keep us."

"Well after the Elektra fuck up, you might be right!"

Ann was not willing to rock that boat, knowing Mathew's temperament and instability.

With all the madness going on within our camp, I decided to call my family and see how they were. My older sister Louise and I were very close and she was always encouraging so I wanted to hear her voice and get a little boost from dealing with all this stuff. It was on a Tuesday, and I hadn't spoken with my mom and sisters for some time. When I called Indianapolis, my sister Armelda answered the telephone and said that Louise and my mother all went to the church. So I called up to the Greater Shepherd Missionary Baptist Church where my uncle Shep Banks was the pastor. My cousin Jeanette answered the telephone.

"Hey, this is Kenny, is my mom or any of my family there?"

"Uh, hey Kenny, yes Aunt Liz is here and Louise is here."

"Well, let me speak to Louise."

Louise came to the telephone and we talked for a good minute.

"Girl, I'm so proud of you."

"Man, I'm proud of you. I love you man. It's been too long, but I know you are doing some great things so I will let you off the hook."

"Oh."

"No Bae, I wanna tell you something. You have been the best brother I could've had. I love you, I love you, I love you."

"I love you too girl!"

"No matter what happens, you gonna be somebody famous, and I know it and I know you know you gonna do great things."

"I love you too. You gonna do good too."

My sister Louise and I left things just like that. It made me feel good and took my mind off of some of the mess that was going on in Houston. It was good to hear her voice and as always she knew the right things to say and when to say them. I hung up the telephone feeling better about things.

That Thursday night, I got a call from my niece telling me that my sister Louise died in a car wreck. I was devastated and in disbelief. I had just spoken with her two days prior. After that news, I flew out to Indianapolis for her funeral. On the flight I was fine, but when the plane went into the descent, that is when it actually hit me, that I was going to bury my sister. I completely lost it on the plane. People were asking, "Is he gonna be okay? Can we do anything for him?"

After the funeral, I went into a state of depression and walked through life during that time in a daze. I withdrew from everyone and everything.

Upon my return, Ann kept calling and checking to see how I was doing. I wouldn't talk to her nor see her. She kept asking Cassey how I was doing and if I needed anything. Cassey would talk to Ann, but I remained withdrawn. Everyone else pretty much left me alone and gave me the space to grieve in my own way. One day, Ann came by while I was moping around the house and the garage. I was pitiful and feeling down dealing with the pain of losing my big sister. I had painted a mural on the entire wall of the garage of what heaven looked like and where I thought she was. It was my way of grieving with the loss of Louise. Ann looked at me and looked at that big ass picture on the wall and had a look on her face like, "How in the hell am I gonna reach this nigga."

I was scruffy and looked like I had not seen the light of day in forever. I had been in a state of depression after my sister's death.

"Kenny, there's some exciting stuff going on. Things are coming around. I need to talk to you. How are you doing?"

"Well Dretta, I'm okay."

"Kenny, you got to come out of this. You just got to. We gotta keep going."

"Dretta, I know, I know."

"Well…"

"But…Louise was always that sister who told me I could do it."

"I understand Kenny. I really do, but you have to keep going."

"Louise was the type that she just wanted me to get on a bus and go to California because she knew I could make it."

I took a deep breath and Ann just listened as I talked about Louise. As I told her how Louise's accident happened, Ann saw the irony of how our lives were truly crossed. My sister was leaving my sister Amelda's house on her way to church when the accident occurred. Ann recalled how she and Dwight were leaving her sister's house after leaving church when their accident occurred. My sister was forty-two when she died along with the driver's seven-year-old daughter. Ann then compared this to Dwight and Shawna dying in her tragic accident. The finally irony was as my sister died at the corner near my sister Amelda's house as my sister and brother ran to see Louise take her last breath. This reminded Ann of stories of her sister telling her of Shawna and Dwight taking their last breath. As I often reflected back on the last time I spoke with Louise, I could not help but to think that possibly she knew somewhere deep down that she was not going to be around.

"Kenny, I know it's hard, but I need you. You gotta come on out of this."

"Dretta, you don't understand. Do you know how my sister died?"

"Kenny, I understand exactly what you're feeling."

"Dretta, how in the fuck do you understand what I'm feeling?"

Ann gave me a looked of disbelief, then said, "Really? Really mutha fucka?"

"Oh, yeah…I forgot."

"Look, its' gonna take a minute, but you can't quit. You can't give up."

I just listened to Ann for a moment.

"Kenny, I know exactly where you are."

"I ain't giving up, Ann, it's just…"

"…Well then get your ass on up. You know she wanted you to do something famous and big. So let's get on up and do something famous and big."

"Okay, Ann…you think you bad mutha fucka…you ain't the boss of me."

After we laughed, Ann said, "Look, I tell you what…can you barbeque for me next weekend?"

"Yeah, let's do that."

"Come by the house this week and I got something to share with you."

After that conversation with Ann, I started to come out of my depression. I got back to the point of functioning and back into the swing of things. Ann was nudging me telling me what was going on with Dwayne Wiggins and the new music.

"We have been working. Things are going good Kenny. We got some nice songs coming out."

"That's good, Dretta."

"Just come over later, I got something to show you."

"What now Ann?"

"You know the song Killing Time, which the girls recoreded?"

"Yeah?"

"Well, that's the one Dwayne Wiggins did. It's gonna be on the Men in Black movie soundtrack."

"What! Okay! That's great!"

I was happy, but I was not as happy as Ann wanted me to be. I was still coping, and finding it difficult to jump for joy. Ann could see right through me and it bothered her because I was not as jolly, and her friend and partner was not as fully present at that moment as I normally would've been under different circumstances. It wasn't "Blackie this or Blackie that." I was strictly professional with her and giving short unemotional answers and comments.

"That's great. Okay, good…"

Because of the promise of having one of our songs on the soundtrack for a major motion picture, things were looking very favorable and everything was in place to make this major deal a success. Teresa was still talking with Columbia/Sony for us, ensuring them we were on point, and still advising Ann on our next moves. She was even ecstatic about it. The girls were happy and hanging out with Dwayne Wiggins and other celebrities from Tony, Tone, Toni. They were also starting to get calls to do cameos in hooks for a lot of the local Houston and New Orleans rappers. The excitement for the album was building. Everything was just starting to fall in place.

During this time, Mathew was trying to wedge his way in between Ann and Dwayne Wiggins. However,

Lonnie was in California with Dwayne and was telling Mathew, "No you taking your ass through Ann."

Mathew could not really weasel all the way in because Lonnie knew he would get kicked to the curb like in the Elektra deal. To protect himself, Lonnie used his connection with Dwayne as leverage. Ann also saw to protect herself, as in the back of her mind she knew that her health was deteriorating. So, she signed a new deal with Mathew to secure her and her boy's future.

"Kenny, I signed a new deal with Mathew."

"What?"

"Well…at the end of the day he is Beyonce's father and she is the star of this group. It's just that whatever happens…with me or with this deal, for the lifetime, as far as the management is concerned, I'mma be fifty percent manager for the lifetime of the group."

"That's smart as hell, Ann."

"Then, Mathew will get his half. Of course you know…you get half of mine."

"Dretta, whatever…when some money come through, we'll deal with that then."

"No, that's the way it's set up."

"Okay, fine."

"Here, Kenny, sign this."

Ann handed me a contract for the first time to sign as all of our other agreements were contracts we reviewed but never signed. In the contract, it certified my twenty-five percent ownership Music World. I signed the contract and then told her to hold on to it.

"No, you take your copy."

"Andretta, we don't have to go through this."

A couple of days went by and Ann gave me my copy of the contract. It was in an envelope and until this day I haven't even opened it to look at it again since signing it. I went home and put it in my box. I said to myself, "Man, this is really finna happen."

Ann and I had gone through everything and we did everything. Our word was good enough for each other. For the first time, Ann was adamant that we sign something. The excitement in me started to build by this time and I started drawing logos for Music World. I would take the drawings to the meetings and show the team our logos. I used to draw a globe or the world spinning on a needle on top of a record and the record was on fire. Our slogan was "Music World is taking over the world."

We had it all mapped out. Everyone was starting to get their place now. We knew that Mathew wasn't going away and we had to pacify him. We knew that he was working with the girls, so Ann and I made sure the rest of the team was strong to compensate for anything he might do to the detriment of the deal and camp. Ann started to tighten things up. She used Lonnie for some of the production so he would be credited on the album as a reward for riding with the team the whole way. David was there as the vocal coach. I was going to be the road manager for the girls and to be her eyes on the road. I really didn't want to do it, but I agreed.

PLAY IT AGAIN

The team was in place and the excitement was building. The girls were back and forth to Oakland recording the album. The results of some of the production were coming forth. Ann received the masters for about half of the album from Dwayne. In her excitement, she called me one day just as tickled, laughing.

"Kenny, Kenny!"

"What girl?"

"I got some of the music!"

"What!"

"Yes, I got some of the masters. I got some of the musics for the recording already! Oh my God, we got some hits, we got some hits!"

"Alright Ann, whatever whatever."

"Get your ass over here!"

"Shit girl, I ain't got time for that right now. I got stuff to do. I gotta cook and shit…"

"Just get your ass on over here!"

"Hell, I gotta stop and get me some beer or something if I gotta come and sit with your Black ass."

"I already got it, come on."

"Oh hell alright... You know you get on my damn nerves don't you."

"Fuck you nigga, just get your Black ass on over here."

"I'm on my way."

When I made it to Ann's house, she was just giggling like a little girl.

"Ann, what the hell..."

"Ok, here, get you some beer first...come on."

She led me into the kitchen. I looked around shocked. Ann had cooked a spread. It was the first time that she had cooked in forever so I was like. "What in the hell is going on up in here?"

Ann had cooked a spread for a stadium which included her famous smothered rice and pork chops.

"Nigga, you done lost your ever-lovin' mind."

"Just get your beer, get your food and sit your ass down."

So I fixed my plate, got the beer and went and sat down.

"Now you ready?"

"Yeah girl, now what."

"Listen."

Ann played the song that went, "Can you say no, no, no, no, no...Can you say yeah, yeah, yeah, yeah, yeah, yeah..."

It was a very slow version of the song from what you hear today instead of the fast rap. When I heard the song, I was shocked. It was on another level from the Elektra tracks.

"That is nice!"

"I know Kenny."

"You can hear the maturity of the girls. You can hear the changes in them."

"There is a big difference between these and all the other recordings. We got something here."

"I have to say we do. Man, Bey's voice is a lot stronger. The harmonies are much tighter than before."

"Let's listen to some more."

"Shit then girl, bring 'em on! I didn't know you were doing it like that."

Ann laughed and then we listened to several other songs on the album. When we got to the last one of tracks, we then listened to a song entitled, My Time Has Come.

"I just love this song, Kenny. Oh I just love this one."

After she played that song, she went back to No No No No No, Yeah Yeah Yeah Yeah Yeah, then back to My Time Has Come. Ann kept playing those two songs over and over again.

"Dretta…Why you keep playing the same two damn songs? You got seven songs let's listen to all of them."

"No! I just love these…"

We kept listening to those same two songs, laughing and talking. She got so excited and we went back and forth between those two songs.

"Ann, I ain't finna listen to these two fucking songs no got-damned more now."

She played No, No, No, No, No again like she didn't hear a word I said. Then she said, "Give me one of them damn beers!"

"Dretta, now you know your Black ass ain't supposed to be dranking with all them got-damn pills you takin'."

"Well, I'm dranking one of them mutha fuckas tonight…"

She was drinking a beer, I was drinking and we were just a laughing. We really were laughing because Ann didn't drink and hadn't drank as long as I knew her. It didn't take much for her.

"Your ass drank one damn sip, Dretta and you drunk as hell."

"Mutha fucka what you talking about I ain't drunk."

"Look at your ass sluring your words, laughing at everything and shit. I told your ass not to be drinking when your ass is taking all those got-damn pills and shit!"

We just laughed. That night everything was funny, and in the background was playing those same two damn songs.

"I know, Kenny, I know…but I'm celebrating. We did it didn't we? We did it! After all this damn time, after all them little bitches spending my money…we did it…we did it!"

"Yeah Dretta, we did it! We did…"

"I told you we were gonna do it!"

"Yeah you did."

"Remember we were in California, I had to get your ass on the balcony talking all that shit! Had to calm you down about Ashley…You wanted to quit then."

"Yeah…if I knew I had to go through all this shit, I wudda quit."

"Your ass talking…I'm Kenny fucking Mo, got damn it…Who these little heffas think they are…I'm Kenny fuckin' Mo…got dammit! Yeah"

"Yeah I remember."

Ann and I laughed so hard reminiscing over all the little incidents and things we had gone through to get to that moment.

"Do you remember when Mathew fucked up the Elektra deal? But we stayed the course didn't we...didn't we?"

Ann was drunk as hell, but we continued to laugh and talk about old times.

"Shit Dretta, he fucked that one up real good, no good dums of bitch! I was ashamed to even come around that mutha fucka! Shit, all my boys in California and thangs and the ones I was in the music industry with was doggin' me out...saying 'Man what the fuck kind of camp ya'll asses running down there and shit?'"

"That mutha fucka was trying to come gansta and shit because of Beyonce being his mutha fuckin daughter. You should've seen his ass almost on his knees when we lost the Elektra deal."

"Naw I tell you who thought he was gangster...that damn Lynn..."

"Ah shit Kenny, don't get me started on his dumb ass!"

"Now that's one crooked ass mutha fucka..."

"His dumb ass gonna write some got-damned hot checks on my account to his ass...You would think if he was gonna steal he would have at least had sense enough to have some of them other crooked mutha fuckas or hoes he' fuckin' to have the damn check written out to them

The Making of a Child of Destiny

where it couldn't be traced back to his dumb ass as quickly."

"That's because that mutha fucka is greedy…he ain't got no damn sense."

"Shit T-Mo is the dumb ass mutha fucka done sold his damn songs for a dollar or penny or some shit like that, then they kicked his ass to the curb…"

I fell out rolling on the floor, as Ann was talking about T-Mo.

"Lonnie and Arne wrote his dumb ass out the picture with one stroke. He's got to be the dumbest mutha fucka of em all. Knowingly signed away all of his damn rights trusting Arne and Lonnie's crooked ass."

"Oh, Dretta, I almost forgot about that…shit. I bet you he ain't gonna do that shit no more."

"Hell naw! He probably knows he can't trust Lonnie's selfish ass. And don't get me started on David. Shit, that short fat ass mutha fucka is trying to be some damn opera singer and vocal coach…with his big ass head!"

"You know you wrong for that Dretta!"

Dretta started mimicking the opera sound. "Ahhhh, Figaro Figaro…what the shit is that!"

"You are crazy as hell, girl!"

"That mutha fucka wanna be an opera singer but teaching R & B vocal…what kinda fuckin' shit is that, Kenny!"

"Oooh weee!" I just laughed. Ann was on a roll.

"Shit though, ain't no got damn body as stupid as or as big of a fuck up as Mathew's retarded ass! He even fucks up fucking up! Ain't that some shit!"

"You know your Black ass is crazy Ann."

"He's a got damned ho! I can't wait 'til Tina find out, cause she gonna kill his ass."

"He's a dirty one for sure!"

"You know though Kenny, it's sad that Nikki and Nina didn't make it this far…now that hurt. I know it was probably the best decision, but it would have been good if they could have continued on the journey with the girls."

"Yeah…but…"

"Those are my girls though. I still wanna find a place for them…but…oh well."

"Same about Ashley. What's going on with her?"

"Yeah…huhm…"

Ann took a deep breath at that moment and appeared to allow her mind to wander somewhere else. Ann and I talked about getting past Carolyn to help Ashley. We talked about Tayste and all the mess surrounding them and how Lynn contributed to the confusion within their group whereas Harlon and Mitch was on one page and A.J. and Tu Tu on another. We talked about several up and coming groups such as Shay Atkins and Flag. We talked about still going after Kathy Taylor who had maintained a good local following. As Ann let her mind continue to wander, for a moment I could tell that she was thinking of Dwight and Shawna. She briefly looked to the sky and smiled and at that moment when she was saying, "we did it," she was not only talking to me she was also talking to Dwight.

We laughed and talked for hours. It became so redundant that each time the song switched tracks and went back to the other one we laughed.

"You wearing them got-damned songs out girl!"

Ann and I have always been professional, but this was one of the few times where we actually embraced in appreciation for one another.

"I love you Kenny."

"I love you too Dretta. You're like my sister baby girl."

"I know what you mean. It's hard for me to say that, but I really do love you man."

"I really love you too Dretta."

After we unlocked from the embrace, Ann hit me on my shoulder, and said, "We did it man. We did it."

I nodded. "Yeah, we did, didn't we?"

"What you gonna do out there on the road Kenny Mo, whatcha gonna do out there?"

"Ann if these bitches be acting like they had been acting all this time…shit…I'mma catch hell. You tryin' to kill me. I'mma have to keep these niggas off these girls.

Hell, four girls, man you gonna have to give me a posse and niggas with guns and shit."

"Yeah…I didn't think about that." Ann said laughing.

"Hell yeah! You gonna have to get chaperones and everything!

We had a really great time laughing and talking that night. We talked about everybody. We talked about the good things and all the bullshit. We had a barrage, discussing everything we had went through and experienced. We talked about friends and so called friends.

When I left Ann's house that night, she was bubbly and happy. Over the next couple of days we spoke and continued laughing about that night. She was still very upbeat. The next thing I knew, she ended up back at the hospital. This time I noticed that her breathing had become very heavy and she was hooked up to a breathing machine.

"Girl, Ann not this bullshit again. What the fuck you doing? We done got the contract and shit. Get your ass up."

"Kenny, I want you to raise my boys if something happen to me."

"Ann, I already fuckin' told you I would do it, but ain't shit finna happen to you okay? Just get your ass up! Come on now I ain't playin' witcha."

"Kenny, I want you to promise me."

"I promise...I promise."

"I got some stuff I need to tell you."

"Great Ann, just tell me when we get your ass back home."

Ann began to tell me about the arrangement with Mathew. She shared with me that she had fifty percent of the girls' management for the lifetime of the group. It wasn't a contract that was going to end and that her estate would get that fifty percent if something happened to her.

"Okay Ann."

"When my boys get up...whatever money that comes in, my boys will still get it. So you will be over that. Make sure my boys are taken care of."

"Ann I got it. What else?"

"The masters...you know where my safe deposit box is up there at the Krogers...it's at the corner..."

"Yeah..."

"I got the safe deposit there...all the masters are there, that's where I'm keeping them until I turn them over to Sony."

"Okay girl...fine Ann!"

I was agitated with her, but she felt that she needed to tell me so this time I reluctantly listened to her go on.

"What else?"

"Well the house and everything…well…I got the insurance that's gonna pay that off. My insurance is a big policy, so the boys should be fine, Kenny."

"Okay…?"

"Yeah…it doubles if it's an accidental death, but it's less if I just passed."

"Okay…Well hell, I need to get your ass out of this bed and take you out and let you just run into some shit got dammit."

We both laughed, but then she began to voice her concerns about another matter.

"Also, Dwight's brother, Keith been coming around a lot more like he expects something to happen to me or something."

"Well that's your husband's brother."

"Naw, Kenny it ain't like that. Like I tell you, these mutha fuckas think I'm finna die or something. They waiting to get my insurance and shit like that. That's why I wanna make sure. Now I done already told my mama that if something happens that you get the boys. Make sure you and Cassey get the boys."

"Okay…"

"You played football, Brian's playing football, Chris is playing football, Armon is playing basketball…so you know all about the sport and recruiting…NCAA stuff so you be perfect you know."

"Okay, Ann that's fine."

The conversation was subdued. You could tell she was sad and somewhat scared. As she lay there from time/to/time I could hear her humming the melody to No, No, No, No, No and another time she would hum My Time Has Come melody.

"Girl, when you get your ass up out of here, I'mma throw you the biggest ass barbeque ever."

"Okay. You know that's the only thing that'll make me happy."

It was a short stint in the hospital. We talked on Wednesday when she was in the hospital. She got out on Thursday, and on Friday, I threw her the barbeque. That barbeque was so big; you might as well have said we killed the fatty calf basically. We had everything from potato salad, baked beans, ribs, chicken, hamburgers, hotdogs, and sausages. You name it, it was there. The one way I could show my love to Ann was to have a barbeque feast she would never forget. Ann, Armon, and Chris came over. We all sat down and said a prayer and ate. Ann ate and ate and ate.

"This some good shit…this some good shit, Kenny Mo."

"Girl you better quit before you trigger something and get your ass sick again, trying to digest all that damn meat."

"Shit got dammit, if I'mma die, I'mma die full and happy as a mutha fucka eating me some of Kenny Mo's good ass barbeque."

We laughed and had a good time. The boys were playing basketball and Ann, Cassey and I sat there talking.

"Kenny, my advance from Dwayne still has not come. So, I need to file bankruptcy or take more money out of the boys' trust. I really don't know what to do."

"For what Ann? Ain't the money came in?"

"No, I'm still waiting on it from Dwayne. But I need to file bankruptcy or something to hold off everything until shit else happens. I don't wanna go back in my boy's money."

We sat there talking about it for a moment. Then Ann said, "I've got until five o'clock to call this lady if I'm gonna file bankruptcy."

"Ann, you a mother and widow! You gotta do what's best for your kids. You have given every damn body ever damn thang. I understand where you at. But hell Naw! Everbody else is sittin' there with money from the advance in their pockets, and if it wasn't for you, none of them would have shit. And you the mutha fucka that's sittin over here broke? Hell, if it was me and my kids…I 'm the type of mother that would go and sell some pussy if my kids were hungry. So I ain't sayin' what you would do or won't do!"

Ann burst out laughing and said, "Damn Cassey, I hear you...I don't think I could get as much as I need to pay them bills in my condition."

They both laughed then Cassey said, "Shit you can stand on the corner with one leg shit..."

After a good laugh, Ann said, "What do you and Cat think I should do, Kenny?"

"Ann, shit...fuck that! You need to go on and file bankruptcy. Hold them folks off; keep a roof over your babies head. Now this is a damn shame. All this damn money you spending and you sitting here in this shit because you helping these bitches! You helping these little bitches' dreams come true and you over her trying to eat and tryin' to file bankruptcy. You call that bitch and tell her you wanna file bankruptcy. Then everything will work out later. Plus that will take some of the stress off you. You ain't gotta worry about folks taking the roof from over your babies' head."

So, at about four-fifty, Ann picked up the telephone to call the lady to tell her to go ahead and start the proceedings for bankruptcy to hold her debtors off. She was not willing to touch Armon and Christopher's inheritance. After that we went on with our evening. We played a little basketball and football, and Ann and Cassey continued to talk. The evening came to a close and Ann left in a very good mood.

That following Thursday, I went by her house.

"Dretta, your ass still lisenting to them got damned songs."

"Man…"

"Dretta…really? I'm sure Beyonce's fucking throat is hurtin'."

"Why?"

"Because that bitch ain't stop sanging since you got that damn cd!"

"Boy…whatcha mean?"

"Hell girl, all of them heffas throats should be hurtin' like a mug. Because they ain't stop singing since you go them damn masters."

Ann laughed. Then I asked her, "What's up baby girl…you good?"

"Yeah, yeah, Kenny, I'm good.

"Okay now. You know the album's getting ready to come out. They gonna shoot the videos. Kenny Mo gonna be in the video. You gonna be in the video?"

"You gonna get in the video?"

"Hell yeah, I'mma get in the video. You let them mutha fucka shoot around here and there's people around here. Hell yeah, I'm getting in the video. Kenny Mo gonna be in the video Ann."

"Well shit, I can get in the video too. I can get up there and be dancing like them girls be dancing. Shake my booty."

"Naw, now we trying to make some money, not give it back, Andretta."

We laughed and hung out for a while.

"Now, I'mma run on to the house. I'll call you tomorrow."

So I left. The next day I called to see how she was doing.

"Hey girl, how you doing?"

"Oh, a little tired."

"You tired?"

"Yeah."

"Ann how the fuck you tired with all this excitement going on? We're getting ready to take over the world like we planned. We need to get everything mapped out."

"Well we're dealing with the label, Dwayne and my money and Mathew's shit. That's enough to make any mutha fucka tired."

"Won't you just get you some rest and I will come on over tomorrow or you come over and I'll barbeque or we do it over the weekend."

"Okay. Yeah, let's do it over the weekend."

We planned the weekend and talked for a little while longer on the telephone.

"You still listening to them got-damned girls?"

"You crazy, Kenny Mo."

"Shit I'm serious. Are they still sanging?"

"Naw I done put 'em down for a while…Kenny boy, I love you. You my friend."

"Andretta, I would say I love you but I'm afraid I might throw up."

"Ah, it's like that huh?"

"Naw, alright nigga. I…I…I…I like you a lot."

"Really, okay okay. You gonna remember that."

"Alright Ann, I love you too. Alright now, I'mma come through tomorrow. You getting' all mushy and shit… I'll come by tomorrow and check on you. But me and Cassey gonna go out dancing tonight."

"Oh ya'll gonna go dancing?"

"Yeah I'mma take her out so she can get her dance on…"

Then Ann gets quiet for a moment, then says, "Kenny, make sure you dance with your wife tonight. You be sure to dance with her every opportunity you get, because you'll never know when you won't have that chance to dance with her."

I paused a moment, then it hit me what she was saying, as if she had the chance to dance with Dwight she would have all these years.

"Okay, Ann, I will dance my ass off with my wife. I'mma do the robot, the bump, funky chicken, the mash potatoes, and I'm slow-grind like in the basement. Now your ass happy?"

"Yeah, okay. Now remember I got all the masters…don't forget what I told you about the partnership breakdown."

"Will you shut the fuck up with that shit? You act like you trying to go somewhere got dammit!"

"Naw, Naw! I just wanna make sure, Kenny, you know…cause that's some serious stuff."

"Ann, I'm serious too. I'mma take care of it got dammit! I got it…we're cool?"

"You know how that mutha fuckin Mathew is. He gonna…"

"Ann, I got everything, got damn…quit trippin woman! What's wrong with you? Cause, heaven don't want your ass and hell afraid you gonna take over! So you ain't going no got damned where."

Ann took the telephone away from her ear for laughing so hard. When she came back to the phone, we bantered back and forth for a little while longer before we finally hung up the telephone. The next day I went to work and when I got off of work, I got an emergency phone call from Charlotte.

"Hey Kenny, come quick, Ann had another attack!"

"She had another attack? What the fuck!"

"Yeah, we had to rush her to the hospital again! Her eyes were rolling in the back of her head and she just passed out!"

"Okay, where she at?"

"She's in the emergency room."

"Alright then."

I took my time. I went and got something to eat on my way to the hospital. After eating I was like, "Damn! This shit is getting old. She is in and out of the hospital. They never keep her ass more than a couple of days, they ain't cuttin' on her no more. One mintue she's strong as an ox, the next she laying her black ass in the hospital."

As I approached the Hospital this time, something felt different. I said to myself, "Let me go on up here. This got damned girl…" I walked through the front of the hospital. I didn't go through the emergency way, I went through the front. As I was walking in, I saw this gurney going from the the emergency room area with people rushing going to the ICU. Then I saw Charlotte run by.

I thought, "Damn that must've been Ann." So I sped up.

"Hey Charlotte…was that Ann?"

The Making of a Child of Destiny

Charlotte was crying. "Yeah…"

"Charlotte, what the fuck going on?"

"Ann eyes fell in the back of her head. I kept telling her Ann stay with me, stay with me. But they kept going in the back of her head."

"Well, where they going?"

"They're taking her to ICU to try to revive her."

"What! Why the fuck you didn't you call me?"

"Kenny, I did! I called you two hours ago!"

"Fuck…this shit going on you supposed to call me back…"

Charlotte and I walked down as close as we could by the door to see what we could see. We were in the hallway waiting and waiting.

"Her eyes just kept rolling in her head, Kenny…I told her breathe, Ann breathe!"

"Shit…"

I scratched my head. All we could do was wait. I called Cassey. Everybody started coming up to the hospital. I walked down the hall to get a soda. When I came back from getting a soda, everybody was crying. Then Charlotte said, "She's dead Kenny…she's gone."

"Girl quit bullshitting now! Quit playing."

"Kenny, she's dead!"

"Charlotte, quit bullshitting, Ann ain't dead!"

I started walking toward the rooms yelling her name. "Dretta! Dretta! I know your ass here me...Dretta!"

The doctors and nurses just looked at me, but said nothing. "Ann!"

Then I looked at Charlotte. "Are you serious?"

"Yeah, Kenny, Andretta is dead."

Everyone else started coming and they just kept coming. I couldn't take it, so I just stormed out of the hospital and went home.

"Man... my friend is dead."

It was hard dealing with it. Cassey was doing her best to console me and console herself. I sat there for a couple of hours maybe longer, playing the same game the night I heard that Louise had died, as I felt myself sinking back into a similar depression. Cassey said, "Kenny, you really need to go over to the house and check on the boys. We need to check on the boys. You know that's what she asked us to do."

"You right. You right, Cat. We gotta be strong."

Cat, Brian and I went to the house. By then everyone from Tyler had made their way up. Everybody from everywhere was there. All the girls, all their parents, and everyone who knew her or liked her were there at the house. Ann's mom Buck had made it as well. There was a hug fest all the way from the front lawn and driveway to

The Making of a Child of Destiny

the inside of the house. People were standing around crying. I went in to check on Armon and Chris. They were dazed out. I was hugging everybody, trying not to cry. I was thinking in the back of my mind, "I can't let these niggas see no weakness."

I hugged Mathew; I hugged Tina, and some of the others. Charlotte was there. Cheryl was there. All of the girls were there. I hugged Beyonce and gave all of them a look that said, "Okay little bitches...you better fuckin' do something great 'cause...she gave her mutha fuckin' life to give you this golden opportunity!"

I walked on further in the house. I looked over at a round table and saw Buck sitting there. As I was making my way, I was saying to myself, "I am not going over there. This woman is hurting and I'm not getting ready to go fuck with her now."

I was kind of walking through the kitchen. As soon as I hit the doorway right by the kitchen, Buck yelled and pointed to me. "You!"

Everybody stopped because Buck was finally talking. They turned to see where she was pointing. "You!"

"Yes ma'am Miss Brown?"

"Come here."

When I walked over to her, she pat me on my chest. Then she put her finger in my face and said, "You...you were my daughter's only friend."

She then grabbed my hand and sat me down in the chair right beside her. I sat there tearing. We just sat there and didn't say anything. She looked at me and I looked at her, and then she said, "Are you okay with the boys?"

"Yes, Ma'am."

"Okay…what we gonna do is I'mma take them back to Tyler with me for over the summer. And…uh…I'll send them back up here to you. Ann said you know where everything is…you have all her insurance information, the music contracts, and the Sony masters?"

"I know where it is…yes ma'am."

"They'll just come back up here with you. That's what she wanted."

Mrs. Brown looked me straight in the eye. "You got all her business handled?"

"Yes ma'am."

"Alright, that's what she wanted."

"Okay."

I got up from the table, needing a serious drink or somewhere to go boo-hoo. I was thinking that maybe I could go down the street, cry and then come back; but right when I was making my way back through the house without tearing up, Mathew came up to me.

"Hey Kenny, man I need to talk to you."

"Matt, not right now man…not now."

"Come on man, I need to talk."

"About Ann?"

"Naw, I need to talk to you about them Sony masters."

"Matt not right now man, please. Not right now."

"Come on Kenny man, I need to talk to you. We can't have them masters getting out to nobody man…"

"The masters are secure. Let's do this later man, not right now."

Mathew grew more persistent and impatient. "Come on man, come on!"

"Matt, Ann had everything taken care of…"

"Come on Man!" Mathew said loudly.

Right in front of everyone, I said with great irritation. "Look, Ann had every fuckin' thing taken care of. She got the Sony contract and your contract with her locked away. She got all the information on how she put the deal together locked away. She has damn masters locked away. She took care of all of it, it's okay, secure, and locked away! So you just chill the fuck out! She always took care of business. You know that. So it's okay. It's handled."

"But…but…what about the masters, Kenny?"

"Mathew, I've got the got damned Sony masters. I have the masters to all the girls' songs. I got them! Ann told me where they were. I have them! I got the damn masters! And for any fuckin' body who got any fuckin' questions as to if Ann was running shit and whether or not she put the Sony deal together! I got the fucking Sony masters now because Ann gave them to me."

I spoke to Mathew loud enough for everybody to hear me just in case there were any questions in terms of what Ann had done. Several people looked in disbelief as to how I was talking to Mathew. I was hot by then and didn't give a damn who heard me and what they thought. My friend had just died, and he was more concerned about where some damn cd's were.

"Dude, not fuckin' now! Not fuckin' right now bro! We'll talk about this later!"

I then walked away from Mathew and headed out of the house. Before walking out the door I ran upon Armon and Chris.

"Ya'll gonna talk to your grandmother?"

"Yeah, we gonna talk to her."

"Ya'll know what you supposed to do?"

"Yeah we'll talk to her."

"Okay now. Ya'll need anything, I'm here."

Then I spoke with Ann's brother Dick.

"All her stuff is in a safe deposit box. We can get together later and go through the insurance policy and everything related to the music."

"Okay…cool."

I told Dick where the safe deposit box was. I showed him which key would open it.

"We need to talk because Mathew is…"

"Look, Dick, let's go through the process, bury Ann, then I tell you everything you need to know and what we need to do."

Dick agreed and we left it at that. I walked out of the house. I said to myself, "Can you believe these mutha fuckas. The woman ain't even cold yet and they worried about some fuckin' Sony masters!"

DRUMS STOP, BUT THE BEAT GOES ON

When I left the house that night and headed back home, I marinated in the fact that Andretta was gone. As I sat there in my chair thinking and replaying last moments in my mind, looking back at how she was going back and forth with "No, No, No, No, No" and "My Time Has Come," I realized that she perhaps knew that she was at a crossroads and through the songs, she was expressing her sentiments of how she was feeling and what she was struggling with internally. She may have known her time was up, but she was saying she wasn't ready. There was something about it that was very spiritual.

I missed it because I honestly thought in my mind it was business as usual and she would get back up as she always had. But this time she didn't. Sitting in my chair, the realization of me having a great task ahead was an ever present reality. As long as the boys came to me as planned, we would have control of her estate and it would be much easier for me to enforce the contract she had with Mathew and that the boys would get what they had coming to them.

The days ahead, I anticipated calls from her, and a few times even went to call her and say, "Hey Blackie, get your ass up and out!" However, no sooner than I picked up the receiver, I realized, she was not there. She would never be there again. I would often ride by the house and see the cars there. Sometimes I just sat in front of the house, thinking, sometimes tearing up, and then pull away. I would go home, expecting a call, but it never came. I pulled out the box and went through the mounds of paperwork collected over the years and looked at all we had accomplished. It was a journey. As I was going through all the "stuff," Cassey would look over her cup of coffee and observe. It was hard to believe that seven or eight years had gone by so fast.

Those who knew that Ann and I were close friends came through to show their support. The Dunsons, my friend Vilia from the airforce, and many more of the Continental airline flight attendants came to check on us. Mainly people who knew us and knew what we were working on stopped by. After a couple of days, the family was making funeral arrangements. I kept checking on the boys to see how they were handling things. Armon drowned his feelings in basketball and Chris pretty much stayed in a daze. Whenever I stopped by the house, I met more and more of Ann's siblings, until I was able to meet the whole Brown family.

It was an uncomfortable situation because I sensed that they were aware of Andretta's wishes for Cassey and me to raise the boys, but us not being blood relatives, you could tell that they were not totally cool with the idea of Armon and Christopher coming to live us. Many of them offered up their homes and lives for the boys, and wanted to know what my plans for them were. Some might have been genuinely concerned that it was something that I was willing and capable of doing, while others most likely wanted to make sure that I was not there to steal the estate.

Ann's estate was the furthest thing from my mind. Buck was very reassuring and made it a point to constantly tell me not to worry and that everything was all good. So, I didn't worry about it. The day before the funeral I actually finally got the chance to release what I had bottled up inside for the sake of being strong for others. This was a tough time as Cassey had a trip to go on and could not attend the funeral. Brian was there, and my friend Vilia kept coming back and forth to see about me, even my boy Rob flew in from L.A. Yet, when I had a moment alone after friends were gone and Brian was in bed, I cried. I finally cried!

It hit me. This was real. We accomplished all this. It was hard because she worked so hard and now she wouldn't even get the chance to see it.

"Man! Life is just unfair! Lord, I'm not questioning you, but why?"

All I could do was cry. The knot formed in my throat. My nose got all stuffed up. The more I cried, the more I cried.

"You lose Dwight and Shawna, then you go and do all this stuff and make all this stuff happen…you fight through all the setbacks and triumphs. We dealt with these parents, we went through all the disappointments…we make it and we're jamming…and then your ass go and die on me! It's just not fair!"

As I cried, I cried for Ann. I cried for the girls. I cried for the boys. I cried for Dwight and Shawna. I cried for Louise. I cried for the struggle. I cried remembering the words of Dr. Martin Luther King, "And He's allowed me to go up to the mountain. And I've looked over. And I've seen the Promised Land. I may not get there with you. But I want you to know tonight, that we, as a people, will get to the Promised Land!"

I sat there crying, shaking my head, and talking to the empty room.

"You knew that Destiny's Child would make it. You always knew and proclaimed that they were destined to be great! You knew that you would not be around to see the fullness of that greatness. You tried to tell me, prepare me, but I couldn't hear you."

I sat there on the couch crying so hard because the drum major who was leading the band was silenced.

The funeral was very difficult. Cassey and I had squared Brian away so he would not have to go endure it. I rode with friends who came along to provide support since Cassey would not able to be there. Eric and Vilia were insistent on going to the funeral with me.

"Look man, Cassey ain't here and there is no way in hell are we gonna let you go over there by yourself man."

"I agree Vilia. Look Kenny Mo, we are right there with you man!"

They drove me to the funeral. Everything was cool in the car. We talked light-heartedly as they expressed that they understood how close Ann and I were. We laughed about how they would see me and Ann playing the dozens and "Joning" on each other.

"Man, I know it's gonna be hard on you, but we're here for you."

"Thanks Vilia man I appreciate that."

"No doubt, Kenny Mo, you know we got your back!"

"Thanks Eric. I don't know what I would do without you two right about now. This is some hard shit!"

"It's gonna be alright.!

We just shot the breeze so I wouldn't cry, which would make them cry, then we all be messed up. The truth was any of us could have cried at the drop of a hat so we just tried to keep it light. Finally, we pulled up to Yale Street Baptist Church located on Yale Street right off of Cross Timber in Houston, Texas. When we pulled up, the front was filled with cars and the hearse, so we pulled around back. We got out the car and as we were going in, we saw everyone standing around. The family had just walked into the church. I told Eric and Vilia I was gonna walk on around to go inside. The last time I saw Ann she was alive. As I started to walk on around, I noticed a tall figure from a distance walking toward me. As he got closer, I realized that it was Mathew.

"Hey Kenny, let me talk to you real quick man before you go into the funeral."

"Huh?"

"Let me talk to you for a minute."

I had calmed down from the last conversation we had. So I said, "Mat, look man, everything's cool, man, everything's cool. Ann told me about the contract. I know about the arrangements. You're gonna take over management. It's your daughter. It's not gonna be a fight man, everything's cool. I'm just gonna help you wherever I fit in…and we go forward…you know…it's no big thing. We'll keep things rollin'."

"But man, I need those masters."

"Mat I got them man. I'mma give them to you tomorrow man. We'll settle that tomorrow. Let's just go in here and pay our respects."

"Kenny man, we can't have those masters…."

"Mat…the damn things are still in the safe deposit box! Ain't nobody listening to them or nothing, trust me. I don't wanna listen to them mutha fuckas no more! I done heard them enough!"

I put my hand across his back and said, "Come on man, now let's go in here and bury our friend."

Mathew violently jerked away from me and said, "Fuck that bitch! I want them mutha fuckin' masters! And I want the mutha fuckas now!"

Mathew turned and stormed off across the street. I was standing there in shock. Eric and Vilia heard the conversation and rapidly approached me in disbelief.

"Now I just done reminisced of all the shit that woman has sacrificed and done for his fucking child and those girls, and he gonna go and say some bullshit like that!"

"Yeah man."

"Shit! She done paid his got damned bills, covered for his dirty mutha fuckin ass when he was lying to and cheating on his wife...and this is his gratitude? What the fuck!"

"Shake it off Kenny man."

I was standing there, and I was honestly looking for the biggest brick I could find to throw and hit him in the back of his "mutha fuckin' head." Then suddenly a peace came over me as I turned to my friends and said, "Look here ya'll, after everything Andretta has done, and all we've been through, if I have to deal with a mutha fucka like that, I prefer to walk away."

So, that is what I resolved to do, that is, until I started to hear Ann's voice in my head and my damn peace was disturbed.

"Oh naw...you Kenny Mo dammit! What the fuck you doing? What about my boys?"

"Ann, but I gotta deal with this nigga. If I get the boys, then I gotta deal with this mutha fucka...shit...got damned!"

I braced myself because I was mad as hell. I looked across the street hoping he'd come back. I was thinking to myself, "Bring your ass back! I'm finna whoop your natural black ass. Bring your ass back here, I finna put a Mississippi ass whoopin on you."

Then I said outloud, "I'mma whoop his mutha fuckin' ass!"

Vilia said, "Man, just calm down, calm down."

Eric said, "Yeah Ken Moore calm down. But…if he come back, we kickin' his ass!"

"Got damn, that Mathew is cold man."

"Look Vilia, that ain't the half of it."

We started to go inside. As I got up to the door, I saw family members standing around and Armon by the door next to Beyonce, Kelly, and Nina. LaTavia, Niki, Letoya were with Chris. I walked up and leaned into Chris.

"Hey, you alright?"

"Yes sir. I'm good."

"Okay."

I then walked up to Armon and hugged him.

"Are you okay?"

"Yeah. I'm good. I'm good."

I then turned to Beyonce, and said, "Finish it!"

She nodded her head and said, "Yes sir. We don't stop."

Beyonce knew exactly what I meant and we have always been able to talk to each other and understand each other. From the studio to that day, it didn't take a lot of words to get a point across. We just understood where each other was coming from. My point was, finish it. It is not over, so make something happen from here and don't stop moving forward until we're the greatest group ever.

They all walked on into the main sanctuary of the church and I walked in behind them. When I walked into the room, everyone looked at me as if I was the preacher. All eyes in the place were on me. Even her family turned to look at me. I was thinking to myself.

"They are not gonna see me show no emotion whatsoever. I'mma going into the Kennedy's mode – like they do when one of them die."

I strutted in with pride. We had done something big and this was my girl, and my time to say goodbye. I acknowledged various family members. I didn't try to speak to them other than when I walked down to view Ann's body. She layed there, dressed in pastel pink, peach, or white. I don't really recall exactly what she was wearing. All I remember was her face because it was swollen. Whatever the trauma of what had happened to her during her final moment had inflamed her face more. When I looked at her, I noticed the hairdo she had, and thought about what she might have been saying.

"You see this shit Kenny Mo? These mutha fuckas didn't even comb my mutha fuckin' hair right. What kind of shit is this?"

Ann's hair was thin from the stress and the medication. I stood there looking at her for a minute, and then turned to look at Buck. She didn't flinch. There wasn't a tear in her eye. I wasn't about to cry. I was still mad as hell thinking about what Mathew had just said, but I was trying to smile. I finally walked on back and took a seat. There was a seat in the family section they wanted me to sit in, but I went all the way toward the back. I didn't want any damn body staring at me. I wanted to observe other's reactions. All I can remember was that after this one up-beat song finished playing, I recall cursing in my mind.

"This mutha fucka! Boy…this low-down dirty ass mutha fucka!"

The preacher was up there delivering the eulogy.

"…as much as it is God's…"

But my mind was on Mathew.

"This mutha fucka!"

In between the scriptures and the preacher's sermon, I was just a cursing in my mind. I said to myself, "Lord, you know I'm wrong…but this…Lord Jesus I know I, I…but this here…"

I said, "…but this right here is some fucked up shit!"

As I was thinking, I got madder and madder, and then the preacher said what his message was for the day.

"My message for today is, 'What do you say, when you don't know what to say.'"

Then he went in to talk about funerals, events like this, life…when you come across things. As he continued to talk, it brought me back to what had just happened with Mathew. It brought me back to the night Ann died.

"People…there are just times you don't know what to say." The preacher continued.

"You want to console somebody…you want to ask for something or do a business transaction in a better way but regardless as to what it is…at moments like this, you don't know what to say…"

I started to listen to the preacher and take everything in. I was angry with Mathew, but I was trying to reconcile that I've gotta take care of the boys and carry on her legacy. I finally came to the conclusion that there was no reason for me to be mad at the girls or anybody else because I had to work with them. I had to be there to watch her money and her estate.

Toward the end of the service, there was a lot of crying. The church became very loud unlike at Dwight's and Shawna's funeral. The girls cried their hearts out. There was no doubt that they loved Ann. Everything else aside, the girls were extremely crushed at Ann's passing. As I watched Beyonce, Kelly, LaTavia and the rest of the girls bawl, you could see that they truly loved Ann and the mask that they sometimes wore was because of some of the adults' mess. I had heard so much and have seen quite a bit, but I realized as I was observing them, that those girls had been manipulated because their tears expressed their pain.

They couldn't know. Yes, they knew Miss Ann was gone, but they couldn't possibly know the behind the scenes tug-of-war of the management team. Charlotte, Tina and Carolyn, I mean all of them came. They cried and appeared to be truly hurting over Ann's death. It was a sad day. The whole thing was sad because of the promise. We all took flight. There were some talented artists who got us to where we were going. They all began their journey at nine, ten, twelve years of age. Yet here Ann was, at thirty-nine years of age at the end of the road. We had some ways to go, but we would have to continue on without her. This was tough and everyone who was a part of the making of destiny knew, she was truly the staple of it all.

As I looked around the church drenched in flowers of every kind, and the choir began to sing the song, Soon and Very Soon, the grieving increased as they were preparing to say goodbye forever. The preacher walked out, the casket was hoisted and carried out, and the family followed behind. I looked on and I spotted Buck. When she looked up and her eyes locked on mine and I stared her squarely in the face, I noticed that she was crying. Immediately tears began to well up in my eyes. I was holding on, fighting to try not to break down.

As each family member walked out, and each person who thought they were close to her walked by, the humor of recollecting the many conversations Ann and I had, was enough to keep me from completely breaking down. I was able to say to myself, "Boy if you only knew what Ann used to say about your ass."

Sha was bawling. The girls were bawling. It was hard watching those who you knew genuinely cared about her pass by. It was a constant battle between laughter and tears. Seeing LaTavia, Beyonce, Kelly, and Ashley crying the way they were, caused me to lose the battle, and tears won out. I didn't break down, but the tears flowed. All of the other partners who had taken the journey walked down the aisle. They were also crying. I did not see Mathew in the funeral at all. I was standing there in shock.

We all loved each other. We fought, but we loved too. When we got outside, people came up to me and asked, "Okay man, whatch you gonna do with it?"

"I got it! I'mma take care of it. I'mma take care of it."

I scratched my head and said, "What kind of people are ya'll. We just got outside from her funeral. Everyone's crying and carrying on…and now ya'll asking what we gonna do? Damn can we get through one damn night?"

It was an evening funeral, so it was dark outside. They were gonna take her body to Tyler for another service.

"Can we just get passed all this?"

Everyone was trying to talk about what's next. Her brother Dick came up to me and said, "Hey man, we need to talk about some things tomorrow. What's all this stuff Mathew keeps asking about?"

Mathew was going around asking everyone he could about what was going on with the masters and other paperwork. For years he had been telling everyone he was in charge. Now, here he is frantic because he doesn't have the masters.

I said to Eric and Vilia, "Here his no good ass, running around at this funeral asking for the masters and he had everybody thinking he was the manager and in charge and he don't have the masters…come on now…he's in charge. This mutha fucka is losing his damn mind over this shit."

Eric, Vilia, and I left the church and headed over to my house. I went to Lou's place. Lou's place was in my garage with the big ass mural that I painted on the wall when my sister Louise died. There's a big card table, and these big high-back wicker chairs that you see in the club that guys used to sit back in during the seventies where the girlfriends used to stand up next to it. I got me some scotch and a cigar and me and Andretta just turned the music on and listened to the music from the first CD we did out at The Plant in California under A & A Production.

I listened to, Teacher Fried My Brain, Take it to Another Level, 63257 is Your Number. It was about ten songs. I just went through the whole damn catalogue. I cried it out to get up the strength to receive the two boys that were coming to the house. I had to prepare my family for what was to come. Cassey called to check on me. Eric and Vilia left.

The next day Cassey came home. She was meticulous.

"Come on, let's go handle it."

I went to talk to Dick. I handed over the masters and for him to go ahead and give them to Mathew and handle everything else how he felt it should be handled. I was not concerned about who had what, because I saw the contract. I knew what the deal was. Dick handled everything from there on out with respect to the materials. I did not interact with Mathew after that regarding Ann's estate. He communicated with Dick because I turned everything over to him. The last time I saw him at this juncture was when he turned his back at the funeral.

Over the course of the summer, Cassey and I prepared for Armon and Chris. We sorted out transportation and everything else that needed to be sorted with respect to rearing them from that point on. We called to check on the boys, but didn't get an answer. We kept calling to check on them, but still no response. The group was getting together from time-to-time so finally when I ran into Charlotte, the two of us started talking.

"Hey, I have been calling to check on the boys and haven't been able to reach anyone. Has Nina spoken with Armon?"

"Well Kenny, you know that the boys are with Keith, Dwight's brother, don't you?"

"What?"

"Yeah. He has them and he's gonna raise them."

After speaking with Charlotte, I called Tyler, but Mrs. Brown was no where around. I ended up speaking with one of Ann's sisters.

"Where are Armon and Chris?"

"Well you know…uh…they're gone to stay with Keith."

"Oh…"

I didn't push the issue. I started to but I didn't.

"You know Ann wanted them to come with me, right?"

She got quiet, and so I backed off. At the end of the day this is their family and that is their father's brother. Yes, he might be pulling rank and while Andretta's family agreed to it, he may have stepped in and said, "Well you're not family, and regardless of what Ann thought of you, you're not family."

I took it as they were all separating me from what Ann had wanted. While Buck might have been attempting to follow her daugther's last wishes, the family possibly could have manipulated the situation while she was in mourning and she didn't fight the issue. I thought for some time that this was what happened, but I came to find out later that it was more of a kidnapping situation. I found out that Keith came to a family outing and tricked the boys into leaving with him and traveling back to Houston to go to his house and return to their school.

Keith told the boys that he would raise them and he fought a good fight with Ann's family and they let them go, ultimately disregarding Ann's final wishes. He had the boys and claimed that they were happy and wanted to be with him in Houston. So at the end of the day, it was Keith who claimed the boys. The word was, when the family was discussing who would take care of Armon and Christopher, my name never came up.

The Making of a Child of Destiny

When I received that news, I was like, "The boys are gone. They did not do what Ann wanted them to do. I do not have the boys, so there is no real need for me to be around. All the money and things going on with the girls and them blowing up didn't excite me because I still have to work with that mutha fucka."

I resolved to get away because I was too close to everything and I didn't want to make a hasty decision. So I went back home to Greenwood, Mississippi to see my grandmother. At the time she was about a hundred and six years of age. She lived to the age of one hundred and seventeen still in her right mind. Now, my granny was a woman of wisdom. I was emotional first of all because I had not seen my grandmother in years, and she was happy to see her Chin, which is what she called me.

"Mama, well…"

"Chin, whatcha doing out there in Texas?"

"Mama Lizzy, I got this hot little girl group, and we're coming out and taking over the world and everything…but…I don't know if I'mma stay with them."

"Chin, why wouldn't you stay with the babies?"

So I went ahead and told my grandmother the story of what I was dealing with.

"Well baby, what I always told you, 'what do it profit a man, to gain the world, and lose his soul'?"

"Yes ma'am."

"...and know this...all money, ain't good money, baby."

"So, what you tellin' me to do?"

"You know what to do...pray on it. You know what to do."

I returned back to Houston after a wonderful visit with my beloved Mama Lizzy. I came in the house and had gotten several calls from different members of our team.

"Hey Kenny, man rehearsal's going on, we're doing a couple of things...you know...won't you come through."

"Naw, I won't be comin' through."

"Huh?"

"Ya'll can have it. I'm good."

"Huh?"

Yep, ya'll can have it. I'm good."

Whoosy, Chauncey and everyone who was in the clique, was trying to suck up to Mathew. Now that he had the reigns, it was like, "I'm Mathew Knowles and this is my fuckin' world."

He started to become the Mathew Knowles that the world ended up seeing.

During this time, my son Brian was about to go to middle school and playing little league ball. So to pass the time, I started to assist in coaching for a little while. Time

The Making of a Child of Destiny

was getting away from me because I was really beginning to enjoy the football.

The irony with the football was that all this time that I was working with the girls, trying to secure money to do what we needed to do, now I'm the head coach for this little league football team in Kline, Texas. We had great coaches and a great team. I did not experience any of the drama that I had to deal with working with Destiny's Child. Now, unbeknownst to me, four of my assistant coaches were multi-millionnaires. The interesting thing was, Ann and I were running all around the world trying to make this dream come true, and get money for studios and so forth, and now there I was in a situation where all the money I might have needed or wanted was right there.

I finally came to the conclusion that in order to wipe the slate clean, I had to move on. I didn't have the boys, everyone else was chasing Mathew or chasing the girls trying to get on. I decided, I didn't want to be a part of that. Yet, that didn't keep people from telling me what was going on with the group. I kept hearing about their successes and how they were climbing up the musical ladder. They were all over the television and in the papers. I was hearing how Mathew had taken over the reigns and how he was actually doing a great job with them. Of course in my mind I was like, "Is Mathew really doing such a great job or is he just standing in the gap and under the light from a fire that Andretta started. Is he just the one giving direction after the conductor who got the train rolling in the first place?"

I really didn't care to hear anything else about what was going on with any of them. It was hard listening to their songs. Whenever I caught an ear full of their music, I flashed back to when I was working with them. From time-to-time I would also get to thinking about Ann.

The news kept coming. Pam and Letoya must have finally gotten to LaTavia and Cheryl and pushed their point home of them needing separate management. Pam always wanted Letoya to be able to do more than just sing with the girls. Well, they must've shaken things up because they were kicked out of Destiny's Child. Both girls sued Mathew using the same lawyer that Pam and Letoya had used early on when they challenged the contract before with Andretta and Mathew, but with Andretta not being around to balance things out, there was no one to save the day.

This was all too much for me. I wanted no part of the continued chaos and drama. I disappeared, became inaccessible, and chose to stop using the name Kenny Moore. Instead, I started using my first name, which is Brian. Even today, I can distinguish from a person who knows me and has history with me, from one who does not or one who is a current business associate, because if they are a current business associate, they refer to me as Brian. People, who know me, refer to me as Kenny. Those who really know me, call me Kenny Mo.

After the coaching situation ended, Cassey asked me, "Baby, other than music and football, what else was it that you've always wanted to do when you were young?"

"Well, I've always wanted to work in computers. I used to always want to work for Hewlett Packard."

It turned out that shortly after that, I ended up landing a job working for Compaq, who was eventually bought out by Hewlett Packard. That job was my segway into "Corporate America." I went on with my life, but I wasn't really able to go on like I should have been able to because I had major issue with listening to the girl's songs or watching their videos. If it was on, I would walk past it. I wanted absolutely nothing to do with it. I had no idea I had so much bottled up anger. I felt it was totally unfair for Ann to die after giving all like she did. I had a problem reconciling with life with that. I really did.

I realized though once I got in "Corporate America" that all the dealings and preparation working with Ann and dealing with Destiny's Child, helped to shape me into an astute corporate business person. I was able to interact with people of all levels of the corporate world and make things happen. On the side, I met a man from Scotland named Michael. I decided that I was going to start brokering oil deals. My attitude was, "Hell, I helped to put the deal together with Destiny's Child, I could do anything so I'mma go broker me a couple of oil deals."

My thought was, "Hell the girls are one of the biggest stars in the world, Kenny Mo helped them get there. I can do anything. Kenny Mo's a bad mutha fucka!"

There was this housing deal that came up in the Bahamas. Michael knew a billionaire from out of New York. So I got with this Bahamian in the government and said, "Hey, I think I can put a deal together."

"Oh yeah? Go ahead…we need it."

"Alright now!"

I took my skills and my 'we can do it' attitude. I thought to myself, "We have talked with Columbia/Sony executives, and all these other folks. This is just another billionaire…please, I got this!"

We put our team together and flew to New York. We met at the NBC studios. Michael and I were brokering the deal. This eighty-year old billionaire, who was not saying much, had the lawyers on one side and Michael and my guy Eddy was there letting the attorneys talk. The old man was just staring at me and I stared right back at him. While all of this was going on, I was playing an entire conversation in my mind of what he was thinking based on the look he had on his face.

"How in the hell is your Black ass sitting at the end of my table negotiating a deal! You got some damn nerve, young man."

"I'm here to get this mutha fucka money, and I ain't takin' my Black ass up out of here until we get a deal done!"

The guys argued for about four hours. Then the man said, "Do you want to do lunch?"

I said, "Yes sir, A.C."

So we all went up stairs and into the legendary Rainbow Room. We walked in and what we beheld was beyond words. It was absolutely beautiful and dining at its best. When I looked to my left, I saw Katie Couric and the NBC news team. I was thinking, "Naw now, I 'm Kenny Mo, they ain't gonna see me sweat."

I whispered to myself, "Hold up hold up" I done arrived. I'm heeah! I done arrived."

I chuckled to myself, cause, I was sounding in my head like a country ass mutha fucka from the back woods of Mississippi from which I was, Greenwood that is. As I walked over, I saw one of the Rockefellers. Then finally we went and sat in the main window overlooking New York City. As we were sitting there, I was watching Mr. A.C. and he was watching me. He wasn't saying much at all other than a little small talk. Everybody was talking about the stock market and shit. I was like, "I can care fuckin' less!"

Finally, they came out with the food. There was seven spoons one way, seven forks another way, and seven knives. I was sitting there looking at all those damn forks and spoons and looking at everyone else and no one was eating. So, "me being me" and learning from Andretta, and recalling the time we went to California, we need to act like we knew what we were doing. My thoughts were, "If they waiting on me to start eating, then they got another thing coming I ain't eating shit until A.C. eat something, then I'mma grab the silverwear he grabs."

I hadn't seen a seven-course meal so I didn't know what the hell to do. Me, I was from Mississippi! "I was just a country ass mutha fucka." I knew to pick up the fork and eat. Hell, I was thinking, "This is too many damn forks! I done seen five, but hell this is seven! Shit! I am not fixin' to embarrass myself."

So I excused myself to go to the restroom. I grabbed my cell phone and called Cassey.

"Hey babe…babe…I'm in the bathroom. I'm in the bathroom I'm at the Rainbow Room."

"Where?"

"The Rainbow Room. You know what that is?"

"Oh my Gosh! For real?"

"Yeah! Listen here. I got something to ask you."

"What?"

"Got dammit, I'm at a table…they got seven spoons going one way, seven forks going the other, and seven knives. Which one do I pick up first?"

Cassey started laughing.

"Baby, grab from the outside in."

"Outside in? Okay. Alright. Look baby. I gotta go, I'm at the Rainbow Room."

I got to the door and shook myself off and got my stroll back on. It was a long little walk, so I strutted back to the table where everyone was sitting. I looked like George Jefferson. I said to myself, "This is probably gonna be the first and onlyest time I get to be in this mutha fucka, so hell make it count!"

As soon as I got back to the table, A.C. reached and grabbed his fork. He grabbed the outside fork, and then I grabbed mine. At that point, we began to have our seven course meal without me fucking up!

This and other great things were going on in my life after I chose to walk away from Destiny's Child, yet God was still finding favor with me. Everything I learned with Ann was being put to use. The education I received in working all of those years in that camp wasn't for naught. We closed a few deals. I was brokering and everything was going well, but there was still something missing. Chauncey had an incident where he had to serve some time in the penitentiary. When he got out of jail, he had this backlog of music. I had these songs I wrote years ago. Chauncey and I were in Lou's place meditating and talking. He had this beat going. When I heard it, it reminded me of a song I had.

"Man, I got a song that might go half way decent with that."

We got to writing and drinking. After a night of total drunkedness, we walked out with sixteen songs. It was an all gospel album.

"Man I used to sing, but all I'mma do from here on out is gospel."

"Yeah, I wanna give something back to the Lord too, Kenny man."

So we put this group together and I named it after my old street called, "Eastlawn Drive." I changed the spelling of the group to Eastlon to give it a more lively sound and look. We released the gospel cd and although we allowed a guy to mix it who didn't do as good of a job as we had hoped he'd do with it, we pushed it anyway. In a three-month period, we had gone from sitting in Lou's place to our songs being played all across the country. Also, if you turned on the radio in Houston, you could hear our songs being played. The music was still there in my heart. Within a month and a half of releasing our cd, we received a call from Cleveland, Ohio.

The Making of a Child of Destiny

"Hey, we play Eastlon a lot on our station. We would like you guys to come up and do an interview. Also, we got a special show that we want you to perform at which will be at the "Rock and Roll Hall of Fame."

"What?"

"Yeah. It's the Rock and Roll Hall of Fame. You do the interviews on the radio station."

"You mean where Ruffin was at, and Sam Cook and all the greats are?"

"Yeah. You know you guys will get to perform on the church service program."

"Alright, I'm in."

So Chauncey and I ended up going to Cleveland, Ohio and the Rock and Roll Hall of Fame, opening up at Kathy Hughes' event for Jeff Majors, a phenomenal harpist. It was amazing. Here we were, Chauncey and I in Cleveland for this big event. The girls were the hottest thing out there at the time. All I could think about was, "Damn, Ann!"

We had some real talent in our stable, and if one of the managers could get to the Rock and Roll Hall of Fame, then, what would our other artists have done? Chauncey and I ended up working together a little while longer, until Eastlon ran its course. We then went our separate ways. The irony of the success of Eastlon was that I used to tell Andretta I was going to be an artist. She would always laugh and say, "The only type of artist you could be is a gospel artist." Once again, she was right.

We moved on with life. Shortly after that, Cassey got pregnant again, and ended up having my daughter Bryanna. When Bryanna came, it totally changed my outlook. It softened me a little bit on Mathew.

I might not have been able to forget a lot of the dirt he did, but I did grow to understand and sympathize with the fact that, Beyonce was his daughter. Having Bryanna opened my eyes to that. Whether he knew what he was doing or not, at the end of the day, this was his daughter and regardless of what mess he made in the process, I came to believe that his intentions were honestly good toward her and his actions were only to do what was in her best interest even though he screwed up a whole lot.

The other thing that softened me on the situation was that my pastor loved Destiny's Child, and one day he pulled me aside and said, "Kenny?"

"Yo, yo, what?"

"Can we have that conversation that you don't like to have?"

"Okay, what?"

"Look! Why can't you forgive that man?"

"Man let me tell you something…listen here…I know you supposed to be protecting my soul…uh…but right now…"

"Man, you can't move on with life if you don't forgive him."

"So what you saying…"

"You holding yourself hostage by not forgiving him. Kenny, that's that man's daughter… you know…Look at Bryanna. Somebody come around here messing with Bryanna…you gonna kill all of 'em! I know it!"

"Huhm."

"Now…that's his daughter. What he did, how he went about it, may have been wrong, but it was a father thinking he was doing what's best for his child."

When my pastor put the situation like that, I softened a little more. I could relate a little better. Then lo' and behold, the first songs Bryanna would sing at two or three years old, she was singing Beyonce. I was looking at her little fast tail behind. I just looked at her and said, "Really? You're listening to Beyonce."

I didn't say a word to her. My little girl really loved Beyonce. As I was sitting there listening to the words, "Let me cater to you…" At first I was ill-at-ease, but then suddenly a peace came over me and as I watched my daughter I thought to myself, "I hear my Bey again. I heard my Bey."

Although I was listening to Beyonce, I was sitting with my own daughter, Bryanna and all the anger of losing

Ann began to subside. It took me all those years to get to the point of having the willingness to forgive. When I was sitting with my daughter, she was saying, "Beyonce, Beyonce!"

I hadn't shared with Bryanna before then, that I even knew the girls.

"I know her baby girl."

"What!"

"I know her...yeah...I know her...that's my friend."

"What! You don't know Beyonce! You don't know her."

"Yes I do."

"Prove it...prove it!"

When Bryanna told me to prove it, I went into the garage and pulled out that old box. I pulled out one of the photos to show Briana.

"Do you know who this little girl is?"

"That's Beyonce!"

"Yeah, that's my Bey...this is my Kelly...Ashley was here, and Letoya...LaTavia"

"But those girls aren't in the group."

"No, not anymore, but they are still very good."

After going through that box, I realized that enough time had passed, it was done. I felt myself release. I wasn't mad any longer. I could listen to the girls. It was time for me to move on. So, I threw the box away. I threw the whole thing in the trash. However, I found out later that Cassey, saw that it was in the trash and dug it out, and hid it. We went on after that. Life was good. My family was doing well. Brian was playing high school sports by then. National recruiters were knocking at our door scouting out our son. We were going to football games. Cassey and Bryanna was cheering him on with their little cheerleading outfits on and their pon poms.

There were no complaints. Things were great. The only thing that was reminding me of my earlier days with Destiny's Child was that periodically friends would call or come by and tell me that Mathew Knowles was asking for my telephone number. These conversations did not concern me as they all were instructed not to give out my number. Then one day Chauncey came by.

"Hey Mo!"

"What Chauncey?"

"Man, I need to talk to you about something."

"What?"

"You know…it's a subject you don't like to talk about."

"What?"

"Man, I need you to sit down, man…and really listen to me man."

"What? Come on now. Stop fuckin' with me Chauncey now."

"Andretta's estate…well… Andretta's estate has sued Mathew for thirty million dollars."

"Okay…and…okay?"

"Well…they can't pin it down because there's some loop holes there where they can't prove that Ann was the real manager and stuff…so…"

"What?"

"How the hell they can't prove that? Why would they have to prove it?"

"Man, Mathew said he started being their manager and he took over it so… they can't prove it."

"Well…shit…if that's their estate…let them go ahead and handle it…I…hell, I don't want shit to do with it!"

"Mo, look man, TuTu… and everybody said they're gonna lose the case if they can't get more evidence."

"Okay…that ain't got nothin' to do with me. They took the boys…so shit, they took the responsibility of her estate. Fuck it! They took the boys from me, now you need my fucking help? Shit, go to fuckin' hell! Deal with it! I ain't heard from none of their asses in six or seven years and now they need help. Fuck them!"

Cassey spoke up. "Chauncey, we have gone on with our lives. We've gotten away from it. That is a chapter in our past; we don't need to deal with it."

"Baby, you're right. You heard that Chauncey? Cassey said fuck it too!"

That night we left it right there. Then I had the weirdest night. I was laying their sleep. It was about four in the morning. Ann came to me in a dream.

"Dretta girl, what you doing?"

We were laughing and everything like old times. She was healthy. She was healed. She had no fingers missing or anything.

"Girl, I'm so glad to see you."

We were talking then she said, "I got something to talk to you about nigga."

"What?"

"Now, if something had of happened to you, you know I would've moved heaven and hell to make sure that Cassey, Brian, and Bryanna were all okay, and had everything they had coming. Now you get your ass up and go make sure my boys are taken care of."

I woke up out of that dream.

"Cat!"

"What baby, what's wrong?"

"Call Attorney Hall, tell him to come on over and I'll do the deposition."

I guess everyone told him that I was the one they had been looking for. He came on over about five to seven cars deep. They pulled up in long black Mercedes Benzs. It looked like Coming to America in front of my house. The attorney asked me, "Are you ready?"

"Yeah. Let me lay the groundwork. If you are here for me to prove that Andretta Tillman was the creator, founder, and manager of Destiny's Child, I will. However, if you are here for me to destroy Mathew and Tina Knowles for you, I'm not gonna do that."

The first question that attorney said out of his mouth in front of my wife was, "It is rumored that you and Mr. Mathew Knowles used to go and have ménage à trois with multiple women."

"What! What you just say... wha...wha...what you just say?"

He then repeated what he said. So I said again to him.

"Sir, if you are here for me to help you prove that Andretta Tillman was the original manager, and got the Sony deal for Destiny's Child, I can do that. But, if you are here to destroy what we created, Mathew Knowles, Tina Knowles, or the girls, or anybody associated with the girls, I'm not gonna do that for you!"

I was also thinking to myself, "Which also includes my mutha fuckin' ass!"

Being a lawyer, he worked his way back around, and asked a third time. I responded for the third time with a little more attitude. He then said to me, "We need a little more tangible evidence than just your word."

I thought to myself, "Damn, I done threw the box away. I should've kept the box."

"Cat!"

"What?"

"Damn, I threw my box away!"

"No you didn't. I kept it. I got everything."

"You got the box?"

"Yeah."

Cassey went to get the box. I told the attorneys to hold on.

"Hold on, hold on. Here's a video tape, and on this video tape there is a showcase. You hear Ashley and Beyonce saying, we like to thank our manager, Ms. Andretta Tillman. Also here's a cd, the album we did at The Plant that Ann paid for. Here, take this. Now here, I got all these contracts."

They looked at the contracts. They must've gotten them in discovery.

"We got these…we got these…"

I gave him Mathews resume and everything else I could think to give him that might help.

"No, No we have enough. Would you be willing to come to court?"

"I shouldn't have to…but…if I have to, I will."

"If you could talk to Mr. Knowles is there anything you want to relay to him since you haven't seen him?"

"Yes. You tell Mathew that I said, just do right. Just do right!"

That was the entire message I left for him. Then the attorneys proceeded to look at the drawings that were dated all the way back to when we started Music World. Then they realized something.

"Are you aware that you own part of Music World Management?"

"Yeah."

"Do you know you can sue him for your royalties and everything, like Andretta?"

"I know it…but…I don't want to. Just tell him I said do right or I will come back!"

They left and never called me to come to court because a week or two later, the case was settled out of court. I heard that the boys received seven figures. At that point, I was done. I felt that at that moment, I completed what Ann had asked of me. I went and helped to get her boys financially squared away which is what I was supposed to do. They got money. Her estate got money. They were fine now. I left it at that. I didn't see them. I didn't know where they were. I did my part to assist in getting the lawsuit settled. So, I felt that this was the purpose and now it has gone full circle. Everything should be done now. There was a burden that was lifted off of me, and I did not feel bad at all. I didn't feel that I had let Ann down by not fighting more or doing everything that I could do.

Later I heard that Mathew sold Music World to a British company. I guess this was his way of ensuring I don't change my mind and come back. This dissolved our partnership forever. Destiny's Child also split to do solo projects. As indiviuals, Mathew would not be required to pay Andretta's estate, because her contract stated 5% royalties for the life of Destiny's Child.

SOMETHING KEEPS CALLING ME

"Kenny!"

"Uh...wha...huh?"

"Bae, where is your mind? Did you see them. They are hot! It's a shame that this is their last concert man."

"Dang!"

"Bae man wake up...where you been, did you see that? Beyonce and Kelly and that new girl tore it up!"

"Cat, these girls took me way back in time, replaying goodtimes and bullshit from the time they were nine years old, to now. Andretta would be so proud of them. Shit, its' just a got damn shame she is not here to see how successful they have become."

"I know whatcha saying. But hell...you should be proud. You worked your ass off too. I will never forget what you told me about that day at the funeral when you were about to whoop Mathew's ass for dissin' Ann. Shit I wanted to tap that ass too!"

Cassey and I laughed and just shook our head. I looked up toward the top of the Toyota Center's dome one last time, and again water welled up in my eyes. "Well,

Cat this is it. I'm sure Beyonce will continue to blow up big. That knappy head ass Kelly ain't doing so bad her damn self either. Yep, whoo…Andretta would be proud of her little girls. These little heffers done made something of themselves. They did good."

"Yeah, Bae, that's something."

"Hell, they was sanging 'Hit me!...Bring the noise, make me lose my breath…Now you wanna act like you don't know what to do,' these little heffers handled their business. I gotta say I'm pretty proud of them if I do say so myself. Shit I'm tryin' to catch my breath after that one…but…I know what us asses finsta do…we finna take us asses home."

"Bae, how do you feel after this concert?"

"Shit Cat, like I said, it took me way back to when it all began. Each song made me reminisce on how we got here. As I watched them performing, shit…I flashed back in time thinking about all the good moments and all the fucked up shit."

"Come on, let's go get a drink and head our asses home."

"Cat, let's go to Lou's Place man."

"The fucking garage? Negro you crazy as hell. Shit…come on let's go party at Lou' place."

Cassey and I left the Toyota Dome, and headed back home. We talked, laughed, and remininced. After a few drinks, we finally called it a night. It looked like Beyonce and the other girls had settled with moving on with their lives outside of Destiny's Child. Yes, the concert was appropriately named – Destiny Fulfilled.

After the concert and after the whole situation with the lawsuit, and with the attorneys and Chauncey insisting that I help Andretta's sons, I finally felt free to move on with my life without hesitation or wondering in the back of my mind if I had truly done everything that I could possibly do. Going to the concert let me know that I had finally moved on. Things were going good in my life. Cassey and I were doing well. We were traveling all over the place and made frequent trips to the Bahamas. We went at least three of four times a year. Brian was about to go to college. Bryanna was growing up. We had no complaints. We were peaceful. I guess you could say, I closed that chapter of my life once and for all, or at least I thought.

Somehow word had gotten out that I had been associated with Destiny's Child. I was quickly able to pinpoint it down to the pastor of my church. Although, he meant no harm, the "cat being let out the bag" caused frequent visitors to my house of people who wanted help in the business. I wasn't much help because I made it clear that I hung up my music boots and it was something I just was not interested in getting involved in again.

One evening, Brian's school was putting on a talent show. We decided to go. When I got there, I found out that somehow word had even traveled to the school. There was this girls group who performed one of Destiny's Child's songs. When they finished performing, they came up to me asking me how they did. I was taken a back and in truth, it didn't matter to me how they did, I was there as a spectator, not a scout.

"Mr. Moore, how do you think we did? How did we do?"

"Well, I think you all did fine. It really don't matter what I think, everybody else is voting."

"Yes it does, we heard you used to work with Destiny's Child!"

These types of things kept happening and I had to let it ride and run its course. It seemed like something one way or another was trying to pull me back into the game. However, I was content and resolved in moving on with my life. I was moving up the corporate ladder, things were fruitful.

Things appeared to also be going well in the girls' life. Beyonce was doing well. Kelly and Letoya had released their albums. Ashley popped back up on the scene using her middle name Tamar and was working with Prince. She was nominated for a Grammy and was with him at the awards. All of the girls seem to be doing great except for LaTavia. So as far as destiny being fulfilled, I thought things had come full circle, and I was proud of them. There was nothing left for me to do at this point; so no matter how many people kept calling requesting help, I was done. Anything the girls were doing at this point was no longer about Andretta giving them their start, but rather about them standing on her shoulders to make their own mark in the world and completing their dream and aspirations for their own lives and careers.

Then all of a sudden, I got a call from Keisha. She is one of Cassey's flight attendant girlfriend's daughters. Keisha has always been around. As a matter of fact, she went to High School for the Performing and Visual Arts with Beyonce, Ashley, Kelly LaTavia, and Letoya. They were all classmates and knew each other.

"Hey uncle, I got a surprise for you!"

"Surprise?"

"Yeah. Are you at home?"

"Yeah, why?"

"Nevermind. Okay, I'm on my way over there."

About twenty minutes later, there was a knock on my door. I opened it and sure enough, there was Keisha standing all giddy.

"Hey girl, what's up with you?"

"Close your eyes!"

"No peeking uncle either."

"Girl, I ain't gonna peek."

"You better not!"

The Keisha yelled, "Surprise!"

Out stepped from around the corner was Ashley. I hadn't seen Ashley in about ten years. So it definitely was a surprise. We hugged, then I stepped back to look at her all grown up.

"Hey Ashley, how are you? You have sprouted I see."

"Okay, Uncle Watermelon Head!"

"Yeah, I remember you and Bey used to call me that. How are you girl? What are you doing here? I just saw you on Good Morning America with Prince on Monday."

"Yeah…Well, you know, I left."

"You left? You left Prince?"

"Yeah, I kind of stepped out to do my own thing."

"Oh…okay…well…good luck with it."

We all sat around, talked, and ate for a while. Then Ashley said to me, "Mr. Kenny, I need your help."

"What?"

"Well, I'm doing my solo album on my own. I got this producer…but I don't have a manager."

"And…what are you saying?"

"Will you come back and manage me?"

"Tamar…Ashley…Shit…whatever your damn name is or whatever they call you now, I've been away from this way too long. I don't do that no more. I'm done with the music and all that."

"Well, I can really use your help."

"How…how you doing an album and you were just with Prince?"

"Well we agreed for me to just go on…go ahead and start making my way…and that's what I'm trying to do."

"Ash…I don't know…I don't know."

"Please…Please help me."

"Okay…Ashley because it's you…I'll help out. I'm not promising you nothing, but I'll just give you my advice and if I get my chops back to manage, then we'll talk further."

We both were fine with that. She then invited me to the studio to meet her producer. A few days later, Cassey, Bryanna, and I went by the studio. Bryanna was thrilled to be in the studio with Tamar because she had just seen her on T.V. with Prince. We met her producer and listend to her songs. They were really nice.

"Tamar, you got something here, girl!"

"Thanks."

"But this one song is interesting…"

She had a song that talked about childhood friends. They grew up together, but then her girlfriend stabbed her in the back.

"Now Tamar... that song can be taken two different ways."

"What?"

"It could be that you're talking about a girlfriend that stole your boyfriend...or it could be that you're talking about Beyonce and the girls."

We listened to several of the songs. As we observed her, it was the typical Tamar to me where it was someone else controlling her. It wasn't like she was in there making her own decisions. She seemed to still be that little lost girl looking for her way. We talked awhile, brainstormed, and begin putting some ideas on the table.

"I wanna go back to this girlfriend song, Tamar."

"Okay..."

"I was just thinking. You know what would be a great video?"

"What?"

"Well, picture this...If we could get Niki, Nina, LaTavia, and Letoya back together to do a video with you for the song, "My Ex Best Friend," and have all of you up on the stage on the video and a silhouette of the two microphones where Beyonce and Kelly would go, with the lights shining down on the space where the two of them

The Making of a Child of Destiny

were missing. Now I think that would be an awesome video."

"Uhm."

Then if you were singing, then all of them came back up on stage with you as you were singing...you would have Girls Tyme back together in the video except Beyonce and Kelly. I think that would be hot!"

Tamar and her producer thought that was a great idea.

"Wow! I can see that."

After going to the studio and listening to Tamar's songs and chopping up some ideas, I started to get excited.

"Shoot girl! Let's see what I can put together!"

So as I began to seriously consider managing her, I looked at the total package of Tamar and the wheels started turning. She had a pretty good producer. The music sound good. It was a matter of re-imaging her, marketing, and releasing her as an independent, then getting someone to pick it up. So when I left Tamar, I went and spoke with Michael.

"Hey Michael, I need a favor."

"What?"

"Now, I know you don't know nothing about the music industry. We done all these other damn deals together...oil, real estate...and all of that...but I need you to go to bat with me."

"What?"

I told Michael the deal and finally told him about my days with Destiny's Child.

"What! You worked with Destiny's Child?"

"Yeah, and Tamar was one of the original members. She started out singing lead for the group when they first got started. She just finished doing some things with Prince, and was nominated for a Grammy. Well, I wanna raise some money to help get her back out there. She's hot! She was recently on Good Morning America. She's hot! So let's roll."

So Michael got some investors together. I met with them, told them about my background, and within a week we pulled a major deal together. They were interested in hearing her. So, that following Saturday, we met Tamar and the producer back at the studio. After the listened to some of the songs, Michael, the investors and I walked out into another room. I told Tamar I would be right back and proceeded to go hear their thoughts. They loved the music and they loved her!

They agreed to invest two hundred thousand dollars to produce the video, do some marketing, regroup, do some pressing, get distribution, and get her back out there.

"We got the check. We're ready to write the check."

"Okay."

The Making of a Child of Destiny

We agreed to meet back at the wine-tasting room to outline the particulars, and then draw up the contracts. We laughed and talked for a moment, and then they pulled off. So I walked back into the studio.

"Ashley...well baby they love it! So what I'mma do is go down here and get it lined up. Then I will have Michael draft up a little management contract for me and you and we'll get everything rolling."

The producer turned to me and said, "Hey...uh...I need to talk with you."

"Okay."

Ashely turned and looked at me and then started to walk out of the room.

"Ashley, where are you going?"

"Uh...he wanna talk to you so..."

She then walked out of the room and went into this lounging area and closed the door.

I said to myself, "Okay then."

"Well, uh...Tamar wanted me to talk to you."

"Okay..."

"...about management."

"Okay...and?"

"Well...uh...I'm the producer of Tamar..."

"Yeah...okay...and?"

"...and Tamar also wants me to be her manager."

"Okay…she wants you to be her personal manager…business manager…manager for what?"

"…Uh, she just wants me to be her manager period!"

"Okay then…what does Tamar want me to do?"

"Well…basically…you consult me on how to manage and what to do and everything."

"Oh…okay so let me get this straight. She came to get me to bring me out of retirement, then I come out of retirement for her, and then I go get money, show her how quick I can make it happen, we back ready to roll, and then after you have me bring my people in here, secure funds for you, you watch me secure the funds, then you are going to tell me at that point that you're going to be her manager?"

"Yeah."

"So I'mma give you two hundred thousand dollars, and consult you on how to spend it and get her back out there?"

"Yeah, that's what we're thinking."

"You must be out of your mutha fuckin' mind! I'm Kenny fuckin' Mo and apparently Ashley or shit Tamar excuse me, must have forgotten that shit! I only fuckin' came and dealt with this shit because of Ashely being who she was and I still felt that we owed her. But I don't know who the fuck you is and if ya'll don't get ya'll fuckin' asses away from me…Don't ya'll every fuckin' call me again with this bullshit!"

He just looked at me looking all stupid.

"Ashley!"

She hurried into the room.

"Ashley, you done hooked up with the wrong mutha fucka. He is infatuated with you and can't see clear because of ya'lls personal relationship. I wish you well, but your ass ain't going nowhere with a situation like this!"

I walked out and went down to the tasting room. The men were all excited about the deal. Then I had to break this bullshit news to them.

"Hey. You ready to roll? Here's the check."

They handed the check to Mike, Mike then handed it to me, and I tore up the two hundred thousand dollar check shreds.

"Mike, we won't be needing it. Some things happened and I just don't think it's worth us dealing with this project. But I thank ya'll for believing in me and for coming to bat, but after you all left, something happened and it's not a good situation and it's too big a gamble."

We then left it at that. The situation though left a very bad taste in my mouth and re-triggered some of those bad feelings. Some people just aren't worth two flies mashed. I said to myself, "Now how are you gonna come…I minding my own fuckin' business. You bring your ass to my got damned house. Asked me to be your damn manager. You just left Prince, you thought enough of me to come and get me to help you, and then you let some mutha fucka you probably screwing fuck it up for you again!"

The more I thought about it, the more I got upset, and the more I talked to myself.

"You haven't changed. Your ass out here and sayin' you're grown, but still being controlled by people who do more harm to your career than help. You ain't a damn child no more. Your ass still acting like a twelve got damn year old. Ashley how could you get caught up like this? You should've just let it ride out and let me get you going again before you let that mutha fuckin' present that bullshit."

When I got home, I was livid and shared the whole situation with Cassey.

"Dammit Cat, why is it every damn time I try to get away from this shit, it keeps coming back up in my face? I just don't understand and why when people need help they don't know how to receive it without letting someone else fuck it up for them!"

Even with this minor setback, I looked up and realized that everyone from the Andretta Tillman camp was having some form of success. Mathew and Lonnie must have reconciled because he was producing tracks for Kelly as well as working with Dr. Dre. Shay Atkins, another artist that was in our stable, had a nice little gospel album going. Even though she came up under Ann late in the game, she was still doing fairly well. T-Moore was doing some writing and producing around town and his name was becoming a regular mention. Corey Moore and his brother, who was from the stable with the group Flagg was doing well. They became big underground producers for Kanye West and others. Chauncey was grooving with his own production company. Whoosy was working with some rappers from out of Memphis. The members of Tayste, although disbanded, were all having minimal success as solo artists. It was great because everyone was having some form of success. I was cool with it because I knew if Andretta had not have passed and we would have kept the stable together, all of them would have been a lot more successful. Even my stint with Easlton in its' rapid success further confirms that belief.

"Cat! I'm out for real this time, and I'm out for good!"

"Okay, baby, I hear you. That's what you sayin' now."

"It's just not for me! It's just not fun anymore without working with Ann."

"I understand."

"The thing that is bothering me Cat is Ashley is with this guy and he has no vision for her, and is only going to further hinder her career, and the poor baby has had enough bad breaks as it is. But everybody's grown, and she's not a little girl anymore so I have to stay in my lane."

Ultimately, Tamar did a few Tyler Perry theatre productions and now touring with the cast of Motown the Musical.

"Sad part is Cat, after she left the group, she seemed to just chase the industry and never really found out who she was as an artist. I always felt sorry for her after she was railroaded from being lead singer at the Plant."

Before I could shake that situation off, about two weeks later, Michael and I, along with some of our business associates were hanging out at the tasting room. Cassey's friend Chris said, "Hey Cassey, I want to go next door to this place and check out these jeans. They are supposed to have these real nice jeans. I wanna take a look."

"Alright then, let's go check them out."

Cassey and Chris went next door. They stayed over there for quite a while, so Michael and the rest of us continued drinking and smoking our cigars. Then, I noticed Cassey come back walking fast.

"Hey Kenny, come here…quickly."

"What?"

"Just come here."

"Alright, hey guys, I will be right back."

So I followed Cassey. When I walked into the boutique, the lady behind the counter started immediately speaking to me.

"Don't you remember me?"

"Well...your face looks very familiar."

"Kenny, I don't believe you don't remember me. I'm Pam, Letoya's mom."

"Oh...Pam...wow!"

We started laughing and talking.

"If you wait a few minutes, Toya will be here. This is her store and I'm running it for her. Lady L."

"So how are things going?"

"Well she's working to get things back on track and working on releasing a new album."

Letoya came into the place and Pam asked her, "Do you remember him?"

"His face looks familiar."

"Do you remember Mr. Kenny, Miss Ann's partner?"

Letoya then burst out laughing and said, "Uncle Watermelon Head."

She hugged me and we all started laughing and talked briefly before Letoya had to leave.

Pam and I discussed what the other girls were doing. She informed me that LaTavia wasn't doing too well because of all the things that went down with her being kicked out the group, as well as dealing with the earlier childhood issues she had. We reminisced for awhile, and then she took me in the back and asked, "Hey whatcha gonna do about all this stuff with Mathew trying to write Ann out like she was not the one who created and managed the girls? Are you gonna do anything about that?"

"Pam…yeah…I'm working on something."

"Well if you need any help let me know."

I told Pam I was working on something, but in reality I had no plans to do anything because in my mind, I thought that I had done all I needed to do.

After hearing the story of the problems that LaTavia was having, as any parent would feel, I wanted to run and try to see if I could help her. However, the Tamar situation took the cake though, and I wanted nothing more than to put that whole situation behind me. With thoughts of my girls suffering or having pitfalls, I made a concerted effort to put the music back in my own life. I began researching and engaging the impact of the internet and social media on the music industry and how it would impact the artists. My thinking was not only to create something to help my girls, but every independent artist trying to make it in the music industry.

Through my research, I developed Dousic, a concept for getting independent artists exposure. I worked with internet radio and got on the cutting edge of the industry transition from terrestrial to the internet. I was very happy with what I was doing. After a while, life was great again.

Cassey had a group of girlfriends that would all get together when each of them had a birthday. This time it was Cassey's friend Jean's birthday and she wanted the husbands to go.

"Girl, I'm not going no damn where with ya'll. Have a good time without me."

"Come on big daddy…Let's go have some fun!"

"Jean, you lucky it's your ass…cuz I would be sitting my Black ass at home watching the game or something."

So after being convinced to go out, we all got in this long black stretch limousine. The women were about ten deep. We rode around town partying and drinking in the limo. We ended up at The Sky Bar. When we arrived, the line was extremely long. Just as they wanted to turn around and leave, I spoke up.

"No, let's stay."

I kept hearing them say Gertner. So then it clicked, one of our business partner's name was Gill Gertner. I called Michael.

"Hey Mike, this is Kenny."

"Hey partner, what's going on?"

"Is Gill related to this cat named Scott Gertner with the Sky Bar?"

"Yeah, that's his uncle."

"Hey Mike, I'm stuck outside with this damn line of about two hundred people, and I got about twenty people with me. I need to break this velvet rope."

"Hold on buddy, let me call Gill."

So Mike hung up and not even five minutes later called me back.

"Look, Kenny…go to the side by the elevator, there's a guy that's gonna come down there in a few seconds."

Everybody was waiting at the elevator because you have to go up the elevator to get to the Sky Bar. So the manager came down and yelled, "Kenny? Kenny?"

"Right here."

I motioned the rest of the crew to get out of the limo. He backed everyone up so my party could get through. We broke the line and as we were walking by we could here some of the comments.

"Who the hell are they?"

"What the fuck…"

"Shit…I'm with them…"

"Can I come with you?"

We chuckled as we headed on the elevator.

When we got on the elevator, Cassey, Jean, and some of the others wanted to know what I did.

"Bae, what did you do to get us in?"

Then Jean said, "Hell, if I didn't no better, I would think you were some fuckin' body!"

Tony was like, "You know Kenny is big time around here, he just don't say nothin' to nobody."

"Jean, I'm Kenny fuckin' Mo. Understand?"

We all laughed as we got off the elevator. We partied and celebrated. There were drinks everywhere. The Sky Bar has an open balcony where you can go smoke cigars. So we were out there sitting, drinking, and partying. Suddenly, Cassey got started.

"Well, I 'm going dancing since you out here with the boys smokin' cigars."

"Take your little fast tail ass on then, girl. We just shootin' the breeze."

Cassey went out on the dance floor. She was just a dancing. She noticed this big tall guy just staring at her. She thought he was weird, but he had a woman with him. As she was leaving the dance floor, he walked up into her space.

"Excuse me ma'am."

"Yes?"

"You gotta know me...you gotta know me."

"Baby, I'm afraid I don't know you."

"No, No, No…you know me. You gotta know me! You my mom's friend. You my mom's friend."

"Your mom? Well baby who is your mom?"

"My mom…Andretta Tillman!"

Cassey looked real close at him, the said, "Armon?"

"Yeah!" Where Pops, Where's Unc?"

"Oh baby!"

Cassey grabbed him and they hugged. Cassey started crying. He started crying. The woman with him started crying. Next thing I knew, Cassey, Jean, and the other women ran off the dance floor and headed in our direction. We saw them running toward us with this big old dude.

"What the hell!"

Me and the boys got up. "What the hell is going on?"

Cassey was yelling.

"Kenny! Kenny! Kenny! Look! Look who it is!"

I looked, and then looked again. That big 'ole dude walked up to me.

"Pop!"

"Armon?"

We both burst out in tears. Everybody started hugging.

"Man, what?"

"Ken Moore, what the hell is going on?"

All of Cassey's friends knew the story. There was not a dry eye in our party. Some of the men still hadn't figured it out.

"Who is that V?"

One of the women spoke up.

"Do you remember Andretta? Her kids were supposed to come and stay with Kenny and Cassey? Well that's one of the boys."

Everyone was talking and crying, but Armon's girlfriend was crying almost uncontrollably. Cassey looked at her and tried to comfort her.

"Baby, what's wrong?"

"Ya'll don't understand. He's been looking for ya'll forever! Ever since his mom died he been lookin' for ya'll."

"We've been looking for them too."

"Armon, what happened?"

"What?"

"Ya'll was supposed to come and stay with us…"

"Pops, somehow Uncle Keith, got us man and convinced us to go stay with him. I didn't even know we were supposed to come and stay with ya'll. Ya'll name didn't even come up from what they told me. It probably would've been better if we had come to stay with ya'll."

"What?"

Armon and I talked for hours that night.

"Man, Pops. Chris gotta see you!"

"Yeah. How is everybody? How's Buck?"

"Well she's old and not really doing too well."

By the time we finished talking, I asked about everybody from TuTu to Mop and everybody in between.

"Okay look, get Chris, round up all ya'll damn kids, my grandkids, and ya'll come on by Saturday. I'mma barbeque."

"Oh snap! Not the world famous barbeque again!"

We laughed and talked briefly about the old barbeques and how much fun they used to be. Finally Armon and I parted ways that evening, but we talked everyday the following week. I also had the chance to speak with Chris. We made arrangements for the upcoming weekend. At that moment, I was so glad I went out that night with Cassey and the girls as it was a life-changing moment. I learned that Armon had one child and Chris had five. I was a grandfather six times over or at least Andretta and Dwight were. I could not help but to think about Andretta and Dwight in their absence, Cassey and I would have to serve as grandparents.

Armon called me the Friday evening before the barbeque.

"Hey Pops, I gotta a couple of people who wanna come to the barbeque, can I bring them?"

"Yeah...no problem...cool."

So like old times, I went and killed the fatty calf and barbeque up a bunch of meat and prepared all the "fix-ins." We were all excited and waiting for the boys to get there. Bryanna was looking forward to meeting them because she heard us talking about them since forever. Brian was looking forward to seeing his big brothers who he hadn't seen since he was really young. All of our immediate friends came by. They wanted to be there to witness the reunion of Andretta's boys and grandkids with our family.

First Armon showed up. He had his girlfriend with him and this little girl that looked just like Andretta. She had such an uncanny resemblance to her grandmother that it was amazing that it almost brought us to tears. I looked at Cassey and she looked at me.

"Oh my Gosh! This is Ann Jr. Kenny look at this."

I bent down and said, "Hey, hey little Ann."

I went and picked her up in amazement at just how much she looked like Andretta. We all started calling her Little Ann. Shortly after, Chris arrived. He had a basketball team with him. he had four girls and one boy which included a set of fraternal twins. As I looked around and saw all of these little extensions to Ann, it was a bitter-sweet moment. All of the children had a touch of Ann in them. So, out of all these grandchildren, there was only one little boy.

"Chris, so what is the boy's name?"

"His name is Dwight."

"Oh, okay…wow."

I paused for a second before I reached down and picked him up. I said, "Well, it is finally good to meet you Dwight Tillman."

As I walked around the room holding him and talking to him, I said, "I've heard a lot about you over the years…Armon give me little Ann."

With both of them in my arms, I said, "So you got a little Andretta over here, and a little Dwight over there…Uhm. Lawd have mercy!"

I just thought for a moment to myself, "Everything has come full circle."

It was a fantastic evening. We all laughed and talked about old times. I shared storied of their mom with them and her grandchildren, maybe exaggerating a little but to the kids to make her seem even funnier. Then I got another surprise when the doorbell rung. It was Nina and Charlotte. Cassey started screaming.

"What is this? Are you kidding me?"

We hugged, laughed, ate, and talked. It was as if we had never been separated. When we finished eating,

The Making of a Child of Destiny

Charlotte pulled me aside and said, "Kenny, I wanna to talk to you for a minute."

"Okay, what's up Charlotte?"

"Well, what are you gonna do about Mathew and them doing all this lying? Whatcha gonna do about them trying to act like as if Ann never existed?"

"Charlotte, well…I'll handle it."

"Well, it's just not right the way they are trying to write her out of history and she did all the damn work."

"Yep, I know, Charlotte."

After this conversation, I began to wonder was there more for me to do. I had not taken the time to really listen to what they had been saying about how the group was created. That evening, as Cassey and I were talking, I wondered what was going on. First it was Tamar, then Pam, then Letoya, Armon and Chris, and now Nina and Charlotte. It was something to think about because all of them pretty much wanted to know the same thing – "What are you gonna do about Mathew trying to write Ann out of the history."

We continued to host barbeques at the house which included Armon and Chris and their families. They re-entered our lives and have once again become a part of the family. I am very grateful for that, and I know Ann is really proud of them. Armon and I got to talking about music. Then out of the blue he said, "Pops…how can we go about getting my mom's story told?"

"Huh?"

"Well, they act like she doesn't exist. They're trying to write her out of the history, like she wasn't nobody when she sacrificed a lot. Come on Pops, my family had sacrificed a lot. All I want is her story to be told."

"Well then, Armon, why don't you just tell it!"

"I can't, because when the lawsuit was settled, we had to sign a non-disclosure clause. We can't write it, and even if I could write it, I don't know everything you know. You are the only one that was there that can tell the truth about what she did. You were there."

"Okay. Armon, I'll think about it."

Armon and I continued to bond. Likewise so did Chris and I. Armon was always pretty upbeat, but one day he had heard something on the news about how Destiny's Child got started, and when he heard it, his mother's name was not even brought up. I guess it got to him.

"Man, we gotta tell my mom's story!"

Armon had this look on his face of pure disgust mixed with helplessness. If I was able to read his mind, he probably was saying, "Shit ain't nothin' I can fuckin' do to tell my mom's story!"

"Armon…you know…"

I really did not know what to say. I took a deep breath.

"Armon…I don' think I can go back down that road."

"I understand…I understand Pop."

Once again, we left it at that. Two weeks later, Armon called me and said, "Hey Pops, I got someone who wants to come and talk to you about how everything went down with my mom."

"Now Armon, you know I'm not just gonna tell anybody about this story. I mean… so who is it?"

"It's David."

"David Brewer?"

"Yeah."

"What!"

"Yeah, he flew in from Germany."

"Got damn! What's really going on? Are these mutha fuckas trying to draw me out? Why is everybody looking for Kenny Mo? Can you tell me that?"

"Well Pop, you the only one that know. You the only one that knows the real story and people are going to keep coming until they can get it out of you."

"Okay Armon, tell David to come on over."

David and Armon came over. We sat down in the backyard and had some scotch and cigars. My thinking was, a man not used to scotch and Cuban cigars will get drunk enough to expose his true motive.

"Well David, whatcha need? What's going on?"

"Well, they are trying to discredit me from being Beyonce and the girls' vocal coach."

"What? What's the purpose of that? You were their vocal coach."

"I don't know. They're trying to discredit me."

"Man, that's a shame."

"It's as if they're trying to write out anybody who had a part of creating the group. It's like Mathew is trying ot take all the credit."

"I see."

"Well, you know I'm writing a book."

"What…you writing a book, David?"

"Yeah, and I wanna include some of the stuff about Ann being the manager. So I just wanna get some information from you because…so… I can add it in the book. No one will really only take my word for it. I need some facts, some contract and different things like that to prove I was there."

"Well David, I haven't said anything to anybody all these years. What do you need?" Why should I start to talk now?"

"Kenny…I just wanna know why you haven't said anything all of these years?"

"To be honest David, I promised Tina when Beyonce was a little girl and we were traveling to California. Tina was crying and I asked her why. She was telling Beyonce she didn't have to do this. I told Tina not to worry, as long as I'm alive and I'm able to that I would never let anyone hurt Beyonce."

"What? For that reason, you haven't told my mom's story?"

"Yeah."

"You worried about not hurting Beyonce. What about all the hurt its causing me?"

I thought for a few minutes, sipped on some scotch, and puffed on my Cuban cigar, and the next words that came out of my mouth was, "What do you need, David."

"Anything tangible."

"Well here are some pictures. I can email you some stuff, come contracts, some dates, and hope it helps you."

When David left, Armon and I continued to talk.

"Pops, now you know that even though he tells the story, he wasn't there behind the scenes. He was living with the Knowles' and worked with the girls, but he can't tell the story like you can."

"Yeah...yeah...you got a point."

"He can only talk about what went on at Mathew and Tina's house."

"Okay, well…Armon, I got one question."

"What?"

"Is this about your mom's story being told, or is this about making some money off of her memory?"

"Pops, it's about my mom's story being told."

"Okay. Now if I tell the story, I'mma tell the whole story. How she came to do it, what happened. I'm not going to leave any stuff out."

"Okay."

So from there, I started to write the book that you are now reading. Often, I was asked the question, what am I gonna do about them writing Ann out of the history of Destiny's Child. I then began to ask the same question. While the first two albums were dedicated to her, gradually after that, you did not hear her name when the subject of their beginning came up. If the truth was told, there would be no need for me to write this book. Yet, I find it necessary to write so that the world can know what my friend sacrificed to get them to the greatest pinnacle of their young lives and careers.

Andretta Tillman opened the most important doors of their lives driven by the dreams of her husband and the love of her daughter. They died in pursuit of the Destiny that these girls are living. So how dare we forget where we came from? I don't know if they just don't remember, don't talk about, or just ungrateful for her as a manager and mother figure in their lives. She is the one who helped to turn on the lights so that the world could see that it was the Girls' Tyme, after all and Andretta Tillman was in fact a Child of Destiny and why Destiny's Child came to be!

For me, the original question still remains, "Do they really know what happened?"

The sacrifice of a daughter, a wife, a mother, and a friend was the greatest love she could have shown. As the Bible says, "No greater love has no one than this than to lay down one's life for a friend."

So, what's the measurement of love when three lives are laid down for a destiny? While we may not know what's ahead, and none of them may ever find the courage to step forward and speak up, one thing is for sure, time will most certainly tell.

As for me, I find myself sitting in the studio again listening to hot new artists wondering,

"Can lightening strike again?"

I don't know if it will strike twice, but while sitting in the studio with my son Armon, the irony is it used to be his mom sitting in the chair. Just doing music again, the feeling, the passion and drive has returned. So, will we be able to recreate the magic that brought the world Destiny's

Child? I don't know, but what I do know is, we will damn sure try. More importantly, however, is that we're back as a family; and that's what the journey was all about in the first place. So my wish for those of you who are on similar pilgrimage is, I hope that you are able to maintain your peace and integrity and in the end find your Destiny!

About the Author

Brian K. Moore is the CEO for Dousic Entertainment, LLC., Co-founder of Music World Entertainment, and former Co-manager of Tillman Management.

Coming from a line of preachers and raised in the Mississippi Delta, for New York born Brian "Kenny" Moore, music has always been a part of his life. After his tour in the United States Air Force, he found his heartsong co-managing one of the greatest female groups of all time – Destiny's Child.

Kenny-MO as he was endearingly called lives in Houston, Texas with his wife, Cassey and their two children, Brian and Bryanna. This is his first novel.

APPENDIX

Ann Walking Down the Aisle

Ann in High School

Ann Home Going Leaflet

Ann Watching Beyonce

Dwight and Shauna Home Going Leaflet

Dwight in Football Gear

Destiny's Child

Destiny's Child

Destiny

Girl's Tyme

Something Fresh

Shawna (Shauna)

Ann and Dwight Wedding Day

"A Picture is Worth a Thousand Words"

Brian Kenneth Moore

The Making of a Child of Destiny

Homegoing Celebration
For
Mrs. Andretta Brown Tillman

Services
New Canaan Baptist Church
Whitehouse, Texas

Thursday, May 22, 1997
1:00 p.m.

Reverend E.L. Lockett, Pastor
Reverend D.C. Brown, Officiating
Reverend Holcomb, Eulogist

Message From My Family
Family Meditations
Obituary and Order of Service

Brian Kenneth Moore

The Making of a Child of Destiny

IN LOVING MEMORY
OF

MR. DWIGHT RAY TILLMAN
and
MISS SHAUNA TILLMAN

NEW CANAAN BAPTIST CHURCH
Whitehouse, Texas

Saturday, November 1, 1986
12:30 P.M.

****
Reverend D.C. Brown, Pastor
Reverend J.T. Holcombe, Officiating
****

Brian Kenneth Moore

The Making of a Child of Destiny

The Making of a Child of Destiny

Brian Kenneth Moore

The Making of a Child of Destiny

Somethin' Fresh

Brian Kenneth Moore

The Making of a Child of Destiny

Brian Kenneth Moore